THE

"IDSTONE" PAPERS,

A SERIES OF ARTICLES AND
DESULTORY OBSERVATIONS ON SPORT AND
THINGS IN GENERAL.

By "IDSTONE,"

OF "THE FIELD."

LONDON:
HORACE COX, 346, STRAND, W.C.

1872.

LONDON :
PRINTED BY HORACE COX, 346, STRAND, W.C.

PREFACE.

"THE Idstone Papers" were originally written for the *Field* Newspaper.

I have consented to republish them for the following reasons :—

First, the favourable and kind opinion expressed by the late Mr. Charles Dickens of the first paper ("The Agricultural Labourer"), which was submitted to him by a mutual and eminent friend ; and, secondly, the repeated requests made by friends and strangers that I would give them to the public in a collected form.

I issue them fully conscious of their many imperfections, but with the hope that they may be somewhat interesting to those who can appreciate the simple and unpretending recital of a sportsman's experience.

"IDSTONE."

Morden Vicarage,
      Near Blandford,
            Dorset.

July 22, 1872.

CONTENTS.

THE IDSTONE PAPERS.

PAPER I.

AGRICULTURAL LABOURERS.

I WAS awoke by the barking of an old fox some winters ago, and, drawing aside the window blinds, looked out into the dark gloom amongst the trees which skirted our village road. The yelping had ceased for some minutes, and my vigilant dogs in the kennel no longer responded to it, nor were they excited by the glimmering light from some lantern which was so dim and uncertain that it failed to show anything of the bearer thereof. It was evidently a common occasion.

As I let the blind fall again, my little forty-shilling clock struck half-past four, and I then understood well enough that the "Jack o' lantern" was a carter going to feed his horses, which were stabled somewhat to the eastward of me.

It set me thinking of the English labourers in general, of their early and late hours, their providence and prodigality, their virtues and their vices. I began to consider how they are represented, say on the stage or by magazine writers; what they appear in the eyes of squire or squireen, especially when he views them through the telescopic lens of a frilled steward. a butler, or his valet—all of whom have very limited views, and the narrowest notions of the bucolic species.

Before I proceed further, let me show that I have a right to be heard. I have lived amongst the labouring classes the greater part of my life. How many years? you say. Well, never mind. During that quarter of a century, more or less, I have frequently acted as their medical adviser, their lawyer, their mediator, and their severe Mentor—the last not often ; I don't like it. In the matter of medicine, if I have done no good I have done little harm, for I use the simplest drugs. I accept as gospel all I read in the "Domestic Medicine," lately published, or in self-evident cases I am guided by the wisdom of a shilling book, which, when I bought my medicine chest, was given in—almanack and all. The only danger is when I am compelled to "exhibit" powders, for I am not very clear about the weights; and as the children have, in former days, made toys of the scales, they are a drachm or two out of square. Yet, as a physician, I am popular; and one of my patients who had eaten too much at a club banquet paid me the highest compliment (after recovery), saying that, "true enough, my doctoring was like hedge carpentering—not *neat-like*, but everlasting strong."

Of all the medicines known, give me those you can guess at, or measure with a spoon, which is much the same thing—Gregory's powder, for example, in which I and my parishioners have the firmest faith. It is not a week ago that one of the stoutest men in my parish (I believe that he exceeds the girth of our largest elm tree by two inches) sent for a dose of my "headache tackle," as he irreverently called it; and the wife, as she held out the bottle (they prefer it ready mixed), said her master hoped I would "*give him a good dollop of it, for he wanted to be cured quick.*"

I had a difficult case some time ago—not the first by several. It was what is here called "hag-rod" (hag-rode), or nightmare. The patient was one of the very ugliest ploughboys I ever saw, and about fifteen or sixteen years old. They told me he was "dying," and, although the messenger had taken her time in coming for me, she desired me to lose no time in going to see her lodger, adding, in a whining voice, "It warn't his body, but his 'sperrit;' and that after supper, when he went to bed, 'the devil played the very wag with un.'"

It is extraordinary what superstitions still obtain amongst our labourers. If one of twins die, and the limbs do not get rigid soon, they will delay the funeral, believing that the dead one is "waiting for the other," and the carelessness of the relatives will occasionally verify the assertion, for the dead one has not long to wait. In their own ailments they have unlimited faith in beer and brandy, and any medicine—even tonics—they believe "makes" them weak.

They look upon the neighbouring magistrate as the embodiment of English law, and are rather fond of "pulling each other up." These quarrels are of a strictly parliamentary kind, nevertheless, and I have frequently seen the plaintiff take the defendant in his cart to a court of justice, and as often bring him back again, or *vice versâ*; whilst the animosity, the swearing, and the conviction, all are buried at the nearest public house.

My legal experience is confined for the most part to the making of wills (agreements or other documents we use none). The few who happen to have a score or two of pounds lend it at "use" or interest without any other than a verbal agreement, and often with no security at all. Generally unforgiving with regard to *assaults*, they are very lax in money matters, and pretty easily defrauded, except the recovery of the sum, or part of it, can be managed for them by the interference of a magistrate. Unless you make a will for them, they are certain to break down, and they have a weakness for letting the testator "sign it," and taking it into other houses for the separate and independent signature of two witnesses as required, generally selecting the man's eldest son, who will be benefited, and a lad of twelve or fourteen years old. I once detected much such a case as this, where the will was, of course, no better than waste paper.

Well, the glimmer of that lantern on a winter's morning determined me to look into the unseen life of these farm labourers, and I set to work. I was not long in discovering the man whose early movements I detected; indeed, I could track him in the snow when I went to my kennel in the morning. I have a fancy for noticing the footprints of all that live in my village, and I can verify the impression made by almost all the men, some of the women and children, and a good many horses and other cattle.

Here I saw the wide, awkward, hobnailed, thick-waisted prints of the old carter's boots, and recognised his wide, lounging, undrilled stride, the outward direction of his toes, and the common practice with those of his genus to tread principally on his heels. I determined to find out from him the course of his daily life, the amount of his family, the hours of his work—to describe faithfully and in an unromantic way what he called "the heft" (the chief points) of his history—one I took notes of as I sat in his cottage, and which with him has ended before I began! I found his home was one of two old cottages which, for economy's sake, were built together, and, picturesque enough for Wilkie or Morland, was nevertheless, like certain whited sepulchres, fairest on the outside, though clean within. There was a small garden or yard, desolate enough in that winter's time, though the margins of it in summer were gay with holly-

hocks, of which he had a famous selection, tastefully arranged
according to their colours, from black to white. He was known
for miles as one of the most celebrated growers of "fancy
pinks" in all the county, so that it was no uncommon thing to
see a smart carriage and bonnets, which set our village in a stir,
stopping with patience until he had returned to set a price upon
some of his new seedlings or old-established favourites. I did
not go to his house by appointment, but dropped in about that
time in the evening when I expected he would have finished his
supper, for just then I have almost always found his class are
most communicative. I need hardly say it was past the hour
known about us as "duckish"—so called because at that precise
time you may indistinctly see, and very easily hear, the rush of
the wildfowl going out to sea, when they pass over you like a
whirl of wind. Indeed, I so contrived it that I got my "flight
shot" just before I "knocked off" for the night ; and as I was
not wet in the feet, I sent home the spaniels, strolled over the
old moor, and took up my station ; gave the flight both barrels,
picked up two and a half couple of ducks (one a mallard), and,
lighting my pipe, sat down as my retriever walked up the swamp
and at last got my cripple. All right : a couple for the home
department, and the other for old Nichols (that was the labourer's
name), whose tracks and lantern I had seen.

He had just finished his supper as I expected, and as he sat
meditating over the fire (he was no smoker) I began to talk to
him about things in general, before I touched upon his department in the farm establishment. It was a large room, with a
chimney corner as big as a small parlour, and a chimney up
which you could have driven a small cart. Looking up it, I
could make out a fine planet and several stars, for the sky was
clear and frosty. Half-way up were two flitches of bacon
"drying," and a pig's "face" or two. A large pot or cauldron
was boiling, or nearly boiling, on the turf fire, which was cheered
up with two sticks to keep the other generally sluggish fuel
blazing. Behind the fire I noticed an iron back, about two and a
half feet square, with the date in raised letters, 1625 ; a floral
cross embossed on the top of it, and surrounded by a "rope
pattern" border. The fuel was kept together by a pair of iron
fire-dogs, which were probably coeval with the fire-back, and
the sides of the corner had been ornamented with Dutch tiles,
giving some Scripture history, the main points whereof were
wanting. A large eight-day clock, a chest of drawers, a kitchen

dresser furnished with six or eight pewter or brass vessels, a bell-metal pot or two, and a row of jugs, filled one side of the room. Esau selling his birthright, and a little table thick with china dogs, glass ornaments, two watch stands, a glass rolling-pin, and a chalk parrot, balanced these first-named articles of furniture; and there were the portraits in black frames of two prodigiously large-eyed spaniels, a bird-cage (empty), and a Dutch oven on the other. The window side was nearly all curtains and geraniums, and the chimneypiece was a mass of brass candlesticks. The bacon rack was as yet occupied with walking sticks, some trimmed, some still in the rough; and amongst them I could see the blue wand which the carter carried as he walked with his club to church upon Whit-Monday.

I found that he had begun life by keeping birds off the corn at seven years of age, "for there was eight of us in family, and bread was terrible dear." What wages he got then he didn't know, but he had none of it. At ten he could "hold plough," but the wooden ploughs with only one wheel dragged him all over the field, and it was hard work he could assure me! Then he had half-a-crown a week, and his mother made his clothes. When his boots got worn in holes it was very hard, and he used to come home with his feet bleeding. At fifteen he had five shillings a week, and in dear times six; but then, especially in summer, he had long hours, from six or even four in the morning until six or eight, or even ten o'clock, because "you see he was with the horses." He remembered how proud he was when he was first made carter. He was about eighteen years old, and from that time until the time I saw him he had been nothing else. So accustomed was he to be up and dressed at four o'clock, that on Sundays he could not lie in bed. In winter he might be a little later, but not much; and "if horses are to look well, the more hours your carter is with them the better." "There is no way of inducing a young tender-gummed horse to eat, or one that has a little overworked himself, like giving him a handful at a time. I sits in the old corn bin and gives 'en a bit each, and talks to 'en (he said), or puts the harness to rights here and there, or anything that is wanted. A carter has always something to do. They work from six to two in summer, from seven to two in winter. Two hours is not too much for them to feed, and between whiles I get my cup of tea. Perhaps I pull up a few minutes at twelve or sooner, and get a bit of bread and cheese, but just as often I don't stop until they come home.

Then I take off their harness, and look round their feet, and sponge out their eyes and 'noses,' and if they are cool enough I take them to the pond to drink. When they come back I tie them up and feed them a little at a time, and cut the chaff if it's winter, or go and cut the vetches or green stuff if it's summer time, and the boy and 1 bring it home. Then what cleaning the stable wants we do it, and keep on attending to them all the while. There's the water to pump into 'our trough,' and different things to do. At six in summer I get my supper, and then I have time to myself generally until nine. I'm almost always too tired to go gardening, and sometimes I have to get water for the missis and fill our pans."

And for this old Nichols got 9s. a week and a house and garden —1l. extra for the harvest month—the carriage home of his fuel, about 2000 of turf, and a couple of hundred faggots. The turf would cost him half-a-crown a thousand, the faggots sixteen shillings a hundred. He would rent enough potato ground at about a sovereign a year. His ready-made suit would cost him a pound a year, and he estimated his clothes at thirty shillings a year, "not reckoning his boots," of which he would require two pairs at fourteen shillings each ; a "slop." or short linen frock, costs five shillings, a shirt three shillings, knee-breeches (cotton cord) twelve shillings, a hat half-a-crown.

At one time six of them had to live upon eighteen shillings a week. His furniture when he first married cost him about five pounds, independent of beds and furniture, which cost five pounds more. His "girls" had nothing until they were fourteen years old, when they went out to service, but they helped to glean corn after harvest. and so brought in several bushels of wheat and barley. As he got on his master raised him a shilling a week, and when he went to a town he was allowed a shilling extra ; but then (he remarked) he had driven thirty-two miles on the road. and several times had his horses in their harness twenty hours out of twenty-four.

"Then you know," his wife joined in, "we were always careful, or we never could have lived. I used to go out to nurse, and make the clothes of other people's children as well as my own. I have been to nurse a poor woman, and at odd times put all their things to rights with my needle, and so I was always out when I could be spared, which was when my daughter was about thirteen."

"Yes," her husband added, "I remember her one time going

AGRICULTURAL LABOURERS. 7

to nurse a woman that kept a lodge gate, and had a number of
things given her, and there was a nice pair of trousers the gentleman had given to her little boy, who was all in rags, on condition that the lazy mother altered them for him, and made them
fit. Of course they were a good deal too large for the little boy,
so what did the lazy body do but cut the legs off the right length ?
and as they were a deal too big behind, she put a skewer through
and tied a string round it, so that when my wife got there he
looked just like a monkey with a tail. You can't help such folks
as them."

"Let's look at the upstairs department," I said, as soon as his
"tale" was ended ; and accordingly we went upstairs. All neat
and pleasant enough ; nothing to complain of in any way. Clean,
well-arranged beds, the carter's suffocating with curtains and
four-posts, which prevented all circulation ; but if he would have
it so, it was not for me to do more than the Oxford proctor did :
"I go my way," he said, "and let the undergraduates go theirs."
Then I asked him whether he had not found two sleeping rooms
too few when he had all those children at home. He owned he
did, but he added : " If I'd had more room I should have taken
lodgers, and so would nearly all of us." And this is my experience. Not long after this conversation with him, he was
"death-struck," as the people called it, in the field—in fact, he
had an attack of paralysis, which carried him off in a few days;
and in my churchyard there lies one more scrupulously honest
man.

My neighbour's horses, under the management of his new
carter, don't look as they did. I don't mean to insinuate that he
sells his horses' corn, or, as he would tell you, " shirks his work ;"
but he has not, like old Nichols, his master's interest at heart.
He is later in the morning. No three or four o'clock for him,
but what he calls " lawful hours." If the horses can't eat their
food in an hour, there must be something the matter with 'em ;
and he can mix up stuff that will make their coats slik (sleek),
and make them eat anything he puts before them.

"What is it ? Well, some of it's vitriol, and there's butter of
antimony in it, and arsenic, and lots of things. He gave an old
carter a shilling for it," and so on.

He doesn't " hold with " feeding a little at a time. It's best
to give 'em what you mean to give 'em, and lock 'em up for the
night ; and if there's any left, or all left, leave it there till they
do eat it. He also keeps his horses "short of water," saying

there is no "proof" (nutriment) in water, adding that to drink water only for a week would kill *him*.

And yet this "hawbuck," who can give you ten thousand reasons for every ignorant, selfish action of his, had ten times the education of poor old Nichols, who could only throw his weekly earnings into his wife's lap every Saturday night, and leave her to make the best of it; but whose arithmetic carried him no further than to tell what he paid for turnpikes three months after paying them ; and this was rather to be considered a feat of memory observable in the illiterate, who have a remarkable storehouse for trifles. " It is well on some accounts that a man should not read or write," one of my ex-dog-breakers once told me. " If you've book knowledge, you've so many things on your mind you gets confused. Now," he went on (pointing to his third waistcoat button with his finger), " I knows nothing in the whole world but dog breaking and making ' bee pots ' (beehives), and so I'm never at a loss."   Certainly, with old Nichols his team—I may say his *teams,* for he had the supervision of all the horses— well, his horses were everything to him, his newspapers, his club, his pipe, and his pocket money. I drew this out of him. He said he was ashamed to own it, that was true ; but he was more *hurt* when master's roan colt died than if he had lost one of his children. " I was," he said, "so took up with him ; such a pair of shoulders he had ! and such a back and *line!* (loin). He was murdered too, that colt was, sir. He fell into a ditch, and I wasn't there. Well, they took down a horse to pull him out, and the boys put the cart rope round his head, and pulled him out so rough that he died a few minutes after on the bank. I wouldn't have had it happen," said poor old Nichols, looking round for some means of expressing his bereavement, " I wouldn't have had it happen *for a shilling.* When did it happen, sir ?—well, my wife can tell you ; she wrote it down in our family register ; oh, I remember, two days before Candlemas !"

PAPER II.

THE ROUGH RIDER.

"Davis," I said, as I crossed my stable-yard the last day but one in November, "I want to know where to find 'The Three Pigeons.'"

"Either," said Davis (who was a London groom), as he touched his forehead respectfully with one finger, " either, sir, in Stratford Green or Bermondsey."

"Nonsense," I replied, "I mean the place where the hounds meet to-morrow ; and you had better go and ask."

However, all attempts to discover the locality proved unavailing, when I thought of sending for old Bertie. " Thirteen miles, sir, from here," he informed me, as he came up at a quick walk, " and not very easy place to find ; a good deal of it is crosscountry road and over the Downs. When you get to the crossroads you take the turn to the left, and then you go straight five miles good, and then "—

Oh ! " I said, " I am inclined no give it up, for I am sure I should never find my way, with my ignorance of the country and all landmarks. Is there anyone going from here, Bertie ? "

" No," he said, as he lifted his hat to rub his forehead, and looked thoughtfully upon the gravel, " unless Enoch's agoing. I can go and see, if you like, sir."

" And who is Enoch ? " I asked, for I had never heard of this celebrity.

" Well, said Bertie, " he's a rough rider, we call him, or a horse-breaker, or whatever it is. He always is riding the young hunters and making 'em handy in the season, and he's got a ' body break,' and uses horses to harness and the road, and such like. His cottage is not more than a half mile away."

" Well, Bertie," I replied, " let us go and see, for perhaps he will pilot me to 'The Three Pigeons,' and if he cannot I must puzzle it out myself somehow."

If the " meet" was difficult to find, Enoch's home was not, for a straight road with heather on each side, and now and then a clump of magnificent hollies, soon brought us to a neat stone

cottage, flanked by a longish stable and coach-house, at the gable
ends of which buildings I observed apricot trees trained with
skill, forming the southern boundary to as neat a kitchen garden
as it has been my lot to see. A "hard lad," his hair cut exceedingly short, and with trousers very tight and wrinkled, was
sponging a harness at the saddle-room door, and seeing us walking up the path he left his work to call his father—for so he
proved to be—who nodded to Bertie with the familiarity of an
old acquaintance, and touched his hat to me.

He might have been any age, from twenty-eight to fifty,
judging from his face, which had a slightly gladiator cast of
feature, relieved by a good tempered expression. The cheek
bones high, the eyes small, black, bright, and restless; the nose
rather aquiline, the lips thin and compressed, the chin large and
close shaven; he gave you the notion of a resolute, bold, determined man, who had his passions thoroughly under control,
whilst his manners were a sort of compromise between the stable
and the parlour; and, without affecting any familiarity, he
seemed as much at ease with strangers as I eventually found him
in the saddle. He had powerful arms, thin, clean limbs, and a
longish back in proportion to his height. " On land " he did not
appear quite to advantage, and he walked, so Bertie said, " as if
he was hobbled."

I soon told him the purport of our visit, which he expressed
himself as most ready to carry out; and briskly opening the
stable door, he said, " Perhaps you would like to walk in and just
see the horses, sir ;" adding parenthetically, "*perfectly* quiet, sir ;
and we have no secrets. as the racing men pretend they have. I
remember once, sir," he continued, " a gentleman as owned a
celebrated racehorse told me to call at his trainer's as I went by,
and to ask how he was going on. So I called at the house and gave
the gentleman's card, and I says my message. The trainer—a
very fat man he was—he looks at the card and held it out at
arm's length ; but I don't *think* he could read it, between you
and I, sir ; and he says to me, ' The horse is very well,' he said,
' but I couldn't let you see him,' he says, ' for forty pounds ; and
if the gentleman came himself I shouldn't wish him to see him for
another ten days or a fortnight, and you may tell him so *from
me*,' he says very loud. ' I'll be sure to give your message, sir,'
I says to the trainer, ' but at the same time,' I says, as I stepped
into my dog-cart. ' I know something of racing stables, and at a
second rate establishment I should feel pretty confident that for a

£5 note I could see any horse in it, or, if I particularly wished it, that I could drive him in a gig.' Here's a nice young horse, sir," he added, as he stripped a dark bay thorough-bred and let his head down; "a hardy constitutioned horse, and no day too long. I shall ride him to morrow, if we find at once; and, if not, I shall ride the black one, or he may be a little too much for my boy—he's hot, terrible hot with hounds."

Besides these two I saw a very smart harness-horse—an iron-grey—and a weight carrier which had just arrived : and having reviewed the merits of these animals one after the other, we accepted Enoch's invitation to walk into his parlour ; and a very neat tidy parlour it was. Over the mantelpiece hung Landseer's white pony and Newfoundland, the dog holding whip and bridle in his mouth. and two or more foxes' heads, well preserved, were suspended around the wall. A box of cigars, a new silver-mounted hunting-whip, and one or two blackthorn gig-whips, evidently kept for high days and holidays, were tokens that he had given satisfaction to his employers. He showed us his "curiosities" one after another with great good nature. Of some he was not a little proud. One of them was a stirrup-iron bent almost into a figure of eight. of which he remarked : " I was riding a young horse. and a Oxford gent let a gate fall back in his face. He plunged and caught the stirrup-iron in or on the gate-hook, and bent it like that. My foot came out at the very moment, and I wasn't hurt a bit." "Here's a curious thing." he said as he showed us a piece of wood nearly as thick as a wine cork, and twice as long ; "this was taken out of a grey mare's hock, after it had quite healed, and she had hunted the whole season. She used to go a little stiff at first, and then it wore off. She belonged to Joe Symonds, at Oxford, and one day old Wilde, the vet., was looking at her, and he says, 'Wot's this 'ere!' so he out with his knife and cut the skin and pulled out this plug." "But this." he said, "I value most of all the things I have." showing me a little gold locket. containing a lock of the red chesnut mane of Eclipse. "That," he said, "there is no doubt about. You can see the inscription on it. and I don't know of anyone that has any except me ; but the lash of the challenge whip at Newmarket is made of Eclipse's tail they say, as well as the wrist-string. Here's a picture of the old horse, too. with his white leg behind, going with his nose close to the ground and his head loose ; and the writin' at the bottom says he was never flogged, nor spurred, and also that he was a roarer. However, he was the making of Kelly, his owner, and some horses ruins their masters!"

With the exception of some bone of a horse's neck, which by the aid of a little ink judiciously applied he believed he had made to resemble a monk preaching, we had exhausted his stock of curiosities, all of which Bertie had seen many a time before, and, as he afterwards told me, with a different tale each time; but this he owned was only said to vex Enoch, and nothing did it so effectually.

I now entered into arrangements for "The Three Pigeons" and the next day's hunting. These were that Enoch should drive me over in his dog-cart, and that his son should ride the young horse to the meet in company with my groom. "That," said Enoch, "will be a good thing for me, because my young horse is a bit rusty at leaving the stable, and he will start very well with company."

Accordingly, next morning Enoch appeared, punctual to his time, in a high cart with a brown harness, and a very promising young animal between the shafts. The height of the vehicle would have prevented much damage from light heels, in all probability, but to make sure a very strong kicking strap passed over the horse's hind quarters close to the root of the tail, and I also observed a sort of rope breeching, which did not come into operation unless the horse lashed out, when it stopped the action of the kicker in a most wonderful manner, or, as Enoch called it, "nipped vice in the bud."

I got up gently into the cart, and Enoch chirruped in a low tone once or twice, but the youngster did not feel inclined to start; upon which he dropped the reins, and his youngest boy, who stood by the horse without touching him, put his hand upon the shaft and patted his neck gently once or twice; the only return for this on the part of the four-year-old being that he tossed his head and viciously blew his nose. Perhaps two or three minutes were thus consumed, when Enoch's second signal was more successful, and after two or three slight plunges he sailed away with magnificent action, something like that of the red deer as he crosses the boulders of a "forest."

"I find that," said Enoch, "so much better than wrestling with them; and after a few minutes they get ashamed of themselves."

We met with no adventures (beyond a wish on the horse's part to cut corners, and one or two narrow escapes of a bolt, owing to some carters cracking their whips as we passed their teams) until we were within a couple of miles of our destination, when, as the Trapper did not go well up to his bit, Enoch dropped him a couple of consecutive sharp cuts down his shoulder, which made him shake himself together.

This is exactly the point in which servants fail ; they let a young horse *slouch* when a trifle weary, and imperil his action or even his safety at once.

We now began to pass the various members of the hunt who were riding to the meet, but in the distance saw a four-in-hand and a very light and graceful mail phaeton. Before we reached either of these vehicles we overtook young Enoch on the black blood horse, in company with my man and horse, and we pulled up to give the young one a wide berth, so that I had a good opportunity of seeing the firm neat seat of the breaker's son, who, hands well down and his back a little hollow, let his nag play and jump a bit without any interference until we were almost out of sight.

" Sending on is a great thing, depend on it," said Mr. Enoch. " The only time I was near fighting was about sending horses to covert. I was bred up in a racing stable, and the trainer I was apprenticed to would have no swearing nor fighting. We used to all go to morning church ever so many times a week, and wear these surplices and sing in the choir, and do whatever the parson liked ; for our trainer and he were great folks, and a piece of his land cut right through our *run in*, and I've heard master say that though he was a clergyman he was as good a judge of when a horse was fit and all that as anyone he ever knew out of the profession. And being in such good company of course we all was respectable, and had evening school, and singing classes, and all sorts ; but fighting wasn't taught, and no swearing allowed. Well, after I left this place, I took to riding young hunters, and married and came into that cottage I live in and a few pounds besides ; and I was up at our squire's on one of the young ones, when the old squire and a great long gentleman came out to look through the stables, and a Catholic priest was with them—as good a man and as good a rider as anyone, let his religion be what it may. The great long gentleman's groom was half asleep and three parts drunk when they got to the stable-door ; but he jumped up from the corn-bin, and made believe he'd been at work for his life, instead of making everybody do his work, and abusing them afterwards ; and he turned over his master's horse for the priest to look at. ' Aye,' said his reverence, ' a rare good one, too, for a heavy man ; but my little blood mare will show you the way to-morrow for all that. I only wish that I could send her on.' 'If master don't mind,' said the groom, 'I can lead her on for you, sir,' and so it was settled. I saw a few words passed between master and man, but I did not know what the plot was till next day. I knew they had sixteen miles to go to covert, and so I got up very early to walk on, meaning to lead my horse a good bit of the way and take my time."

"Well, perhaps I had got about two miles, when I saw this great fat rascal riding the poor little blood mare and coming along at a good trot, pulling his master's great sixteen-hand horse behind him; the poor little mare warping and twisting under him, and strained all to pieces. It wasn't my business, you'll say, but I took a share in the concern at once, and as soon as he came up I said, 'You get off that mare directly, Mr. Yorkshire-man, and ride your master's.' He gave me some of his sauce and was very liberal in bad language, but when I rode up alongside of him and shook my hunting crop over him—for I was riding a big vicious thorough-bred Birdcatcher chestnut, and could look right down on him—he gave it up, and I took the mare away from him and led her myself. He was a *mock teetotaller*, the worst of all impostors; and a week after he tried to give me a thrashing for my interference, but found he was no use, I could walk round him like a cooper tightening the hoops of a cask. His master found him out at last. He shared the corn with the horses, but took the biggest half himself."

By this time we had reached "The Three Pigeons," whereat were assembled twenty or thirty hunters and servants) whilst the hounds, huntsman, and whips were under an old oak on a green hill about two hundred yards beyond, surrounded by a "field" of perhaps fifty or sixty, and twice that number of pedestrians; in the midst of whom I saw a carriage or two, and an old gentle-man on a clever pony, who they told me had kept hounds for over fifty years at his own expense.

There were plenty to help Enoch get his young horse clear of the shafts, and to wash his feet and make him comfortable; and, as many hands make light work, he had his nag all right in the stable, and was able to refresh himself somewhat, before his boy appeared in company with my groom.

Very shortly there was a general move, and we were proceeding at a leisurely pace to the first covert, which was at the back of this old and well-known hostelry, formerly the residence of what

Enoch called " these 'ere Catholics." To all appearance it had been a monastery, or one of those offshoots to a religious house which you so often see diverted from the original purpose of its founder.

As I settled myself in my saddle and signalled Enoch to come as near to me as the restless eye and "skittishness" of his "young 'un" warranted, I made the few observations I have jotted down ; but, a stranger amongst this very large "field." I desired to gain some information as to the names and characters of the various men who were bent upon the same errand as myself.

" Who is that on the grey, Enoch, with the patent boots and the large cigar in front of him ?" I asked, as a youngster. almost all nose, and with anything but a good seat, thrust forward through the muddy lane as though the fox had broken. " Some-body's nephew, Sir," said the rough rider, as soon as he could steady himself, for the young one was " raking" at the bit, and trying to jam himself between the two men in front of us (men it wouldn't do to ruffle, for they wore the button and subscribed).

" That." said my companion, as he put his forefinger to his black felt hat, the movement making the horse he rode wince again, "that's some midshipman, sir. He's at most meets, but no deaths. That's 'Will o' the Wisp' just afore you," pointing to a chesnut, " gridironed all over for spavin. curb, ringbone, and clap of the back sinews ; but, for all that, a difficult horse to catch with the M.P. up." Then we had the whole life of the ex-M.F. on the clever pony. given spasmodically ; for the clatter of the horses' heels in this narrow lane, and the constant thrusting for-ward of some lad just off the shop-board, gave Enoch enough to do, so that his biography was something of this kind :

" Woo, now—he's had four wives—quiet with you—and buried three of them—come up. hoss—and this last, they tell me, she likes a drop—I must alter my curb chain about one link—there's the horn ! I do believe. sir. they've found—yes, there they go—no—yes—back again. out t'other side. That midshipman's headed the fox—that's all he ever does. Gone away ; I thought so ; I see the master take off his hat ;" and letting his horse, who had been going all this time on his hind legs. have his head a bit, the rough rider touched his hat to me, and for the present I saw him no more.

As I got on to secure a good place, I noticed the middy's horse loose, and the patent leathers higher than their owner's head, much begrimed with mud, his hat as wrinkled as my top boots and just after I came to grief myself. "What are all these fellows halloaing to me for?" said I, as I went at a very negotiable hedge and ditch this side.

I knew the next second, for I jumped flop into a bog.

Up to the girths in mud and ooze, the cold water filtering through your boots, and your horse changed suddenly into a walrus, and getting, by his vain plunges, deeper into the mire, is a trying change for any man who has just left his hotel without speck or blemish, expecting to sail away and take a line of his own.

How I got out I don't know to this day; but, escape I did, and I was at once surrounded by half-a-dozen of those pedestrians who couldn't run.

One of these Samaritans—an exceedingly "high blower"—at once extemporised wisps from the rushes, which he cut with his knife, and commenced grooming my boots and knees with the hissing sound peculiar to his calling, which, from his complexion I at once perceived to be that of a tipsy "odd man," or helper. Two or three merely stared at my muddy hunter, and took no part, until one of the number, who possessed the sense of the whole meeting, appeared with a cart rope borrowed at the inn, and made a noose at one end of it, which even Mr. Calcraft would have commended.

When this catastrophe occurred I had seen very little of boggy land. I have learnt since to discover it at a glance. I find that any horse well used to the moorland will avoid those bright green patches of short moss which, to the unpractised eye, look so substantial; and that nothing will induce a heath-bred pony, known as a "heath cropper," to set his foot upon that tough but quakeing fibrous peaty carpet, on which I can walk up snipe or widgeon with impunity, although the vibration, as I stop suddenly, is apt to disturb my aim.

To the clump of rustics who prepared to extricate my nag, a stranger's horse in a swamp was no new thing. The chief difficulty, a groom (who had joined us from the "Three Pigeons") told me, was "to get his 'ead round the right way, 'cause," he added, "you see, sir, his feet haven't got no purchase." When this was accomplished it was not long before he was on firm ground again, and, though shaking nervously and much begrimed, little if at all the worse.

I had scarcely distributed some loose silver and remounted— not knowing, I confess it, which way to go—when I thought I heard the horn ; and at the same time I observed a move in the cluster of pedestrians, who had not lost sight of the hounds, or the scarlet welter-weights which hang on the skirts of most hounds when running. Yes, there, a mile away, I catch sight of the huntsman, conspicuous in the bright gleam of sunshine through which he is passing at the moment, in his scarlet, which contrasts forcibly with his old white horse ; and, black and saffron and white spots, all around him are the celebrated lady pack—the descendants of Jasper, Duster, Furrier, Comus, Trojan, and old Hercules. As I make out so much, huntsman and hounds mount a knoll or hill, and, with the light strong on them, their forms stand out clear and sharp against the dull and rainy sky ; the pinks soon show behind them in little groups ; and, as I turn to get to them, I meet at a bend in the sandy track the second whip coming along at a smart canter upon a blood chesnut with a vicious eye—he is a wiry, thin, beetle-browed lad. To all appearance a well-suited pair are horse and man ; a fellow with not many words to spare, and those few he throws out at me as he goes on without turning his head, or noticing, as it seems to me, that I had come to grief.

They say a fellow-feeling makes us wondrous kind. But it has no effect on him. I can see he has had a nasty fall, for his head is cut, and his " hoss," as he calls him, is stained with mud like mine. " Goin' to the Decoy," he blurts out, as he breaks out of the track for me, and rides over the moor where ruts and anthills are hidden by the long grass and heather, pulling up on the crest of another barrow, whence he could command a view of the old decoy, as I imagined—and I was right.

I had not gone far, leaving this disciple of La Trappe to quarrel with his vicious horse alone, when I came upon the rough rider, who had turned to look for me. I could not ride very near him, for his young pupil was full of excitement, and, with his "nostril all wide " and every vein showing, required the best of hands and a good balance, especially as his head was now just turned away from the hounds.

" We only had fifteen minutes," the rough rider told me, "when some shepherd and his dog headed him, and he ran into a little copse, where they mobbed him to death. Now they are going to draw the decoy out in the heath yonder, among those little oaks and alders, and one horse here is as good as another. Nothing for this country," he added, " like a pony bred on it ; they never fall down among the ruts, and know the safe ground as well as

C

you do." He might have said much better, for I had just made
my first acquaintance with the softest place in the country ; and,
as I now know, about a pole further on there was mud enough to
bury a load of hay.

The Decoy has always been a favourite meet. On this heath
you always get a scent, let the weather or state of the atmosphere be what they may. I suppose the fox brushes against the
heather and leaves his fragrance upon the stems ; at any rate,
hounds can always run there breast high. Nor have I ever
known that decoy drawn blank. Wet as the ground is, there is
grand lying for a fox on the grass hassocks, which stand on firm
stems a foot and more in breadth, three, four, and five feet high,
supporting a bed of long grass a yard in diameter or more.

These strange vegetable productions are the resort of many a
wild animal or bird, and when they grow close together, or so
near that the fox can jump from one to another of them as they
stand high and dry above the flooded swamp, they are admirably
suited for his protection. Here he listens for the faintest splash,
and, selecting as he does the highest and thickest for his siesta,
he can lie *perdu*, and steal away upon the first alarm of hound or
horn. Upon this occasion we caught him napping, and, under
the guidance of my friend the rough rider, I was able to get a
very good view of the draw and find.

We got to our post of observation long before the hounds,
who with their huntsman, had a considerable circuit to make
that they might escape some treacherous ground, and, by crossing
ten or a dozen hunting bridges made of rude fir poles and sods,
reach the inner circuit of this old-established preserve of
wildfowl. Before they passed the last bridge the sky was alive
with ducks, which whirled over our heads, swept into the fen and
out of it, whistled among the yellow reeds, and presently were off
in shoals towards the seaboard and harbour, far beyond the range
of any shoulder gun.

The teal did not take the alarm until the hounds were waved
in and they heard the huntsman speaking ; nor, I think, did they
all get up until they actually saw him over the screens, and his
red coat was reflected in the still water. Then they rose in
separate bodies of three or more sections, and, flying low, swept
the pond from end to end ; not like the ducks getting up high in
the air, though, but keeping within shot sometimes for a minute
or more together. A couple of ducks or so would now and then
join company with the teal and widgeon, which last would settle

outside the decoy, two or three score together, until a hound drawing close to them would put them up again.

It was a sight worth seeing, that cold, dull, hungry-looking heath, holding the lonely decoy aloof from all that could disturb it, awakened by the crack of the whip, the splashing of the hounds, and the musical voice of the master ; whilst the little groups of scarlet and the various-coloured horses sprinkled about, made a picture which Davis, brother to the late royal huntsman, appreciated and painted well.

Close to us sat a plethoric country gentleman, very purple in the face, weighing perhaps twenty stone, who kindly described to me the various landmarks, and especially the point the fox would steal off for, unless he made for the squire's park ; " and to prevent that you see, the master has put a whip on that barrow to head him back." I should have learnt a good deal more from him, but that just now the midshipman came floundering to us at a gallop—his horse very nearly done, as he had been " bucketing " him whilst the hounds were drawing, and yet he would not let the poor brute stand still one moment, or, if he did, was striking him on the head, wrenching his mouth, or trying with his short legs to spur him ; but here Providence interfered, for his little fat legs scarcely came below the saddle-flaps.

" I can't think what's the matter with the brute," said the little " salt," hoping to attract attention to his equitation. " Why," said the country squire (scarcely turning his head to look at him), " I should think he's like Billy Butler's horse, going to have an ' F I T.' " I did not hear the rejoinder, for just then, at my feet as it were, there was a rustle amongst the long grass, and a fine dog fox, ears close to his poll, stole away, his long brush scarce distinguishable from the ground ; and, as in a few yards he reached the bare short grass and peaty land, he put on the steam and trusted to his foot.

Just then the whole pack opened, and were on the line like lightning, " No use to ride here," said my fat friend ; " you'll see it all if you keep with me." I thought of what Jem Hill said of men who can't ride. " They are," he used to tell us, " the most affablest men as is." Whatever twenty stone thought of not riding, there were numbers of a very different opinion. Here comes a lady on a dark brown mare nothing can stop, though she makes no fuss about it, and never talks of hunting. " The very best hands in England !" says the rough rider, as she puts the mare at a bank and goes along in about the best place for choice. "There's a lawyer as used to always want to put her life in the leases when she was first married, thinking she'd be killed and make him another job; but he's given it up as a bad speculation, and picked out a consumptive family for his lives now. That's him," he added, "with a glass in his eye, atop of the dark bay roarer, with a boot on each hind fetlock." And now we wended on together. I own it, in fear and trembling, for a fog was coming on; and to be *fogged and bogged* was anything but a pleasant prospect. One moment we were crossing a turnpike road, the next breasting a hill, then going down a valley; and all these varieties of ground occurred in semi-darkness.

Occasionally the fog would lift, and my pilot, listening a moment, would turn sharp right or left, and we were close to the ruck again. The way we got over banks and "grips"—there were no big places hitherto—was quite a lesson to me. He seemed to let the young horse go how he liked, only stipulating that *go he must*. This was the rough rider's *sine quá non*. "No surrender—go somewhere; plenty of time to do it, only no turning." "In or over!" he said, as we could see in the distance a moderately wide brook brim full, and sent the young 'un at it forty miles an hour. "Over it is!" I heard him say to himself as he landed on the other side; and just then we heard "Whowhoop!" The lady and dark brown mare were up, so was the master, and presently the middy at little over a walk, his poor nag sobbing audibly. Then one of the rough-riding fraternity, on a colt (he was little more) well known as the worst of buck-jumpers, who had broken more girths than any horse in the county. When I saw him he had a double girth, another above that, one long girth round the saddle and breastplate, and, if I forget not, a crupper also.

After they had broken up the fox, we joined a company, and as we rode back to the Three Pigeons, these girths and the tackle the buck-jumper wore were the text for a homily from Enoch, who tried to describe to us a girth he had at home which a brother of his sent him from Australia, "made, you understand, a-purpose for these buck-jumpers, or what you call 'em. It is made of brown leather, plaited into thongs. It's a double girth, and each girth has four thongs of three braids each: that's eight thongs, and twenty-four strands, each thong as stout as the lower part of a hunting whip. When you girths up the horse, it isn't only that you gets so much strength, but each thong gets bedded in the hair, and the buck-jumper can't get his saddle forward, and with a breastplate he can't move it backwards, and if you can hold on he's beat." Although he proffered the use of it to the rider of the buck-jumper, it met with no response, except some objection on the score of new-fangled notions, and the assertion that "they foreigners knew nothing, and was full of falseness ;" with which fling at anything and everything not English-born the buck-jumper turned down a lane, and a few moments brought us to the inn. One glass of ale apiece, and Enoch's trapper was set agoing, and well in his stride for home.

PAPER III.

THE FIRST OF MAY.

FORMERLY I used to break my own dogs, and I was rewarded for my trouble and hard work; for dogs, as a rule, perform best with the man who made them.

Given strength, activity, and patience, and plenty of ground and game, and I know no healthier or more interesting occupation; and several times my good friend, the Doctor, has pulled up by the side of the quickset just breaking into leaf, to watch my young team backing and standing; and let me observe (as I walked from one dog to the other, giving a word of caution to one, or commendation to another, and holding up the cat o' nine tails to one a little inclined to creep in) a sort of simulated despondency appeared in his countenance at the prospect of no professional call—for some time, at any rate

When the season came to a close, as all pleasant times do, I use to watch the birds and rejoice to see them pair. Then I took as keen an interest in the green wheat and clovers as the most energetic farmer, and used to dream at night that there was plenty of "holding" for the birds, moist ground, and a burning scent. A little cloudy the sky used to be generally in these dreams, and a fine breeze, fresh, but neither cold nor warm; and some old favourite pointer or setter performed again, which I woke up to know had long turned to dust again beneath the ribstone pippin trees in my grassy orchard!

Old Belle, out of the famous Staffordshire Queen (the Edge breed of pointers, dark liver and white), who, in form, and goodness and grandeur, and style of going, equalled her glorious mother, has often reappeared to me, and here is her history.

She was sent from Staffordshire, a young thing full of life and sense. Better than a gift she came to me, if possible, for my friend Mr. Henry Meir, of Tunstall, the owner of Queen, who knew how I admired his team, and Queen most of all, put so moderate a price upon her that he just tried to make me think I was under no obligation to him; but there were men I think then, and certainly there are now, who would have given the price of a covert hack apiece for all the litter.

I had a speckled pointer (Julie) with a liver head, of which I had a very high opinion until Belle came ; but, when Edge's blood stood by the side of that Berkshire one, there was as much difference as a connoisseur would discover (though I should not) between "20 port" and rough Worcestershire cider.

When I had got each separately to range to hand, I put them together, and for two days, from emulation, they ran up everything. although separately each seemed "coming." The third day I had hopes, for I was determined to fag them down by sheer walking. and neither seemed in peril of going wide ; and as I came back and got my brace to point and back for the first time, I own that I felt a pang as I reflected that the next day was Sunday.

That day of rest upset everything ; they came pretty well to whistle on the Monday, and crossed each other merrily, but after four hours' work I could do nothing with them, so I went in to lunch and then I set off again.

If I took one out alone, I could handle her pretty well, but the other would be getting fresh meanwhile ; and I had got nearly half a mile from my cottage wicket when I thought of a new plan. I therefore returned, and told my man to let Julie follow him briskly four miles along the sea-shore, then to come back and meet me at a wheat-field I pointed out ; and Belle and I worked our way towards it, and got some good steady points, and two or three grand ones too.

It was a hot, or rather a close, afternoon on that fourteenth of March. and the Staffordshire pointer began to go much slower, though she still quartered and carried a high head, and her stern was full of action. I was just beginning to think I might stroll along two miles an hour and yet kept up with her, when she gave a short turn, and with her eyes dilated and nostrils all wide, up went the flag. and she drew herself together in as fine form as ever warmed a sculptor's heart.

I stood and looked at her with much pride and satisfaction, and, raising the whip. began to talk to her and caution her to be steady. for I caught sight of a form, and a hare in it, twenty or thirty yards ahead.

Gradually, I was able to get up to her, and, as Rarey would have said, to "gentle" her, and whilst I patted her I slipped the spring swivel of my check cord into the D link of her collar, and, giving her about twenty or thirty yards of line, I stamped, or rather trode in the peg. I then walked round (very cautiously, I admit), with my eye still on her, and very quietly put up the hare.

"Ho! 'ware hare, Belle!" but all of no use. She shot after puss with a plunge that would not have disgraced a "Bedlamite," and nearly as soon was brought up all standing. I took her back, and, though I didn't like to do it, I gave her half a dozen strokes. After well rating her and taking off the line I let her hold up again. No sulks with that breed: she made three turns as lively and cheerful as though we had not been on bad terms, and all at once, in the middle of her fourth turn, she dropped from her light, airy gallop to a walk, and in three paces pulled up close to some deep old rushes and looked at me over her shoulder, and then with her mouth half open seemed to champ the scent. The same routine again; but this time I went more carelessly up to her, as if I knew she could not do wrong, to give her confidence, and I again slipped on my line and pegged it, upon which she dropped somewhat reproachfully, and I went on to put up what I felt certain must be a hare, although I can't tell how I knew it. Before I did this I stood between Belle and the game, and very slightly menaced her with the whip held up, and then, as I carefully trod the clumps of rushes, I was full of misgivings lest it should be a mistake. Not so Belle; for whilst my attention was thus occupied, she had crept on, and was standing in as good form as ever close behind me.

I gave her a slight stripe for "creeping," and put her back, and as soon as I left her she stood again, not quite so grandly this time, but yet well; and exactly where I took her back from —at any rate, in that line—up jumped the hare. "Wo, ho, Belle!" and down she dropped as though I had shot her; and now I had but to go and caution her and praise her in the same breath.

We found four hares after Julie came, and the first they chased together to the fence, when Belle caught it pretty warmly, and Julie, who got a throw up from the peg and trace into the bargain, felt the weight of my man's arm, and required it twice more that day. By the time it was almost too dark to see I had them both pretty well in hand; and as I put my feet up on the mantelpiece that night in my bachelor's home I felt that my hard work was not thrown away.

It is the rule of barbarous nations when they have an opponent down to keep him there; and this is a good maxim for the breaker. So next morning I was up betimes to get a clear four hours, then luncheon, then professional duties in the prime of the day, and a hard two or three hours in the evening; for dog breaking is not light work, and can't be neglected at the critical moment.

After the second day I had no trouble with Belle, and little with Julie, although she would, it is true, occasionally follow a hare a few yards—an offence I always met red-handed; for I knew she would never blink her birds—a base act that baffles a breaker more than anything.

At the end of March my dogs required simply a walk three days a week, and in the beginning of May, I could have sold them for Norway for a pretty handsome sum, and a worthless brace of shy pointers would have been thrown in; but I expected an old acquaintance who liked good dogs, and the first day we were on the moors together, he told me as we rode home that they were quite as perfect a brace as he had seen for twenty years.

Soon after, by great good luck, I recovered a black-tan strain of setters which I had lost for years, and next spring found me with four brace, which gave promise of furnishing me with many a night's rest of one long sleep and an appetite for breakfast; and when my old friend the Doctor heard them wailing and racing round the yard in February, he told me his spirits sank within him, for he knew there would be no "pills and draughts, as before," for "Idstone" *that year.*

"Urgent private affairs"—of which we heard so much years ago, and which really meant so little—prevented my giving so much time to dog breaking as in former springs, and I took out with rather a heavy heart what I thought the best combination of beauty, pluck, and intelligence. I could hear of no breaker worth his salt. One poor old fellow offered his services, but he had some heart disease and could not walk, therefore he depended on lead collars and heavy chains. The first of these I allow are useful, as equalising *pace;* but give me the man who can walk his dogs down. I was hard at work with this No. 1 pack of Gordons, as people call them (though for that matter they might as well, or better, call them "Elwes' setters," for the old miser Elwes had them, and one used to hunt every field as his master rode to London; afterwards the breed came, in 1795, into the possession of Mr. Pinfold, of Thaxted, in Essex.)

Well, I was hard at work with this brace, which were driving
everything out of the field, and I had just made up my mind
they required no encouragement to hunt, and would do, when I
observed a tall man with a red face watching me with curiosity
as he stood upon the step of a rough wooden stile.

" Think they'll do, sir?" he said, touching his hat as I got
near him and saw that he had but one eye, a rather heavy whip,
a whistle at his waistcoat button, and three or four pointers and
setters with puzzle pegs in their mouths. "I suppose, sir, you
don't want to put out any of your dogs to break," he continued ;
" but I have room for three or four dogs, if you like to let me
have them, sir."

As this was exactly what I did want, I whistled up my two
boys, whom I hired for a shilling a day to walk by the hedge
sides and turn the dogs to me—a course I prefer to "pulling
them" to the whistle (by the way, they ought to learn to come
to whistle before their breaking begins)—and turned for home
with my new acquaintance. I very soon saw enough to convince
me that my blunt, honest, good-tempered dog-breaker knew his
business. I let him take a brace that evening, and in a week he
had the others. For some years he has broken all my setters
and pointers, and as long as he can do it I want no better hand.

It takes a good breaker to make a good dog ; and when you
have a difficult temper to deal with you want genius as well as
patience. Two men have this pointer and setter creating
genius to my knowledge, I mean Bishop and Jim Shave ; and
Adams, of Wardour Castle, in his day, was perhaps as good as
either. I have had scores broken by Jim Shave--good, bad,
and indifferent ; but when there was a fault, it was in the dog,
not in the man.

I have seen Bishop's education of a dog ; and I believe
what can be done with a dog he does. This I said long ago,
when I recommended a friend of mind to entrust a dog of my
breeding, and as good as any I ever did breed, to this Scotch
keeper for a little drill and practice.

Ever since Jim has broken for me I have taken very little
trouble with my dogs ; simply they follow me about the road.
go back with my feeder through the fields to breakfast and
dinner in squads of four or five, are broken off sheep if they
incline that way, and are kept clean and well exercised from day
to day.

If I have a favourite dog, or even a favourite brace, I enter

them or finish them ; and (sad as it may sound to those who are
nice about the law) I even knock down an old cock bird to a
young novice before the season, rather than spoil his temper by
disappointment.

Every year, about the first of May, I go to see the youngsters
when they are as far completed as may be, and have to wait till
the end of July for those finishing lessons which are supposed
to turn them out complete and educated for the hills.

Passionately fond of the gun, and everything with the name
of sport, I care nothing for gun or guns unless dogs go with me ;
and had I the choice of guns and no dogs, or dogs and no guns,
I at once take the latter conditions, and enjoy the walk.

So thoroughly do two friends and neighbours share in these
feelings, that we look forward to this annual holiday, I verily
believe, for weeks ; and Jim (an enthusiastic lover of the high
style of shooting)—" *dree* (three) *dogs or nothing to see*"—dates the
birth of his calves, the marriage of his sons or daughter, the
grafting of his apple trees, and, I think, the death of one or two
relatives, from the " weeks before or after *the gentlemen come
down.*"

Perhaps in the middle of his breaking, some accident may
happen to his "fore man"—the steady dog which leads the
youngsters, finds birds for them, and lets them pass him, or
teaches them to back ; or he wants to consult with me on some
point where two heads are better than one ; and then we have an
hour's walk and a bit of breaking, which I much enjoy ; but, for
my part, I can rely upon my breaker, and when he says he is
ready for us, we know that there will be something to see.

Last week I was not surprised at receiving the annual summons,
and the last first of May we met at the breaker's house. We had
plenty of time to look over the various pupils chained up in his
large orchard to kennels, casks, and thatched hurdles, before we
took out the first team.

There were good, bad, and indifferent. We unbuckled them
and went up the hills across the trout stream, to get the wind,
but " what came of it " I must leave for a future time.

With what various feelings we look forward to the several
seasons of the year ! I recollect as a child, and living amongst
the venerable cloisters of a cathedral city, I expected with keen
interest and a musical taste of a certain sort that sonata of tin
horns which ushered in the 1st of May, and waited with impatience the ballet of the sweeps circling round Jack-in-the-green.

A little further on in life, and the 1st of May ushered in the bathing season in the Cherwell fields, presided over by young Holloway, and in the evenings we sculled to Sandford Lock, or "went down in the eight," for the boating season had set in. When that time of free pupilage had passed, and Thucydides and the rest of them had gone to the hammer (the marginal notes and illustrations in these classical volumes were given in), we used to go with charming simplicity to see the lilacs in London, and join the gaieties of that capital until there was nothing for it but the moors. Tired long ago of all these first-named amusements, or unfitted for them by the stern decree of Anno Domini, I have long ago expected the coming of May Day with an interest centred in my next season's team. Savages have no almanacs but the pole star, and the moss upon the tree stem tell them north from south. I imagine they are not much out in their time of year for all that, nor should I be far wrong without the "Freemason's Calendar" or "The Rural Almanac."

It is an old story that a clerk who looked after his master's garden always expected to cut asparagus the day Balaam and Balak were read in church, and many a country gardener has his operations directed by some as rough criterion. Around me cottagers' wives sow Brompton stocks (or what they call "gilly-flowers") before the sun is up on Good Friday, *to make them come double*, and cover up their peas until the blackthorn is out of blossom, or *has* been white a fortnight. I am rather addicted to this rustic calendar, and I have accustomed myself to fix dates by things around me. "Snowdrops is out, sir," my man has said to me more than once (for he knows every notch in my calendar); "I suppose Jim will soon be coming for the dogs." He does not depend, I may remark, upon the wheat being forward enough or the clovers deep, for he wants first to let the young ones chase and drive, then he has to teach them to range and come to whistle, by which time they will have got some sense, and have given him many a weary walk, sometimes desponding and at others elate, with the hope of showing me something we can talk of and compare others with for years to come.

As Danebury or Woodyate names years after certain winners or favourites, my breaker and I have our Robin year, or Tim year, or Don year, or Ranger year, or "Young Kent" year, or the year "when the gentleman bought Moss and Rhine right out here on the heath, sir, you remember, of the captain, whilst they was a pointing, and wanted to be off the bargain when the lark got up;" for I need

not say that, with all Jim's care and work, we don't make all
good, some, as he says, being bad at heart, and there's no use
denying it." Generally we have a brace or perhaps three, worth
a monarch's ransom. Often we have *one* which would be dear at
no price, and as frequently as not we have "nothing very particular." This is my experience. There have been exceptions.
I once saw five magnificent setters broken of one litter ; all of them
are still alive, and scattered over the British Islands ; but I never
before knew of five in one litter turning out super-excellent.

To proceed with my almanac. When the yellow marigold is
first in bloom, and the buds of my large westeria are forward,
and the cowslips cover the meadows, it is time my dogs were
broken, and I see them gallop annually at about this season.

Jim Shave would rather walk sixteen miles or make a score of
wattle hurdles than write one letter; and a few days before the
appointed time I am awakened a trifle earlier than usual by a
vigorous barking in my kennels. It is without surprise that I
find, as I go to look through the stable before breakfast, a dog
chained at every ring of the kennel outer wall, some of which I
know and some I don't ; and close to the last tied up I discover a
coil of line and a breaker's whip, which proclaim Jim's presence.
He has probably gone the rounds of the kennels (for he alone of
all men is intrusted with the keys) to see some of his old favourites ; and although some of them were broken by him years ago.
I have never seen a dog forget him, nor have I observed one that
did not greet him as something more than an old acquaintance.
So it was this year ; so it always has been ; for he has the knack
of "gaining the respect of a dog," as an old keeper explained it
to me, "and unless (he added) you gets this 'ere respect out of
'em, you'd better throw up the dog altogether."

"My gooseberry trees are coming into leaf," is Jim's general
way of intimating that breaking operations must commence. and
when the apples are in full blossom, or Mrs. Jim's lilies of the
valley are blooming and scenting the air, Jim's kennels are
deserted, and there is silence in the village until July.

As usual, one morning late in April, I find that Jim has
walked eight miles to save a penny, besides which it all goes into
the day's work. For twice eight miles we could walk each way,
east or west, and find no ground unpreserved, and I think that
my honest breaker would be welcome to drive the birds out of
the clover for as many miles at any point of the compass, whether
he met squire or keeper. Be that as it may, here is Jim and

several of his pupils, as I said before, and he has freed them from
their "puzzle pegs," and allowed them to slake their thirst and
rest beneath the trees which overshadow my kennel wall.

The same morning, as he gets his breakfast, I receive a letter
from my two friends, and we fix the meeting for the 1st of May,
two or three days ahead. A fresh breezy morning succeeding a
wet night, and a wind south-east, give me hopes of a good scent
as I drive over to my breaker, and for a part of the morning
we are not disappointed. Jim shows us several teams, most of
them broken, but one or two are not, and never will be. "It
isn't in 'em." Jim tells me, and it "can't be put there." And
yet, as I look at one or two of these failures, I can assign no
reason for it. In appearance there is no lack of blood and
quality. If I observe any want it is in the intelligence of the
eye, which looks dull and desponding, and speaks of hard treatment and the lash, which I am sure they never met with here.

But it is no great amusement to me to look at this beautiful
setter, that can't find or touch a scent, or that pointer, with his
graceful lines. sting-tail, and polished coat, his ears "like bank
notes," and his faultless fore legs, if he won't use them, and
will "only follow and hunt the other dog." "Let us see a little
pedigree and performance combined," I remark to Jim, who, after
a few moments' thought, picks out "four of the best, sir ;" then,
touching his hat, says, "This way, gentlemen, if you please,"
and leads us up "The Hill." We climb this steep ascent to
catch the wind, and, once up it, have a wide fair table-land of
green corn already waving and rippling in the wind, with here
and there large plains of clovers, and (down wind some way
ahead) the yellow flowers of turnips gone to seed look like fine
"holding" for the birds.

Patiently we keep away, that we may have a good stretch back
again, for I need not say to go down wind with dogs is far
more pernicious than to stay at home. For all that I have seen
one or two cases where, with a young dog first upon game, it
answered to let him come upon and *flush* them down wind, for
decidedly he was almost overawed by the body scent of the
partridge if their wind was given him. Let that be how it may,
we went to get the wind—all Jim's team, which I shall not
particularise, following him as patiently and apathetically as
so many colley dogs, which spring to life and action when they
get the signal from the shepherd, and are passionless before.

At length we reach the confines of a wood or covert. dotted

with oaks about forty or fifty years old, where the underwood was of about a year's growth, and some twenty acres had been cut in the past winter. "If you will stand here, gentlemen," said Jim, "I will work round to you;" and as on these occasions to hear is to obey, so we leant on the old grey field gate, as Jim hunted his dogs down the decline in front of us.

Directly he waved his hand to cast them off, they sprang away right and left of him like greyhounds, but, young as they were, they did not go wide, only about what might be called enough ground for three guns. They were all high rangers, and, as I am given to understand, the offspring of one kennel. When I call them high rangers, let me observe that no other dog suits me; that not only does low ranging show an inclination to potter, but that I believe it induces it. High ranging is as much a gift as high or grand action; and though a puzzle peg may improve bad rangers, it won't make good ones, any more than magnifying glasses, which they say the Germans fix on the eyes of their chargers, will make them step up when applied in England. I expect this story of the magnifying glasses to be about as correct as that of the green glasses the miser put upon his ass to make him eat shavings instead of grass.

I saw the team cross each other independently, and their sterns going as Jim walked on. Gradually as he turned in a line with the covert we lost sight of him, and I had time to notice the beauties of the wood by the side of which he posted us.

What a variety of colour! The young oak shoots growing from old mossy stools were a rich brown, not green at all. In patches, the blue hyacinths looked like a carpet. Here and there were spots of pink, caused by the bachelor's buttons in full bloom, and relieved by pieces of the freshest verdure, where the green spurge shot up. Further on were the ash-coloured stems of beeches, then thick underwood, and a number of chesnuts nearly in full leaf and certainly in full blossom; and two or more nightingales, for which these parts are famous, were having a little concert to themselves, and practising that deft ventriloquism which I never observed in any others of the feathered tribe.

I had time to make these observations when I turned to see what had become of Jim, and my companion on the right, touching my arm, pointed out to me one of the team backing a pointer which had got the scent, who was standing in grand form below us.

Jim was standing with affected unconcern, but taking a glance

with his solitary eye first at one and then another of his pupils.
and, as it seemed to me, quite at his ease, and confident that not
one of them would " break."

You seldom, if ever, get such fine attitude in the backing as
in the pointing dog. He who backs has none of the pleasure
which appears to animate the keen-nosed pointer. To him it
would seem a delightful sensation to inhale the body scent of the
bird, and one which, in a *foot* scent, animates hound or spaniel.
because he hopes to overtake and kill.

This pleasure the backing dog *wants*. and we see it in his
posture. At first there is an air of inquiry about him. He
stops, or is stopped by degrees, as he approaches the dog which
has the point, or he learns it by being permitted to run on until
he settles the matter by experience. Very soon the slightest
gesture on his breaker's part gives him the cue, and, presto! he
is cataleptic, or (though not so good) he drops, gazing upon the
dog that winds the birds with suppressed envy.

Thus in *backing* we see the stern not so grandly held, and
most likely trembling excitement restrained by discipline, and the
training, let me say, of a sweet disposition and refined intelligence. If you want an example of self denial, obedience, self-
sacrifice, and amiability, you have it in the backing dog. He is
an amiable loser, and deserves consideration quite as much as
that lucky dog who has won the game !

After standing, perhaps, five minutes, and making sure the
dogs were firm, Jim walked on and put up the pair, when his
team dropped, all but one, and as Jim approached him he fell
too. That dog got a word or two of caution, the rest were
simply commended in a few sentences, and Jim waved them up.
Hullo! before they are well on their legs one stands stiff as a
midshipman, and two eye him and stop; the other does not see.
and has turned for his first sweep across again, when his eye falls
upon his three kennel friends, and he stops, too.

A hare bolts right through them at that moment, and Jim
looks anxious, especially at the dog furthest away, who has
evidently a great deal of dash about him ; but, to Jim's delight
and glory, he drops, although, for that matter, he turns his head
and eye after puss as she skips away, and once or twice stops
provokingly before she pops through the hedge, as though she
would challenge the best of the team to a trial of speed or a
slight flirtation with fur. This time Jim goes to each of them.
and reads a severe homily to them individually on the sin of

chasing. "War hare! will you! War hare! Very well! War
hare!" and when he reached the last, who rolled over on his
back as Jim got upon him, I was rather sorry to see that
appeal for mercy made in vain, for Jim give him two or three
decided, quick, sharp, cuts, which, however, called forth no sound
whatever.

Coming back to me before he let them up, he apologised for
or explained his severity : "He knows what it's for, sir. He
wants to chase, and we've had several quarrels lately. I see
him turn his head, and for the next four or five hares I flogs
him whether he chases or not, until he can't bear the sight of
one."

Not disputing Jim's authority, nor provoking discussion (for
flogging a dog always can be backed by sound arguments), I
told Jim to let us have one more find, and then to fetch another
set out. I could see pretty nearly enough of these, and I wish
I had them now as my *aides de camp* for the moors, but I shall
not.

Before we dropped into the bottom, where the trout stream
ran, we found again, the three dogs close together, and the fourth
away some distance. After a good spring and drop, Jim let
them have a bath in the running water, shake themselves, and
follow him home.

The two brace we next saw were only mediocre dogs ; no tail
action ; heads low, and the pace indifferent ; but they were as
well broken as such cattle could be. "Fit," as Jim said, "for
an old gentleman to puddle about with," but no use for the
moors.

"Why," said Jim, "a gipsy could boil a kettle and steal the
wood, whilst they go across a ten-acre field." And I need not
say we soon saw enough of these.

"And who do these dogs belong to, Jim ?" I said. But Jim
did not seem to hear. I therefore repeated the question, and Jim
replied,

"A foreign gentleman, sir ; and I hope he'll like 'em, for I
don't. But there " (he went on), "they know as much about
good dogs as we do, they tell me, and actually have English
keepers to keep 'em straight! I know," he said, " you would
soon see enough of these ; " and as he spoke one found, and
stood looking as depressed and gloomy as though finding game were
a melancholy affair, and only fit for misanthropes. "There,"
said Jim, "there they be! head down, tail down, like a under-

taker and three mutes ; only wants the bell a tolling, and you'd be a pretty picture, you would." This, however, was not in a tone of voice to dispirit these black pointers, one of which would not keep his tail steady, and seemed to be marvellously suspicious of his funereal brother. Jim soon cut short this appalling spectacle, and put up the birds, when the sable quartet dropped like automatons, but evidently were ignorant of the design their breaker had in thus drilling them, and might have considered it a sort of rehearsal of the funeral rites to sink into their graves.

At this crisis Jim's son appeared with five which Jim called " middling." "This (he continued), must end it for to-day, if you please, gentlemen ; " and we again broke ground.

Hitherto we had not got over fifty acres—perhaps not twenty, for I am a bad judge of space—and we came to some good deep clover, the wind in our teeth, and the air cooler. A few drops fell and just sparkled on the grass as we began to beat this ground, and the scent must have been brilliant, I know. Not one of these dogs hunted another, but as each turned I saw that he gave a wistful glance at what was going on, as though he knew he was but one of a company, and not to do as he would.

I was looking on the ground and did not see this find, therefore I had got two paces in front of my companions when I observed one of the five almost close to my feet, and in grand attitude, close behind a bitch, with her mouth drawn a little aside; behind her, her brother "backed," shaking like a leaf, but stiff, and two dogs at the extreme distance of the field, were perfectly rigid and firm. One I thought was very grand indeed for a backing dog, standing upon tip-toe and making the most of himself ; although but a moderate size he looked quite fine and large.

Jim gave us time to see the point, and then put up the birds, and the three I first named dropped ; but Jim's monitory signals failed to drop the other brace, which we now saw at the same instant must have found another pair. So Jim walked on, leaving his three pointers down, and we went with him. In a few moments we were near enough to notice the birds running before us, and close to the young dog, who followed the direction of his game with his head and eye, and gradually settled on his haunches, but then stood again. His companion lifted one foot, and meant to creep, until Jim's voice brought her up firm again, and then he stood and cautioned her against any such heretical proceedings for the future.

As the birds made for the hedge, I went and sprung them for Jim, and he took the dogs away ; for, as he says—and I agree with him—nothing so destroys the range of dogs as a desire to poke into hedges, or is so likely to create a love of rabbits. One more grand find as we cross the wheat, and then another, each of the dogs getting it and seeming to me level in pace, and nose, and temper. One of them, however, I observe has a coil of chain round his neck—*I should say three fathoms*—but he held his own, and delighted me with his perseverance.

"Whose dog is that, Jim ? " "Why, sir, it's a dog named Sauce, and I think it's the best dog of all my lot."

When the sundew was in flower and the yellow hawkweed, and when the starwort or blue chamomile blossomed, and the white lilies were floating on our lake, Jim brought down his team to run about our heath, and Sauce performed again ; this time with such effect that a friend of mine bought him (chains and all) and has him now. We called that year the Sauce year, and it's a good dog that bears comparison with the Admiral's Sauce, as he would tell you if you asked him.

PAPER IV.

"STRICTLY CONFIDENTIAL."

Nothing is considered complete and well done amongst my countrymen without a dinner ; and. after a walk with a breaker in hard condition, who has been training for six or eight weeks about as many hours a day, none of us are very squeamish as to the quality of the viands, provided the materials of the repast are clean and wholesome.   Indeed, the crisp but succulent flavour of that home-baked bread, the roast leg of mutton and cauliflowers, in which we rival Cornwall, with an appetite and zest produced by meeting the fresh May breeze and climbing those green hills which surround my breaker's freehold cottage, have more charms for me than a far better dinner and the attendance of stately waiters, who resemble beneficed clergymen (at " Willis his rooms " let us say), with Willis *in propriâ personâ* silently inspecting the arrangements, as he moves spectrally and silently behind my chair.

So, annually we have a dinner after our inspection of the young dogs on the first of May, and, when the cloth has been removed, Jem, who has been dining with the coachman who periodically drives his master to this solemn ordeal, or perhaps balancing the table with his presence opposite to me, takes his usual two glasses of brandy-and-water, and relaxes from that silence and solemnity which so well befit him in the field.

He is never mysterious as to dogs of his own with any stranger who comes to him commercially, at the same time that he is a man of few words. I have known him to possess dogs it would be very hard to match, but he would never describe them as more than "middling ; " adding as a rider to this statement, " The best proof, sir, is, if you like the looks of him, to see him out."

With one of these highly-gifted performers, he would thoroughly enjoy himself, and as the dog stood or backed I have known him, led on by the enthusiasm of the moment, put the question to his customer : " Do you think that will do, sir ? Can any gentle-

man wish for anything *stiddier* or grander than that, sir ?"
Generally, however, he is taciturn to a fault, and keenly alive to
want of system in hunting, style in going, keen nose, or *staunchness*. *Stiffness of stern, and his hackles up, and a frown on his
face*—that is Jem's idea of a point ; and going with the head
well up, and lashing his ribs with his stern, is Jem's idea of
style.

A casual visitor, as I have said, would hear very little from
Jem, and his replies to our observations are made with a touch
of the hat and cheerful acquiescence, or a firm but courteous
negation, in which the hat symbol of duty is not omitted.

After dinner, and in the middle of his first glass of brandy-
and-water, Jem relaxes. True he turns his solitary eye to the door,
and if it is ajar he carefully closes it before he unburthens himself
of the fact that " That young dog, sir—begging your pardon—I
hope you'll tell your man, sir, he mustn't have no whip, and beg
him to be sure not to huff him ;" or he may express his fears that
that other one won't have hunt enough, and goes with no
"sperrit ; " and once I considered him quite stubborn about as
good a bitch as I ever had or ever shall. The rock we split on
was *style*. "No style, sir." " Well, but Jem, did you ever see
a setter so quick, or with such a knack of finding ? Here is this
bitch finding every bird, and your grand stylish dogs backing
her ; then you put one of her legs in her collar, and she beats
them still ; you give her the wind, and she hops on her three
legs straight up to her game! " and to this Jem agreed ; but he
added, " A curious-tempered thing, and a *snake* " (sneak). So
she was, but as a finder Jem never had her equal, and, in my
opinion, he never will.

He calls to his aid some of the old ones, after whom we named
the year. " You remember Bob, sir, that fallow dog? That
was the dog! And Robin, sir—him the navy captain took to sea
for two years, and when he came home the gentleman at Liverpool gave him thirty guineas for him?" Then there was this
pointer, and that setter, and the other ; but Jem would not allow
anything in favour of *Rhine the snake*.

" And what do you think," one of our party said—" what do
you think of Droppers, Jem ?"

" Very good dogs some of 'em, sir," Jem replied readily ;
" but "—and here he stopped until the landlady retired, on
bringing in his second glass—" but," Jem continued, after trying
the door, " you can't breed from 'em, and so if you have a first-

rate dog you only have *him*, and can't get a succession; and
then," said he, his eye still on the door, that none of his oracles
might ventilate, "then they ain't gentleman's dogs; and anything but true-bred dogs," pursued Jem, as he moved away his
glass with an impatient gesture, "anything like mongrels, good
or bad, I can't abide. If I don't like a dog, however much I try
to hide it, the dog finds it out, and he don't like me, and we
don't try to please each other. Some dogs," said Jem, "I have
pretty near parted from with the tears standing in my eyes, as I
shook hands with 'em and put 'em in the train; *but they was all
well-bred ones.* The greatest trouble I have is with dogs that
won't hunt. I can't love 'em, and it's no use to waste my time
with them. If a dog looks fat after I've had him three weeks,
depend upon it he is a unprofitable servant."

"And what do you like me to do with my young dogs before I
send them to you, Jem?"

"Nothing at all, sir," replied he, "except exercise. Whatever
you do, don't let them hunt hedges, and don't try to break them;
anyhow, only get them to come to whistle. No down charge, no
nothing. I recollect some fifteen or twenty years ago a gentleman from Manchester wrote to me to take his dogs, and I agreed
to do it; and so he sent the dogs and their names. Nice dogs
they was, and they had the queerest names you ever heard! It's
a fact, this is, and the gentleman's name was—well," Jem said,
after rubbing his head thoughtfully, "I forget his name, but he
had something to do with cotton, and I remember he sent a lot
of calico prints to my missus to make the children frocks, and so
on. However, he called one dog Mule Twist, and another Jute,
and a white one was called Cotton, and he wanted to call the
best of the lot Shirtings, but I didn't—I called him Twist; that
is, I give him half the first dog's name.

"Well, they was rattling good dogs; but I thought I never
should have done nothing with 'em, for you see he'd been
a-breaking them hisself, with tame partridges put into a round
wire rat-trap under cabbage leaves in his gardens, and all sorts of
capers, and they were always looking for my whip and hand.

"Twist (the one he called Shirtings) always would creep a bit,
else he was a good dog, *he* was; and Mule he was the finest of
the lot; and Jute he was very steady, he was; and Cotton, the
white dog, he'd stand for two hours. Well, after a deal of
labour, I got 'em to this, and sent 'em back, and the gentleman
he sent me ten pounds and a lot of this printed calico into the

bargain, and he said 'he had clipped his tame partridge's wings, and had given the dogs the wind (as per your advice of yesterday) and let them find them amongst the strawberries, and they performed as follows : Shirtings,' he says, 'advancing, Mule Twist held firmly, Jute quiet, Cotton firm.'

"This was the funniest letter I ever had about dogs," said Jem, "except one I had this morning. Perhaps " (Jem said) "you'll read it, Mr. Idstone."

"With pleasure, Jem :

Birmingham, *April* 29.

Sir,—Your favour just received. I am glad the dog has turned out well, and a gentleman has purchased him from your description. I beg to inclose cheque. I have done fairly with him, having received in exchange 24½ gross of *best black japanned coffin plates!* "

"Oh !" Jem added, when we had done laughing at this singular idea of a bargain, "I've had all sorts of things offered me for dogs—ash poles for sheep cribs, and a summer's run for a cow ; and once I had thirteen Cochin China eggs, and a new great coat, and four pound ten offered me for a dog, by a gentleman as come from Whitechapel in London. Is there much game there, sir ?"

"Did the gentleman have the dog, Jem ?"

"Yes, sir, but because the dog wouldn't run hares, he wanted the great coat back again ; but he never had it."

Our old acquaintance then began to enumerate the breaker's grievances : Dogs sent as untried which know the check-cord and puzzle-peg as well as their breaker ; these dogs, if represented as unbroken, Jem sends back at once. Others sent to be "made," which have hunted every street in a city until they are two or three years old, having a wholesome dread of boys and stones. Sheep biters, and now and then resolute dogs which no power on earth can prevent from running wide, and which pay as little attention to a whistle as a hare. Dogs with wide thin-soled feet, or tied in their shoulders, "with no gallop in them." Others that go with drooping flag and nose on the ground, and are only fit to follow a hearse. Some with no nose, no taste for game ; and that loose, flabby, slack-loined lymphatic animal which is a delicate feeder, with no energy or spirit, and which no physic will put right, unless it be the water cure—say the Cheltenham waters for ten minutes, a foot above their heads.

"But," said Jem, cheering up a bit, "a nice fresh warm rain, and good deep laying, and a brace of cheerful, active, sensible young ones that don't regard punishment, and plenty of birds—

and I forget all my troubles, and go to work with a good heart."

A sturdy, honest love of truth is one of the sterling qualities of my old breaker. No disguising faults, no varnished statements, no shirking work and excuses after it. If the dog fails it is not his fault; and no man is more discriminating with the whip.

"Nothing spoils the dog like *that*," Jem tells me, as he telegraphs with a Burleigh nod to his old whip, which lies upon the sideboard, close to two china dogs and a knife-case which probably gave Mr. Mechi his first hint for making a cabinet for envelopes.

"You want," he says, "a light whip for a thin-skinned pointer, and a heavy one for thick-coated setters, and you want the gifts to use them. First make the dog understand where he has done wrong, and then see how much he will bear. Many a dog is ruined with one flogging, and many are ruined for want of one. I deliver my dogs steady, and never overlook a fault; at any rate, I talk to them about it, and take my time. Perhaps the new owner don't know or don't care, and the dog 'trains off' to nothing, and then I get the blame. I like to let the gentlemen see them when I take them home in May, and again in July or August, and to work the dogs the first day they shoot over them. If they knock down the birds and leave the dogs to me, there is no more trouble; and if there is, they must have the blame between them.

"Well, Jem, we will come over and see you give your finishing lessons if we can; at any rate, will you promise us to come out with us the first week in September and work the dogs?" To this Jem civilly agreed, and as his second glass of brandy-and-water was finished, our horses were brought round to the porch, and we dissolved the meeting.

"You won't mention anything I've said, gentlemen?" said Jem, as he picked up his whip and hat.

"Certainly not."

PAPER V.

SHOOTING DRESS.

ALTHOUGH reports of grouse disease are very prevalent, I doubt not most of us are already thinking seriously of our annual migration to Norway, Ireland, or the North, hoping by great good luck, superior generalship, hard work, excellent dogs, or all of these means, to get a fair month's sport. The Wizard of the North never fails to attract a full company; and, as I am told, the London gunmakers are almost overdone with orders. I went into two or three of the principal *emporia* for breech-loaders the other day, and found that these cunning craftsmen had a busy time of it. Stacks of gun cases reclined against the walls of their shops, branded with the accustomed and some new names; and guns in every stage of manufacture—some " in the rough," others far more advanced, and a few engraved, browned, and complete—were awaiting the inspection of their respective owners. One of the fraternity handing me a very masterpiece of art, a snap-action treble-grip central-fire gun, which he saw had great attractions for me, whilst he reached the " sister gun," as he called it, with his other hand, remarked,. " That pair of guns has been ready for this three months I should say, and Lord —— never puts off his orders. I'll be bound that he has everything ready, from his hat to his boots; and he always has."

I was set thinking of the various things required for an August migration by this gunmaker's observation, and especially with regard to clothes. I know very well that there are lucky members of society who are always ready for the North after putting off their orders to the last moment; who, on all occasions, get their railway ticket in the nick of time, jump into their seat as the train moves on, perhaps as the guard whistles, and think it a clever thing to do. But these hurried movements and late orders are most perilous and inconvenient to purchaser and vendor, frequently resulting in annoyance, inconvenience, or disappointment.

A tight hat, or a loose one that blows off ; a pair of boots that

won't go on, or that pinch the instep, or press a favourite corn ; a
coat that chafes or wrinkles; gaiters or leggings that won't meet ;
a whistle that won't rattle ; a gun too straight, too much bent, too
long, too short—all these little vexations may crowd themselves
upon you, far beyond the reach of railways, gunmakers, tailors,
or bootmakers, and it is just as well to ensure your comfort and
to have your outfit complete a week, or even a month, before you
book yourself by the Great Northern, or swing from your moorings
at "the Wight."

Old Osbaldeston used to say, "Hang deliberation ; it's only a
long name for craning at a fence, and going round for a gap or a
gate." But, as far as shooting goes, if you are deliberate you are
"all there."

Some years ago I got an unexpected sudden summons to
Perthshire. It was something stronger than an invitation, so I
call it a "summons," and there was no time for making ready.

The party had assembled (it was about the fifteenth), and it
was not possible that they could keep the best beats for me.
"You need not bring a dog," my friend said, "we have plenty
here ; " so I thrust what clothes I thought necessary into a portmanteau, filled a leather bag with boots and gaiters, rushed to
the metropolis, took the first Hansom I could see, of course got
a spavined horse, caught the train on the post, and landed myself
at Perth accordingly.

It was a weary journey, and it always is, especially if you have
long legs, and are subject, as I am, to the cramp ; and, to make
matters worse, the train was full all the way to Carlisle, whilst
opposite to me sat a plethoric old gentleman, his wife's dressing
case for a footstool, forming an effectual barricade to his half of
the conveyance ; and he made matters worse by periodically
refreshing himself with the breasts of cold chickens, French
rolls, and pale sherry, whilst I starved in the corner. As he
threw the bones of the first chicken out of window, I began to
reckon up my "traps." There were no breechloaders in those
days, and I was pretty sure that I had forgotten my loading rod
—one constructed to shut in two, with a joint like the stick of a
parasol, and which, therefore, never got between your legs like a
court sword. I could recollect now, as we whirled along, and
got a little vertical vibration—the train was about forty minutes
late—I could recollect that I left it, case and all, on the sill of
the study window ; and, worse than that, although I had my
double gun case, I had put but one gun in it. The last straw

that broke the camel's back had still to be laid on, for it came to pass next day that I discovered the stock of No. 1, but the barrels of No. 2. As they were not sisters, only cousins, they did not naturally fit, and therefore I had to shoot for five or six days with a borrowed gun, which killed well enough when it would go off ; this was the exception, not the rule.

I don't know what my old acquaintance would have said about "deliberation" as regards preparing for the North, when he found himself, as I did, with a pair of odd gaiters—both right, but in one sense only ; or whether he would have thrown himself into the joke and enjoyed it, had he heard, as I did, the Scotch keeper asking in his native brogue, as he held up the said gaiters derisively, "whether the gentleman who came last night had only one leg or two." Certainly the little miseries I brought upon myself by my precipitate flight from home were lessons to me, not for the first, nor do I think even the hundredth time.

You may think that all this has little or nothing to do with shooting dress, but it has all to do with it. There was nothing exactly right ; boots, hat, under-clothing, coat, all more or less wrong.

I don't mean to inflict a repetition of these troubles upon the public ; but my misfortunes shall be the text of a homily upon dress for the moors, and the home shooting from hot September to the frost and snow of Christmas.

I looked over some old engravings the other day, representing the sportsman of 1793, and gradually bringing me to within a perfect remembrance of those sportsmen who preceded me.

In 1793 the coat was tolerably comfortable, I should say— short in the skirt, loose in the sleeve, rather grotesque when you come to the collar, which looked more suitable for the neck of a cart-horse than a Christian. The nether garments consisted of breeches, white stockings, *shoes*, and short gaiters, which left the calf of the leg exposed after the manner of the Pickwicks. The "hat of the period" was like the soft wideawake adopted by invalid or overworked clergymen at the seaside, high in the crown, large in the brim, and flaccid. It gave a sombre and pious air to the most pious "varmint" examples of the day ; and the old original Mr. Tattersall, who is painted in such a headdress, appears more than semi-clerical, in spite of the merry twinkle of his eye. It was by no means unusual to walk the stubbles in top boots ; and what we now associate with the turf or the covert side was the get-up universally for pigeon shooting.

From this date to 1815 the hat began gradually to assume its stiff, hideous proportion ; and although Abraham Cooper's well-known picture of a sportsman on his pony, called " The First of September," represents him as wearing a soft hat of much more graceful outline than the best that André or Lincoln and Bennett possesses, we may infer that by that time the rigid "chimney-pot" obtained in most circles.

From about 1822 to 1847, or thereabouts, few soft felt hats were worn, except by the lower orders, and it was at the latter date considered *infra dig.* in a professional man to shade his brows one inch more than the letter of fashion allowed, or to put on a covering containing in its fabric one ounce less of glue, shellac, or stiffening than of yore.

In 1825, I observe a picture by Cooper of a pheasant-shooting party, where the single gun is exchanged for a double, where the hat is more easy and useful, the coat more like a shooting jacket, and the legs are protected from the thigh to the calf of the leg with gaiters. the lower part of the leg and foot being encased in boots. In covert, or " outside the palings," this dress would suit one, and at the present time it could scarcely be improved, *except in material. There were no Scotch tweeds then.*

I plunge at once into my subject after fencing with it so far, and I determine to begin with the hat.

I can only say from experience that in August and September there is nothing better than straw. A straw hat, if it is a good one, is better than any other. I confess that it is not without its defects, or rather its *one* defect. It is not a protection against rain. In all other points can you tell me anything that will equal it ? If you get a good one (which you can do by going to a good maker), it will last you two or possibly three years, after being annually cleaned, lined afresh, and stiffened, at the cost of eighteenpence ; and if I get one I like I am very chary of getting rid of it. The black-and-white answer best. They don't get brown like the unstained ones, and don't attract the sun like a self colour. They should have nothing thicker than gauze for lining, and a ring of flannel or serge where it touches the head.

In a broiling day you may get a young cabbage leaf tacked inside the crown ; and if you forget this comfortable arrangement you can put a handful of grass instead. The brim should not be more than $2\frac{1}{4}$in. wide, and I seldom have mine over 2in. If the straw is moderately coarse the wind will not affect this margin, and the eyes will be thoroughly protected.

The crown should be $3\frac{1}{4}$in. exactly. This allows enough circulation above the head, and is not acted upon by the wind. I have been out in very heavy rains with such a hat, and have experienced very little inconvenience from the percolating of the water ; and as soon as the storm passed away I gave my hat a shake, and felt no inconvenience.

If you don't like a straw, you have to choose between two evils —the soft wide-awake and the hard one.

The soft one is by far the most comfortable for the open, provided there is no wind ; but when there is even a breeze, if the brim is a couple of inches too wide, you are always put out by its flapping in your face. As these soft brims are made to turn up. you can't very well shear them down without making yourself "an objec'," otherwise a sewing-machine and a pair of scissors would put all right. These soft hats do not attract the sun so much as the stiff ones, even if they are black ; and we have our choice from white to brown or grey. White are too great a contrast to the heather ; and for fishing. which goes hand in hand with the gun in Scotland, a white hat is most objectionable. Well, certainly, it is advisable to have as few traps as possible on our expeditions, and it would be well that a hat should answer all purposes if possible : suppose we say neutral grey or lavender is the best colour of all.

For covert, the stiff, hard hat will do, as the brims slip through the underwood ; and. though objectionable in the sun, they are cool enough beneath the leaf in October, or when the heat of summer is past. Yet I prefer much the soft skull and stiff brims ; and I have worn them with great comfort even in September.

"Coats for the moors," "suits for the moors," "heather mixtures," "grousings," and various materials, are advertised all the year round. All of them, perhaps, are good in their way ; possibly, and more probably, they are good, bad, and indifferent. You must remember as you go North you don't take the English climate with you; and if you did, it is so variable that you would do well to take clothes suited to all weathers. You must be prepared for chilly mountain rains, damps, and fogs, and all varieties of climate and temperature. In a general way you may

·expect great heat and some wet—more rain in proportion to the hot weather than you experience in England.

You want for the moors and hills something *flexible, soft,* strong, and elastic, and *not too thin.* There is nothing better than tweed, so far as I know. The flax coats absorb the rain, become very heavy, are a long time drying, and when damp they are very cold and chilly. They will do for covert in dry days, as they resist thorns ; but even then I should prefer strong tweed.

In the old days he possessed the best coat for shooting who could boast of most pockets ; now few pockets are required. Formerly the crack shots, such as the late Lord Mexborough, Osbaldeston, or the forgotten Colonel Thornton, wore Quaker collars to their shooting coats, thinking the roll collar in the way of the gun ; but " we know better "—this was all affectation.

The loading rod was frequently suspended through a pipe attached to a belt which crossed the back on one side, whilst the shot pouch crossed the other shoulder. The right-hand upper pocket held wadding, the lower pocket the flask—unless it was in the left inner breast-pocket, close to the lighted cigar or pipe bowl, as I have seen it—and the other pockets were encumbered with nipple wrenches, screwdrivers, and the general *répertoire* of an amateur armourer.

Now you have not forty or fifty times a day to expose your fingers to the explosion of a gun, whilst the action and mechanism are simplified to the last degree. You therefore require simply an easy garment that does not confine your shoulders, and which is loose under the arms ; moderately close fitting at the wrists and along the forearm, or perhaps an unsightly wrinkle may start up between you and your aim ; and, above all things, *a skirt not too long.* Any of the admirable Scotch mixtures will do, if not too much pronounced in colour ; and it is well that *hat,* tie, coat, and the whole dress should be to a certain extent " matching." The general tone of a partridge or of the egg of a pheasant, perhaps a little greyer, is as good as any ; but anything which is like the heather will do. The "three-seam" coat is the most cool, and at the same time the best protection from rain ; and it is as well to have the fabric waterproofed, because this is a guarantee that it has been shrunk. Waterproofed or not, the rain is sure to find its way into the seams, especially the seams of the sleeves.

I think we shall be pretty well agreed as to knickerbockers. They are the most comfortable garments possible for stalking or

grouse. In the first case, the fold at the knee is a great protection, and they do not *chafe* like other garments. Knee-
breeches are not only hideous in appearance (except in the
saddle), but they are close fitting and uneasy things to walk in,
and are now very properly exploded. Shetland stockings and (if
required) a leather gaiter will render a grouse shooter independent of any covert he will meet with, or *ought* to meet with, if
(as I shall soon ask him) he is well shod.

Before I go so far, we will consider the best way in which
these knickerbockers can be retained in their place ; and I must
say that I think, for a long day, and to get the free use of your
arms, there is nothing like getting rid of your braces. A few
loops (two before and three behind), through which a leather
strap will pass to buckle in front, will answer well. You say that
this will cut your hips, but it will not. The strap should not
be less than an inch and a half wide, and the portion which goes
over each hip should be sewn together, and stuffed with some
soft material. I have found a roll of chamois leather the best
thing. This method is not only advantageous, as it takes a load
from the shoulders, but it admits, by having a swivel or two on it
or a blunt hook or two, of your carrying a bird or two until you
meet your man, or of your attaching a flask of brandy or a sandwich case to you in a most convenient way.

Buttoned gaiters are the most trustworthy, but they are tedious
to put on, and are, when wet, difficult to take off. I have of
late years patronised those which close with a spring, and I have
never found them otherwise serviceable. If you use leather
ones, those made of " hide " are better than sheepskin for keeping
out the wet, but they do not allow of ventilation. A far better
gaiter is made now of canvas strapped behind with leather. It
resists thorns and it is porous, If you desire to protect the knee
and thigh from thorns, it will be best to have this upper legging
in a separate piece.

As to boots, every man who shoots has some plan or model or
make of his own ; but I think we almost all of us take refuge in
the lace-up boots at last. With many modifications, this is certainly the shooting boot, and there is none other. It ought not
to be hard to get a good one, but it is. I advise any man who
is hard to fit, which I am not, to get a " last " made, and he
will surmount much of the difficulty. Then you will say he
wants good leather and good workmanship. So he does ; and
first as to leather. I used to have my shooting boots made of

what are known in the trade as "kips"—the skins of animals which have died a natural death. But the boots were always hard, and for tender feet (which mine are not) they won't do. If you want *watertight* boots, you must have them made of cow-hide, or of two leathers, having between them a bladder or a thin skin of gutta-percha. Boot-makers will tell you they can keep out the wet. I never could get a pair of boots which kept it out for long. I have tried various compositions ; the best was made by a man of the name of Jones, who used to attend the various cattle shows with his tins of this material ; and I have now used it for several years with complete success.

The form of boot I have described. Well, it should have a toe-cap and it should fit you : but it should be wider than your usual walking-boot, and thick in the soul to receive the hobnails, which are placed about three-quarters of an inch apart all over the sole, including "the waist," so that you don't slip as you spring at a bank or get over a gate or stile. These hob-nails should be of wrought iron, and of the sort called "star hobs"—1000 of them should weigh 3lb. Years ago I used to get hob nails of either gun metal or bell metal, I forget which. They wore well and did not rust when laid aside, and so rot the leather. I think these nails were made in Belgium.

I have thought that leather dressed with the hair side outside kept out the water better than when dressed in the usual way ; but these boots cut and scratch with the thorns, and presently become very shabby and defaced.

A man living in town, and accustomed to thin boots, will do well to shoot in the lightest boots which will stand the work. For my part, I like strong ones and a thick sole. To attempt to walk all day in new ones is a very rash proceeding ; it is advis-able to get accustomed to them by degrees. I make it a practice to wear all which are destined for winter service without the hobnails until they are *thoroughly easy*, and, as my man calls it, "broken in." I then have them nailed ready for work, and have only to assure myself that they have no projecting points within. It is well to have what shoemakers call a " beak-iron " to beat down these points, if you live at a distance from the " cordwainer," otherwise you may be very much inconvenienced or permanently injured.

Nothing is so tedious, you must bear in mind, as a chafed or galled heel. If you are not careful you are sure to get one, partly from chafing, but also from want of condition.

If you can get boots made like Wellingtons to meet the knickerbockers, and do not tread them over at heel, you will find nothing more enduring or convenient; for, though lacing boots is to me no trouble or inconvenience, many dislike the task.

There is no better way of fastening the lace than by giving it a *single hitch;* and if you burn the end of the lace slightly in the flame of a candle, you will want no "tag."

For a jersey, if needed, there is nothing like silk. Winter or summer, hot or cold, wet or dry, I have found it so; and they are economical as well, if that is an object, for they hardly ever wear out. I need hardly say flannel shirts, the thinner the better, and as soft possible.

Three things more—straight powder, unfermented liquors, and early hours. No man can walk and shoot well unless he attends to his condition.

E

PAPER VI.

SOME OLD PORTRAITS.

IT is amusing, and I think profitable, to notice the changes that take place in fashion, and to trace our improvements in many particulars, if not in everything.

I recollect some years ago turning over with a friend the sporting treasures of his grandfather. At that time my host was a grandfather of some twenty years' standing ; and the old bureau had come to him by the death of an elder brother, with what was of far more consequence—the Elizabethan house, the park, the deer, and the broad lands of his bachelor relative.

With the care and hoarding nature which seems equally the mark of the unmarried and of magpies, he had religiously preserved these old household gods, and they had not been seen by their new possessor for many years.

The old ancestor had been a very mighty Nimrod in his day, and his son had been charged to preserve and never dispose of these hunting chattels, which, with the self-conceit of an old, uneducated squire, the failing huntsman believed no future science could replace. Thus we rummaged out from the old " press " that morning many a quaint old vestment, a wonderfully hard square-cut saddle, topboots with about as much shape and make about them as a dried sole-skin, and a coat which would have encompassed most water-butts, but was more remarkable for its uncouth and desperately inconvenient collar.

There was the old hunting whip, fashioned like a short carter's flail, having a large boss or knob at the handle, and adapted for frays with highwaymen, or the destruction of " upper bars " if the short-tailed hunter, pumped or stale, refused timber at the end of one of those terrible long days, lasting from dawn to dark.

At those times the "orange tawny" of the Berkeleys was more fashionable than the pink, and a long-skirted frock coat (a huntsman's) turned up amongst the treasures, threadbare on the shoulder from carrying the long curved hunting horn.

Leaving these moth-eaten garments and accoutrements, we had come to the old bureau, where we found snuff boxes, one or two of exquisite manufacture, wrought in gold, and adorned with jewels, in the fashion of Louis Quatorze, one of which a good judge declared to have cost at least three or four hundred pounds. Here are the spurs with which Nimrod rode ; here again a small parcel of " kennel whipcord," which never was required ; and a morocco case, much faded and battered, impressed with the gold effigy of a fighting cock (trimmed and spurred) without, and holding four pairs of silver spurs within.

The cockpit (long since turned into a fernery) adjoined the billiard-room, and had been constructed to accommodate upwards of 100 persons.

Looking round at the old portraits of dogs and horses, growing obscure behind a coating of yellow varnish, I am struck with the ingenious cruelty of these times ; I see the portrait of Colonel Thornton's pointer, who had but the stump of a tail left, and who, as a puppy, in all probability was " wormed."

Here are two of the old black waggon horses with no tail at all. No—my friend corrects me—those were the *coach-horses* which were used on grand occasions, named, perhaps on account of their docked tails and crops ears, " Crop " and " Stump." " I can remember " (my friend added) " seeing George IV. riding a roan horse which he purchased of old Tattersall, and which the barbarous fashion of the times had deprived of both his ears."

The barbarous votaries of fashion always had some excuse to urge for these savage " customs." Thus they argued that worming a dog (the cutting some imaginary nerve from the root of the tongue) prevented rabies. Docking a horse strengthened the back, and the same operation performed on the pointer did away with self-inflicted flagellation when Don came upon the body scent of game.

I never could discover any excuse for cropping or nicking horses ; nor can any palliation be offered to the miscreants who not unfrequently, by their severity, superinduced lockjaw.

Unwilling as we may be to confess it, the sportsman and the brute were too commonly synonymous terms, and this antiquated belief descends upon some persons to the present day.

Bear-baiting (the bear's eyes put out occasionally, to deprive him of half his power of opposition), badger-baiting (five dogs at the badger altogether), bull-baiting (frequently on a Sunday afternoon), and cock-fighting in the public streets—these were the tastes of the pigtail period ; and advocates for the suppression of these " pastimes " were met with the even then stale argument that on such scenes we depended for our national bulldog courage.

To this end princes of the blood were present at prizes battles, and in one or two instances conveyed one or other of the heroes to the arena. A " captain " trained a pugilist for the encounter, and once, I believe, himself fought for and won the stakes. Fifty times the property was required to kill partridges as to enable a man to vote for a knight of the shire, and those who were qualified to shoot did not blush to sally out at night and slaughter whole coveys at a shot " at the time they jugged."

Coarseness, cruelty, and unmanliness did not cease with Queen Elizabeth and the princely pleasures of Kenilworth. More than two hundred years after her day the blasphemous letters of pugilists, all unshorn of their bad spelling and want of grammar, were printed in the *Sporting Magazine,* and its pages were further garnished with *"crim. cons.,"* elopements in high life, and " the valour of a ginger-red."

Veterinary science was another name for barbarity. Horses labouring under glanders were subjected to unheard-of barbarities. Drinking was chronicled as a great feat, and at Cambridge these " bottle combatants " sat *vis-à-vis* on the floor, pledging each other in tumblers, until they had consumed more than eight bottles a man ; " Lord B." exclaiming with an oath, " I would I were the arch of a bridge, and liquor always running through me ! "

Badgers, fighting dogs, " fair Cyprians," and bears, gamecocks, pugilists—now and then of the " fair "(?) sex—duels to the death after a severe night's potations, made up a sportsman's life, and shared the attentions he bestowed upon his pigtail, his powder, and his " ginger-red."

Gaming was looked upon as a relaxation from the fatigues of mind and body, but it was not uncommon with the loser to forget to pay ; and Elwes the miser, who " would never ask a gentleman for money," was first and last a loser of fifteen thousand pounds.

In 1795 " cock-squailing " (throwing at a tethered cock) was the common practice at Ipswich, and " knights of the fist " fought their battles in the Lyceum. Highway robbery was the rule, and not the exception, and sportsmen loaded their guns to return from Lewisham.

Cock-fighting was not suppressed in the city until 1795, but then the sport still continued at Cockpit Royal, St. James's. "Ladies of title" played fraudulently at faro, and were convicted, though not much punished ; but shoplifters expiated their crimes upon the scaffold.

In 1802 bull-baiting and bull-running were attempted to be stopped by Act of Parliament. Mr. Windham declared this system of reform arose out of jacobinism and religious fanaticism. "Were gentlemen certain that the bull did not experience pleasure from it ? Bulls once baited (he said) were called *game bulls*, for they were more anxious to attack the dogs than others ! Gentlemen would not deny that the *dog* had pleasure in the contest. In his opinion it was the least cruel of all field sports, and cherished those feelings which were the best support of loyalty, *and the greatest protection both of Church and State.*" Colonel Grosvenor followed on the same side, declaring that "if a treaty was signed between bull-dogs and bulls *the death warrant of the country would be signed.*" Mr. Courtenay proposed bringing over Corsican bulls, which he understood were "particularly adapted for the sport," and wound up by "trusting that, as bull-baiting had been proved so conducive to the happiness of both the human and brute creation, and so essential to the preservation of our constitution, our national character, and morality, the House would never consent to abolish so invaluable a practice." The bill was thrown out by a majority of 13.

Twenty-one years after Parliament interfered again, and still the pastime had its advocates (being defended by Brougham) ; but even "Vox Humanitatis," who expostulates with the Scottish barrister, does not dare oppose badger-baiting and dog-fighting.

These sports remained until my school days, although cock-fighting was on the wane.

A Worcestershire village feast was not absolutely complete without a badger. When a schoolboy I have seen the whole performance on the banks of the Severn. There was no interference on the part of the magistrates, and police there were none. The village constable was selected (like a London watchman) as the most decrepit who could be found, and in this particular instance he assisted in the badger's toilet, fastening the rope with "wax ends" to his tail, and getting a good foundation for the clock case, which, placed lengthways, did duty for a "holt" or "trunk." Down this the terriers rushed to the fray—one or two, with rueful countenances, coming out a great deal more precipitately than they went in ; until a vixenish terrier, with sharp cropped ears (she was white with a smutty nose), walked deliberately down, and there was "a deal of drumming" at the lower end. Presently the turmoil extended towards the mouth of the den, and out tumbled dog and badger, but the white terrier had finished the poor victim. He opened his jaws once or twice upon the sward (as one of the bystanders, probably a florist, observed) "like a pair of garden shears," and in spite of cold water and brandy administered with a bottle—rather a ticklish operation as it seemed to me—the poor brute breathed his last, and the parish sexton, turning to a bystander, exclaimed ruefully that all the sport for that feast was over.

Nominally forbidden, cock-fighting was tacitly sanctioned at some schools ; and I recollect hearing of a village priest who eked out his income by pupils, and was remarkable for his grim views ecclesiastical, whose only remonstrance with his pupils was, one Easter Monday, "I hope, young gentlemen, there's nothing wrong going on in the barn, for I *can hear a deal of crowing.*"

Drinking—how long ago shall I say ? well, thirty years ago—was a very venial crime at our universities ; and well it might be, for all *my* dons but one were three-bottle men, and what could they say to an undergraduate ? I can tell you what one *did* say as four were carrying off an invalid who was biting fiercely at the cuffs of those Samaritans who had picked him up helpless in the " quad," " Don't hurt him, poor fellow ! he had better have had another bottle, and then he would have sobered under the table."

With a great deal of the immoral. we did not want for wholesome lessons in the capital punishment line. We hung then for arson, horse-stealing, and, if I am not wrong, for sheep-stealing.

We did not excel in cleanliness. There were not many advocates of cold tub in a morning. and many a student might, as far as his ablutions went, have got a degree in Germany.

Then how tight the clothes were ! Far tighter than the skin. The tailor tapped the chalk upon every little crease in the sleeve and across the back, until the force of tailors could no farther go ; and when we owed a very long bill he left in the basting cotton—much such a hint of non-payment as the old painter's, who put a pair of chalk moustaches upon the unpaid portrait as it hung in the Academy on the line. This puts me in mind (pardon the digression) of a story that went about, not long ago,

of a modern schneider, who was accosted at the covert side by
one of his customers, a terribly particular one as to fit, but
having, as regarded payment, the best lungs in the shires.
"I believe," he said, accosting his robe-maker, "You are
Mr. ——, of —— street?" "Yes, sir, I am." "Then," said
the customer, "just look at my coat. Doesn't it wrinkle in the
back?" "Decidedly," the tailor answered, not the least discon-
certed; "allow me—got a bit of chalk in my pocket," and,
leaning forward, he drew a large chalk mark across the pink.
"Send it us, to-morrow, sir, and it shall be remedied;" and with
that he made off, the whole field roaring with laughter at the
rebuke administered.

I go back to the old days again. Athletics! They were few,
and athletes scarce. Boating with in-rigged eights, sculling in
heavy skiffs or flat canoes, with partial training, and sometimes
with a discipline regarding only the morning's run and mutton
chops. I remember a capital eight being sent up to contend for
victory. It is as long ago as I can remember; and they won it
too, but they were so beaten that two or three had to be carried
out of the boat, and I think it shattered the constitutions of the
whole crew. Late hours, bad wine, smoking, and all that, won't
do, either in training or out of it, for long; and though we had
men who could row a mile or two, say from Iffley to Oxford, they
could not "stay."

But I have not half completed the list of implements in the
press and the bureau my friend and I turned out. "Badger-
tongs;" a "bull-iron," for hauling the unhappy animal to the
stake; "branding irons" for hound or horse; a copper abomina-
tion for burning down what the ignorant call "lampas" in a
horse's mouth, a process aggravating the pain under which the
colt suffers when cutting his teeth; a pulley and weights (the
ceilings of the old stable still retained the hooks in them) for
keeping the wounds of the nicked tails gaping, and so to prevent
the tendons from uniting; the saw for amputating the natural
spur of the cock, and which was contained in a pocket-knife;
and several dozen "dog-spears" for the protection of the coverts
—all these were there.

I don't say there is no ferocity in the present generation;
but it is not to be found in the polished or educated classes.
Anything like ruffianism or barbarity meets with something
sharper than rebukes; and I don't think that in all London
nowadays you would find a cock-pit in the upper story and a

band of music, whilst the hostess, with a bland smile, would telegraph you towards the cock-pit in the garret, and reassure you with the remark, " Our neighbours thinks as we've got a dance ! " It was so not much more than a score of years ago.

No man would dare to paint what Hogarth painted, supposing —vain notion, truly—that he was Hogarth's peer in genius ; nor to write as Fielding, even if surrounded by that novelist's contemporaries.

There is a rooted contempt for cruelty and coarseness, which leads to the disuse of the cock-pit, or oaths and curses as expletives in conversation.

I think most of this improvement had taken root at the very commencement of this reign. I am sure the purity of the Court, and the example set by " the father of our kings to be," did a great deal for the present generation. It is true that we did not agree with him in all his ideas of sport, and some of us had a far more fiery ardour in the chase : but we learnt a great deal of refinement from him, not only in the form and colour of the commonest themes, but in our manner and expression.

I recollect, very soon after the Royal marriage, the Prince came to Nuneham, where they stayed as guests of Archbishop Harcourt, and what a crowd from young Oxford rode out to welcome them.

I remember the Duke came about half-an-hour before her Majesty—a little man, in white trousers (badly made, my tailor said), in a yellow postchaise, his old Waterloo valet on the box ; then four greys and the Queen and her Consort, a very young man then ; and by each of the carriage-doors a yeomanry officer, with a very red face, then, galloping on hired screws, and a few on their own horses, all the men who could ride, and a good many who could not.

Next day the Prince came to " the grand commemoration," attended by Anson—" George Anson " I think they called him —and some one else, who stood behind his chair ; young, grave, sedate, handsome, in a dress-suit, with the garter on his knee ; dark hair and moustaches, and a melancholy though intelligent look. A great contrast to the tremendous waistcoats, the loud-pattern trousers, the claret, blue, drake's-neck green, and snuff-coloured coats, with their basket gilt buttons, which were there to greet him—many of them, I fear, still unpaid for ! And the next day he was seen visiting College gardens, Museum, College chapels, halls, and quadrangles in a dark frock-coat and the

remainder *en suite:* a very good exemplar to our "fast men,"
upon whom, by the way—some at least—the Prince's appearance was not lost. I can answer for one, at any rate, who came
an unlicked cub from Australia, and, having "gone the pace,"
and bolted from the course, fell in the Indian mutiny. "If," he
said, "I could venture to give an order, I would come out in a
dark suit, and I shall give my crimson velvet waistcoats to my
scout." There must be something in an example, for proctors,
doctors, and dons of every degree had attacked these waistcoats in
vain.

The impression of example was felt more year by year, and I
have always regretted that the author of our improvement as a
people did not live to see what I look upon as the completion of
a work which all true men watch with interest.

I could quote many instances of the benefit from this Royal
example ; but as I consult my notes my ear catches the sound
of altercation in my yard below, where I heard the postman (two
minutes and three-quarters behind his time) exchanging compliments with my servant, and asking him, with strong adjectives
and adjurations, if his "so-and-so" master means to detain *him*,
Her Majesty's servant : finishing with an anything but bland
permission to me to take my bag myself unless it is instantly
forthcoming.

Verily, he has lived beyond the reach of a good example ; or,
wait—perhaps he is a sportsman of the old school !

PAPER VII.

DENS AND SANCTUMS.

IF there is one picture of Hogarth's which enlists my sympathies more than another, it is that of "The Enraged Musician," beset by drum, horn, clarinet, milkmaid, ballad singer, screaming child, cleaver grinder, and dustman close at hand, whilst the cats are serenading him in the distance. What would not such a musical genius have given for a lone quiet room, apart from all these false notes and that cunningly-painted discord!

There is no doubt that some temperaments are so happily constituted as to be undisturbed by any sounds, musical or unmusical. The Battle of Prague (with the common accompaniments), those eternal "scales" (I know the very part where I may expect a break-down, a pause, and the usual expostulation of the governess); the measured thump of the rocking horse overhead, varied by a sudden fall, momentary silence, the scuffling of feet, and a prolonged roar; the crash of the crockery, the announcement that there is an end of the vegetable dishes, which can't be matched—these domestic catastrophes fall lightly enough upon some tough dispositions I could name; whilst street bawls, peripatetic organs, Punch (in more senses than one), and the various street bands of London murdered John Leech, and nearly drove Mr. Babbage wild.

When you have anything to do, it is a great blessing to be able to escape into some quiet place to do it—a den where none dares to follow you, where you put on the coals yourself, and without that crash which sends all your blood to your heart, and what is of more consequence, disarranges for ever that last neat thing in paragraphs.

At certain fixed seasons every Englishman's home is more or less a Pandemonium. When the "carpets are up"—especially the stair carpets—I can say for myself that I believe in the transmigration of souls. I am the camel fainting beneath that last straw, and I rejoice that I can "make tracks" for my home in the wilderness.

It has always appeared very strange to me that a man's

dressing room is for the most part so contrived as to be at once
the smallest, darkest, and most uncomfortable cabinet in the
dwelling. If he lays out the house himself—which nine times
out of ten it is a weak thing to do—he is satisfied to put up
with ten feet square and a boot rack, devoting one corner to the
shower bath, the other to his towels and lavatory; and very often
there is no means of lighting a fire or making things look cheerful for "master," on his return wet through after "drawing
blank" from "eleven thirty" to "three fifteen!"

! rue enough, the splash and slop of a dressing room is rather
discouraging, and 'tis an apartment which finds little favour
with any of us. After it has served its purpose, we gladly
throw the window open, and look for the neatly appointed breakfast room.

But supposing you are a restless spirit, that you come down
before they have let light into the hall, or that the house is as
yet involved in a sort of common ruin, or being sacked by housemaids and the footman out of livery ?

Here I blunder over the boots of yesterday, and in my lady's
drawing room I can hear as I listen the throbbing and long
pulses of the "carpet broom." Here, as I live, is a cracked
platter of tea-leaves ; and, as I run the gauntlet amidst domestics
who seem just as desirous to escape me, I stumble over a dust-
pan and coal scuttle in this darkened "atrium."

I have made it my business to notice quiet nooks and
corners lately, and to mark their excellences and defects—these
private rooms, apart from the sound of the school piano, the
slamming of doors, the harsh voices of vigorous servant maids,
and the rough dialect of groom and helper—where the ejacula-
tions that "Robert have a bin and throwd down the horse," or
that the youngest child but one "would have been burnt to death
but for," &c., &c., come upon you sobered and softened by time
—wherein it is death without benefit of clergy to appear (except
by proxy of the "Missus") with requests for the loan of a
hammer, an axe, a list of all the trains that stop at Swindon, a
teacupful of cod liver oil, or the well grapnels—where village
news breaks upon you by degrees, and you don't jump in your
chair as that loud ploughman proclaims like a stentor, "Brown's
five boys is got took down with the fever, and four on 'em won't
live the night !"—the door of which dwelling room shall be impenetrable as a portcullis to persevering wine merchants, peripatetic dentists, and Solomons with crystal spectacles, which

"cool" the eye, preserve the vision, and are recommended by
"the faculty,"—where that clamour and Babel of tongues which
maddens me, and which I fancy must much resemble in its inarticulate confusion, 500 or more excited Welshmen at a national
"Eisteddfod," is deadened into a murmur like the sound of the
aspens by the side of my favourite carp hole. So much for the
preamble ; now for the particulars.

You see in most country houses a good hall, which airs the
whole dwelling in summer, and warms it in winter. There is to
a certainty a good dining room, a drawing room, replete with
bric-à-brac, ormolu clocks, French polish, and possibly a sewing
machine to balance the "Erard."

For the most part, the library has a deserted appearance,
Above the books, including topography, Dugdale's "Monasticon,"
Burn's "Justice," and other light reading, it is very common to
suspend your ancestors. I know one room of this description
wherein frown innumerable militia colonels, backed by thundering
cannon and murderous engagements. In one large county house,
the library is also the lumber room, and the prospective barley
for future pheasants rests in sacks against folio Shakespeares,
and a veritable original edition of Ben Jonson. When I was
last there several volumes of rare value were displaced to make
room for twelve vases of blacking and six Bath bricks ; and the
most beautiful spider's web I ever saw in my life was suspended
from the ceiling to the corner of Gisborne's "Whole Duty of
Man."

Apart from the library, and generally remote from the most
select parts of the house, magistrates have what they call a
"justice room." It is a dreary apartment for the most part, and
the furniture is of the coarser sort. Sometimes there is an
official deal table, tolerably well stained, and above it numerous
pigeon-holes filled more or less with what, to the uninitiated,
resemble "briefs," but which a "justice's" wife pointed out to
me, in one instance, as "dummies." There, too, is the professional Testament with brass hinges, on which the "haw-
bucks" are sworn, after it has been ascertained that they know
the nature of an oath, and are prepared to be sworn accordingly.

One of the rooms I saw last has remarkably high windows,
and was entered on one side through the "still room," on the
other by the "butler's parlour."

In country houses—yea, even in "a villa," which I detest—
you want some room for yourself : a sanctum with a latch key,

and an approach *through* the house, and by way of the garden, if you will. It is of the utmost importance for your comfort that it should be away from the sounds of a family, and so contrived that those you desire to see may be ushered in and out without much trouble. You want a room cool, *light*, well ventilated, easily warmed, and fitted up to hold what you are constantly using, whether guns, fishing rods, or the smaller agricultural instruments, in a compact and even an ornamental form.

I have seen a good number of these rooms adapted for their purpose moderately well; some of them could scarcely be surpassed. Almost always they were *after-thoughts*—that is, they were built subsequently to the completion of the house; they had nothing to do with the original design.

I have seen one which, raised twelve feet or more above the ground, gives space for a keeper's gun room beneath; whilst above, with sofas round, and from bay windows, you can see the long reach of a trout river, and everything going on in the stable yards below. This room is thoroughly detached from the "manse," but it might very easily be approached by an ornamental bridge. It is fourteen feet square, and a great proportion of the sides is taken up with glass. You go up to it by an outside flight of steps, and there is a capital Swiss balcony or verandah all round. If they had put a ventilator in the roof, it would have been a perfect bachelor's room, fitted as it is with many of Negretti and Zambra's best instruments, and on the seaboard side as excellent a telescope as I ever saw.

I saw a room the other day which I thought excellent. This room, eighteen by twenty-two feet, is about two feet above the surface of the ground, and looks through two large French windows upon the croquet lawn, flower garden, and background of home coverts and deep woods. You can get to it through a long and winding passage without going through any of the suites of rooms, and you can leave it by the French doors, and be at once in your saddle room or stable. You can slip away from a bore or admit a friend, or ring up a servant to administer a caution about the way the oats are disappearing, the dull polish on those saddle bars, the scratch upon the carriage panel, the way they shut up and stifle the horses in the stable, or correct these various offences which cost a man of average income about two hundred pounds a year, to the advantage and benefit of no one on earth, but which a bad servant thinks it "impossible to prevent."

Now the ventilation of this room is *perfect*—although it is

covered with tiles, which to my mind are the next bad thing to
slates—for there is a double skylight in the top, with the power
to let a current of air through it at will, a large chimney and
chimney corner, and plenty of "head room," the middle of the
ceiling being twenty-one feet high at least.

The beams or rafters, or whatever builders call them, are of
varnished deal; the walls are covered with books of reference
and of imagination—I didn't see any law, physic, or philosophy;
and there were stuffed birds, preserved reptiles, and a few
antiquities, which would have raised the envy, some of them, of
Scott's "Antiquary." You could get by a short flight of stairs
into a very comfortable and pleasant dormitory, which the owner
thereof irreverently termed "The Barracks," for it had been the
home quarters of a younger brother, who had played heads or
tails with his life in the Crimea, India, and I know not where,
returning to this "roost" a full colonel, and I don't know what
besides.

However, let us leave this den or roost—and upon my word it
is a good one—to look at another, which is to my mind perfect.
I believe that it was built by a railway contractor, who rented a
house near me whilst he made that line, which has swallowed up
the fortunes—the *large* fortunes—of more that one good old
sterling county family.

Mr. Railway Contractor wanted more room for his wife's landau,
his mail phaeton, whitechapel, and private omnibus. He had a
largish family, and they were brought up to deny themselves
nothing. Some one said they were as improvident as a West-
end butcher—at that time beefsteaks were something like 1s. 6d.
a pound. At any rate, the contractor deserves well of his suc-
cessor, for he made him a fine set of coachhouses on the ground
floor, and first-class den *and ante-room* above.

These rooms are separate from the house, and on both sides
they have as much glass as you would desire in most conservatories. The top storey is about twenty-four feet wide, and fifty
feet long, approached from without by a wide flight of steps,
which leads to the first room, about fifteen feet long, and separated from the inner room by folding doors. It is now occupied
by a country gentleman who owns the estate, and who uses it as
his morning room and smoking room. As he is also a county
magistrate, and employs a great many hands, he has a good deal
of intercourse with the labouring classes, and he tells me you
can't possibly imagine the advantage he has over the men with long

and imaginary grievances. "I never admit them," he tells me,
"beyond this ante-room. I always get a warning that some one
is coming, for as they pass that footbridge there it lets off this
little trigger, and I get a glimpse at the comer before he can see
me. I go out and see him in that ante-room, and I can say as
soon as I like, 'Very good, I will see you again,' or 'There is
nothing to be done,' as the case may be, and I come through
these doors and am beyond his reach."

Whilst he was describing these arrangements the simple contrivance I have described was set in motion, but we had to go to the
window to see who was coming. I thought this a clumsy arrangement, and suggested one of those reflectors which give you a street
in miniature; and when I was last there he had adopted and was
pleased with my suggestion.

If you combine the writing room, justice room, gun room, *and
workshops,* you should have a good deal of space ; and everything
tending (like a lathe) to make a litter should be *far off,* and
beneath a skylight if possible.

I don't advise placing tools, which are portable, or a lathe,
which tempts meddlers irresistibly, in the ante-room. If the part
of your den appropriated to work is covered with oilcloth, litter
is soon swept up, and especially if in one corner you have a spout
or "shoot" leading to a dust bin below. Don't build it by
preference on the ground floor. The rooms under a den are
available for so many purposes, and it is so pleasant to have a
good "look-out." Have a verandah all round, and sacrifice
anything or everything to a *good draught* for your fire. Window
glass is cheap enough, and don't spare it. The contractor had
balancing shutters to his, which came up and went down almost
of their own accord. Take the season through, I think floorcloth
is better than a carpet. If you must have a carpet, there is
nothing like a Turkey carpet for economy, and I never saw one
worn out. One of the prettiest rooms I ever saw is panelled with
varnished deal ; but this was expensive—it cost over 30*l.* A
speaking tube to the house or stable need not cost much, and it
is a very convenient thing. If you have made your sanctum
comfortable, especially if it can be got at without difficulty from
the house, it is a famous place for those fellows who, when it
rains, smoke all day long ; and when they are in it, it will be
wise to take care that your house is well found in "soda and
brandy."

I have not said anything of one den which I have in my mind's eye, looking out up a ghost walk—a terrace, stone balustrades, and peacocks—where of a still evening you can just hear the wash of the sea upon the distant shingle beach, with its white closets stacked with havannahs. I speak feelingly of that " cool grot," as I write here with the thermometer at I don't know what !

Nor have I mentioned that room, half library, half work-room, and, an Irishman would tell you, half a dozen other things besides, which leads into conservatories, peach-houses, photo-graphic sanctums, pigeon-lofts, and poultry-houses where arti-ficial mothers act the entire part of hens (except, I believe, laying the eggs). For the once I shall not say anything of my private room, or the well-used ink-begrimed table which has been my support in many a struggle to get to the bottom of the second column of the *Field* in my writing, and yet to catch the post. My maid of all work says the boy's waiting for " the bag." All right ; here you are !

PAPER VIII.

THE RAT-CATCHER.

ON some occasions everything goes wrong. Whether it is "the planets that are a working," or what the evil influence may be, I suppose we shall never ascertain. The first reason my old laundress assures me is the correct one, and I accept it as a fact. At any rate, so it was one 5th of September, when two of us had prepared to start for a day's shooting about five miles away from home. I broke two boot laces ; I had a tender heel ; my groom, as we breakfasted, "wanted a word" with me, and stated his intention to marry our light-handed abigail, and to better himself. As he turned away he advised driving the bay instead of the brown, for Brown Stout seemed off his feed ; to make it worse, the bay had done twelve miles that morning, and was a four-year-old, hot in harness, and fretful unless he could snatch at his bit and do all twelve miles an hour. The prospect of unmitigated happiness had produced its effects upon my man servant, and as we drove along in my pet Whitechapel a faint squeak on my side of the cart intimated a hot wheel. There was no "spanner" in the driving box, though at the Squire's stables, which we were passing, we could have obtained oil ; so driving slowly the last two miles made us late by forty minutes all but a few seconds.

I could see that we had been the subject of animated discussion when we found our party at the trysting place, and, though our host was all that was kind and polite, his keeper looked glumpy and stern as he touched his hat and helped down my young setters. His subordinate wore the aspect of an injured man ; and "the friend from Oxfordshire," who had come down from the midst of his shorthorns and superphosphate, merely touched the brim of his white hat in recognition of an introduction which he evidently could have dispensed with, and at once put in his cartridges—a hint that there was no time to lose.

"Them dogs," the keeper ventured to remark, as he jerked his thumb towards my lemon-and-whites—"them dogs," he said (in a stentorian voice, which made them shake again, and intimated

F

his opinion that they were useless brutes), " arn't agoing to do anything to day. If master had some sandfoin, the birds would lay ; but I don't believe we shall get anything at all except in the hedges." And so I at once returned them to the custody of my servant, and my retriever, for all I cared, could have gone with them.

We spread out to walk, and we might as well have tried to shoot the emu—a bird the Irish naturalist described as " *extinct*, and therefore only to be obtained with difficulty." We fagged on for two hours. Such long hours they were to me and to my friend on the right !—him of the shorthorns, in the long-waisted coat with the large buttons, with that long waistcoat of the same material, the white wideawake hat, and the red face beneath it, a face that seemed somehow associated with " one cheer more " and a chorus. Two brace of birds and a "rail," no hares (my friend keeps greyhounds, and aspires to be the winner of the Waterloo Cup); coveys of twenty, coveys of eighteen, get up at sixty, seventy, and a hundred yards. I limp along wearily, and rejoice to see the little waggon and the luncheon.

Leaning on the tailboard of this primitive vehicle is the superannuated carter, very old, very long in the body, and particularly short in the legs ; in his present position he much resembles a greyhound eating off a kitchen dresser, and he has the same suspicious look. As we get nearer I make him out to be perhaps eighty, with a face indicating natural humour, and withal unconsciousness of the fact. His " boy," a son of fifty or sixty, is holding the horse, an active though coarse-bred hackney or roadster, who seems a little fretful, and is caparisoned with harness that has seen a deal of service. " The tugs," the old man tells us, have broken once as he came along. The old man has but one eye ; the other, I learn, "master's grandfather " shot out for him years ago, and he has never given his mind to shooting since. " Now," he adds, with much loquacity, as soon as we have done luncheon and he has driven us to the next ground (two miles away), " we shall turn back and kill them rats in the barn with master's old greyhound," which he states to be "the best dog as is."

As we discussed the good things from the waggon, he waited with what, considering his age, I might call alacrity ; regretting that his last daughter had died a couple of years before, who would have served us better, for she was " as handy as a horse about a house."

" Twelve children " he had reared, but the six girls all died ;

and he supposed if that boy holding the horse had been a girl, he would have died too.

"Better than eighty," he was, "last Lammas." "Work? Yes, with any man ; and it was because he had taken care of himself and stuck to cider. Someone had told his missis that he was hearty because he hadn't worked his mind, and that was the first time he had ever known he had one. He thought such things belonged to gentlefolks."

"No school when he was young," he said, "nor yet gas, nor any of these engines." "Now," he added, "there's brandy, and penny papers, and lucifers to be had in our parish ; and they *do* say we shall have a policeman, but of course he'll have to keep the parishes quiet and help the gamekeepers for miles round."

You want the man and his manner ; words of mine won't represent it, nor explain the way in which his good humour, patience, thankfulness, and quiet wit dispelled the feeling of mortification which we had been undergoing until the lunch began ; and I have a suspicion that somewhat of our improved feelings may be ascribed to that hamper of cold soda-water, each bottle of which we just flavoured with brandy to "kill the insects."

And when he went on to tell us of his terriers and ferrets, which by the aid, assistance, and co-operation of his master he possessed in numbers, and which state of things he considered affluence, the gloomiest man of the party cheered up, and suggested an adjournment to the barn, and calling for the ferrets and terriers on our way.

We had a level "down" to cross, covered with the scars of cart-wheels, and one track was marked with heaps of flints to guide night travellers making a short cut to Old Sarum ; so we got into the waggon in a body, the old man asserting his privilege to drive, though with many misgivings as to the old harness, which had been treacherous for years, but now was a trifle worse than perilous. We did very well on a dead level, but the young horse broke the "tugs" going up the very first incline ; and, what with anxiety to stop him, and misgivings as to the reins, old Bob, the driver, looked something like a large S reversed upon the footboard.

I can't say his cottage was picturesque, though it was ruinous. The bailiff had not been to school for nothing, and, having a careless squire, it was his way to whitewash the outsides, and make out a good long bill for mending interiors. Sometimes they

F 2

whitewashed that side only next the road, like the lazy coachman who cleaned that part of the body and those wheels of the
landau which faced his mistress as he took her up. She used
to tell all her friends that he was "quite a lady's servant! So
he was.

Inside Bob's cottage everything was neat enough, though he
said, with grim politeness, " he could not ask us upstairs, as he had
lent his ladder ; and then," he said. "you must go on all fours,
or your legs will break the flooring."

"Which is best ?" he said, with naive simplicity, "to sleep upstairs and tumble through, or to sleep down here, and for them
to fall atop of you ?" Not waiting for a reply, he crept through
the low back door, and reappeared with three or four white
terriers, which he carried in his arms much as I have seen a
gardener carry flower-pots, whilst an old blue greyhound limped
behind him.

" The barn, gentlemen," he said, " is only just across here, and
perhaps you wouldn't mind walking ?" Remembering the exploits of the coarse-made hack, which had manifested some
restiveness, and the brittleness of the harness, I was spokesman,
and acquiesced.

"Give me my gloves, missis," he said to an old woman, but who
might be ten years younger than her husband. "Barn rats ain't
poisonous like town ones if they bites you, but I keeps 'em from
doing it 'cause I don't like to gratify 'em. And now I'll get the
ferrets," which he proceeded to select, from a ferret box of his
master's which stood at the end of the house under the eaves,
four or five "rippers" as he called them—pushing them about
with his naked hands as a fish-woman might handle sprats, or a
lady would scrutinise a tray of ribbons.

" Oh, dear," he said, raising his voice that the old woman might
hear him, " where's that little white ferret with the rings in his
lips ? That's the handiest way to muzzle 'em," he told me confidentially, giving a spasmodic jerk to the lid which had no eye
beneath it ; and at the same time remembering that he had the
animal he asked about in his pocket, where he had been all the
morning (as he would work in a line); then he put about four
or five white ones, the favourite included, into a box something
like a bird cage, which he slung over his shoulders, whistled to
his terriers, which had remained around his cottage fire, and
walked across the down much more actively than I should have
expected.

"You'll see a lot of rats, I expect," he told us; "most of our farmers have thrashed, because they think wheat's agoing to fall; and you should hear what excuses they make. Sometimes they tell people they want the straw; but there is one of 'em that always makes his ricks on furze faggots, and when he sends for ' the steamer ' he always says the same thing—that his wife wants the bedding of the rick to heat the oven!

" Here's the barn. sir. Lor, what a lot there must be here! Don't make no noise. I thinks," he said (looking round with his one eye, which seemed to expand under his suppressed excitement), " I thinks lots of rats, and some cider, and white terriers, and ferrets, when they bolts quick—why, it's better than being a king. I'd sooner be here," he continued, as he busied himself to untie a knot in the ferret bag with his nails and teeth—"I'd sooner be here than in that place you was talking of to the young lady, Master Henry. when I came round the corner, and you said I was always where I shouldn't be. Oh, oh," he said, " that's the place —Paradise ; well, I'd sooner be here than in Paradise. I'm always more at home with dogs and ferrets than women, specially _gen_teel ones. Come on Slippery "—this to a white terrier, which he took under one arm, as he held a bouquet of ferrets, all white ones. in his left hand, and contemplated their red eyes and writhing bodies with much pleasure. " Stop, though," he said, offering the bunch of ferrets to the visitor nearest him ; " perhaps you wouldn't mind holding them one minute as I put down the dogs. This old greyhound. he must have his own way ; and if he's huffed he won't do nothing." But. seeing his proffered loan of the ferrets was declined, he handed them to a labourer, who was the widower of his daughter deceased, and caught up three or four terriers before he reconnoitered his position.

Slippery he dropped outside at a bolt hole, where a great deal of earth had been " drawn," as he explained, since Tuesday, and made him lie down at an angle about a foot from the wall. To me the dog seemed rather stupid, and somewhat over-broken, probably stubborn also, for he left his place and moved off a couple of feet, when he crouched and looked with a slight want of confidence at old Robert, whose one eye just observed the movement. But it was at once evident to the old man that this faithful servant of his had "shifted " to watch and command two holes instead of one, and the rat-catcher gave him an approving nod.

Carefully going round the old building, and dropping a dog at

each likely place, he had disposed of all that he brought with
him, and was short of dogs at last. "We must have the young
ones," he remarked, as, without ceremony, he walked briskly to
his cottage, whilst the dogs remained stiff as pointers on game,
never turned their heads, and stood motionless till he returned
with three young white terriers, all of one litter, white with blue
or black-blue ears, and a terrier with too much bull about his
head, which he declared had killed a badger in his earth.

"Never mind his head, sir," he replied to my objection ;
you reminds me of master finding fault with his best cow because
she has ugly horns. I tells him we don't get milk out of her
horn. I took him once to show a gentleman as had been a
Queen's messenger, and he wouldn't believe in him, though I
only asked a pound for him ; but a gentleman as is in some
grand soldier regiment gave me five pounds for him and asked no
questions, and he is to go to London next week."

This second sample of terriers, though neat as the dogs I had
already seen, were by no means so subdued. They were all life
and animation, and were only fit to work under old Robert's eye.
One or two required several cuffs and whispered admonitions
before they would be persuaded to guard a hole, and one milk-white
bitch of 10lb. or thereabouts insisted on gambolling to the last
moment with the lame greyhound, who had taken his post close to
the end of the barn, which was half full of barley in the straw,
trodden in hard by my friend's brown shooting pony, who, after
eight hours' hard tramping at this work, and sliding down, was
bridled, saddled, ridden, and made comparatively quiet for the
gun.

They were all fox-terriers, inside the barn and out of it—a
good straight-legged, active, sensible, punishing sort—level-jawed,
with black noses, and ribs and shoulders which would have
caught the eye of Captain Percy Williams or Jack Russell.

As soon as two ferrets (called by the ratcatcher " The Doctor"
and " Old Stumpy") were in action, there was a marked
difference in the position and expression of the dogs. Burke, a
white one, named after that great surgeons' purveyor who was
the terror of my childhood, turned his head from side to side, and
as he detected, after giving the matter keen attention, a sort of
rumbling noise as though a train of rats were coming express
that way by "the underground," opened his teeth a little and
prepared for a rush. A brown streak on the floor, a snap, and a
large mother rat is dying, and the dog is motionless as before.

Outside there is a scurry and a squeak, and through the barn
door thrown open I see Slippery and a rat roll over, the rat left
dead, and the dog in hot pursuit of something in the straw.

The old greyhound shows some excitement too, and presently
a rat, as it seems to me, jumps into his wide jaws, which close
and open to drop a " buck" rat (as Bob calls it), cut in half, and
dead before it reaches the oak boards.

Here we have a chase, three dogs all after him as the
" varmint" slips under the winnowing machine, dodges beneath
the " barley booby," and is lost behind the bushel measure and
half a dozen harvest rakes. He is not gone far, though.
Worry, the white terrier, with the rich foxhound tan cheeks,
stands sentry and won't move. Two of us move the *impedimenta*,
as Livy calls such gear, and, though the eye can't follow the
game, the little bitch is after him, and he pays forfeit.

Here a whole bevy bolt in desperation, and in unpleasant
proximity to the last peers the face of the white ferret, " The
Doctor, and it is hard to say whether his eyes or lips are reddest.
He has evidently been operating successfully, and has cut his
patients about a good deal.

Attracted by the chase of these, I don't observe the greyhound
for some ten minutes : but presently, as Bob nudges my elbow, I
see him within a few yards of his first position, and seven or
eight rats dead around him. One has scarce expired, and is
gasping his life away. The old dog casts a look at him, and
would say if he could, no doubt, " Don't make such a fuss about
it ; get on with your dying ; you will soon be all right." (I have
heard " Christians" comfort a suffering human creature in much
the same way). A rat runs between my legs, and the white dogs
are round my feet like a swarm of bees. There is a sort of scurry
and disturbance round about me, which somehow makes me think
of the coming elections, and presently a dead rat is left within
five or six feet of me, gasping like—what shall I say?—a rejected
candidate.

There were intervals between these incidents, and deep consul-
tations between master and man as to what hole should be
operated upon, and what ferret should be used ; but they were
not long. The great thing is, old Bob observed, to keep on
worrying 'em—don't give 'em no " let up" (rest). Master
Henry put in The Butcher, a white ferret, who was supposed to
exceed all the family in atrocity and intelligence ; " he'll nurse
'em up!" And at another spot where there were suspicions of a

family, I might call it a domestic circle, of young rats in a nest, there were many proposals, the last being acceded to—to let 'em grow until they were big enough to afford another day. " If we are lucky," the old man said, " we shall have swarms of rats by October, when the rest of the ricks are thrashed ;" and with this promise we were compelled to be content.

As the rats seemed sensibly diminishing, we were inclined to stop, but the old man declined moving his dogs until the ferrets, especially " The Butcher"—declined business. " They've got a few favourites inside, bless you !" said Robert, " and won't leave them ;" and so it proved. There were a few desultory " bolts" from time to time, when, with a little trouble and patience, he collected his ferrets, counted and cut off the rats' tails, and whistled his dogs away.

" All your traps and poisoning and what not," he said (as he touched his hat and pocketed the half-crown I gave him), " all your traps and drugs is no use whatever, compared with terriers and ferrets—provided," he remarked complacently, " as you've a man who has patience and never makes no noise. I only wish I had taken to it when I was a young man. I should have been pretty near a professional ! Shouldn't I, Master Henry ?"

PAPER IX.

EARLY MORNING IN LONDON.

WHAT do you call early ?—That is the question. In the Albany, twelve o'clock perhaps; but in this instance I am thinking of sunrise, 3.57 a.m.

How many are astir in the great city at this hour—in Kensington. Bayswater, Notting-hill. or the fashionable squares ?

These questions occurred to me as I heard a mixed party talking of what they had seen in London. and what remained to be seen ; and I discovered the experience of the majority was confined to the boundary of certain hours. A plethoric old gentleman, "something in the City," restricted his observations to what he saw through the windows of his brougham, between Acton and Bread-street, and had seen nothing else "this nine year." "Seen the Derby ?" Not he ! "John Parry ?" Certainly not ; but his "son Tom there at the bottom of the table" (with the expansive dinner shirt and brilliant studs ; his hair parted down the middle, and up again ; with moustache, and scarlet geranium at his button-hole), " *he seen it. he did.*"

Two of our company had seen the sun rise from Waterloo-bridge after a late dinner and an equivocal party, consisting of dancers and musicians ; but having witnessed this " glorious sight," as one of them called it. which he added he never expected to see again, he resumed his cab, drove home, and buried his head beneath the sheets.

So there was nothing for it but to get up myself next morning, and to take observations on my own hook.

At half-past three a.m., on the thirtieth day of May last, I threw up the window of my bedroom and looked out towards Lord Holland's park. The very morning for my purpose, and the aneroid barometer steady and inclined to rise. No treat, remember, to feel yourself locked out at such an hour as this, and to have to stand under archways in the rain, or sit in a four-wheeler and while away five hours ! To tell the truth, I should have been pleased to observe a cloudy sky as an excuse for

turning in again. As it was, I followed the example of our
Continental heroes—I smote myself on the breast and cried
" courage," and so dressed myself.

I crept down the stairs, feeling somewhat, I fancy, like a burglar,
and narrowly missed the coal-skuttle on one landing. I unbarred
the front door "gingerly," and stepped out; the door slammed
behind me, and, like my friend Fechter, in the " Duke's Motto,"
" I am here."

In the utter solitude of a fashionable Bayswater-street! A
solitude relieved by the presence of two policemen—one in the
foreground leaning against the area palings, through which he
has received many a pound of cold mutton ; another is walking
towards him, from what painters call the middle distance, with
slow and measured tread.

The white houses on their own lawns as I come down the hill
answer "Mrs. Fuggleston's" description of a suburban villa to a
nicety, they are " so like poached eggs on spinach." And the
cats ! Every green is occupied by two, three, or more ; and
occasionally I hear their refreshing melody.

In the extreme distance I observe (it is four o'clock now) a
four-wheeler at breakfast, and I make sure of an easy ride into
the heart of London. To my dismay, as I approach him he
acknowledges the hail of a young late gentleman, with disordered
hair, his white waistcoat dashed with claret ; and I have to walk.

Never mind : a little further I shall find a cabstand. I *do*
find it, but there are no cabs. Nothing for it but to turn into
the High-street ; but there, too, all is silence, excepting a distant
sound of wheels. I walk on enjoying the fresh cool air, and
presently I am overtaken by a greengrocer's cart, drawn by a
bright. broken-down chestnut thoroughbred, over whose hind
quarters I observe a substantial kicking-strap.

I hail my friend the greengrocer, who, as he arranges his blue
serge apron, curtly demands " What's up ?"

I blandly request to be driven to Covent Garden, whither I
presume that vicious chestnut and he are travelling.

" Well," he rejoins, " so I am, yer see ; but how is it you're a
walking ? Haven't you got a van ? I suppose (glancing at my
watch and chain)—I suppose you're in a large way ?"

I put my friend right on this point, and explain that I am
actuated solely by curiosity. I believe that he considered
curiosity to be some herb or vegetable, for he remarked that he
" never saw none there, and if there was, he couldn't bring it back

'for me;" adding (I can hardly s y as a rider) that "for that matter I couldn't bring *you* back neether, for I shall be chuck full of cabbages, and you'll spile 'em." Then his better feelings overcame his scruples, and he permitted me to "jump up."

As we approached the Marble Arch a few postmen, singly and in pairs, were hastening off to get their letters, and a large flock of sheep, driven by a dog (the man in front), passed in a leisurely way along Oxford-street. Regent-circus was desolate, excepting one or two shivering figures huddled on a doorstep, and a man and woman, decent and sober, who were to all appearance walking at a very slow pace to while away the time, with a despondent aspect which it was sad to see.

Arrived at King-street, Covent-garden, we came upon huge waggons of greens which blocked up the thoroughfare, and close to some hotel the vicious chestnut pulled up. "He won't go no further," said my friend the greengrocer; "and what's more, I don't want him to. Now, if you will tell me what you want, I'll help you to buy it; I can get it cheaper than you can."

I assured him I simply desired to see the market, and, having given him an admirable bas-relief likeness of Her Majesty wrought in silver, I left him with my best thanks.

A striking contrast to the quiet and stillness of the London streets as I turn into this vegetable market, which I have in former days contemplated often enough at mid-day from the windows of the old Tavistock.

Here, in the thick of it, are crate-like waggons of young onions, and loads of carrots, as big in bulk as a labourer's cottage, discharging into vast round baskets held by men with porter's knots, who, as soon as their dozens are told off, run with them to the carts and vans of the wholesale dealers; these will shortly disperse them, by means of their fast-trotting ponies, amongst the retail shops of London.

A costermonger, one of the better class, a well-to-do man apparently, from his style of dress—possibly a sort of middleman or go-between, who buys for the trade—is contemplating a pyramid of rhubarb, his eye wandering thence to a stack of red radishes and lettuce packed in layers on a chair waggon which hails from "Wickham;" and to his left I observe a breakfast party *al fresco*, the materials for the repast being young onions, bread and cheese, and porter. Further on I see geraniums and pinks all in bloom, but of a coarse and gaudy kind, mixed up with flaring yellow wall-flowers and Brompton stocks.

By the church palings men, women, and children are sitting, or in a half-recumbent position, making showy little bouquets with practised taste and elegance.   One rather pretty Irish girl of about thirteen—not more—is surrounded by a group, who copy her, and evidently she is an adept, for older hands wait to see what she will take next, and look up to her as an authority. Little creatures of four or five years old are assorting the flowers if they can do no more, and thus dividing the labour with older hands.   The flowers are as fresh as though just gathered, and cannot have come from far, nor have been long in transit.   The roses have the dew on them still.   Here roses and geraniums are the principal combinations, with a sprig of lemon plant, and perhaps a spray of myrtle.

Leaving the bouquet-makers, I find Russell-street jammed with " empties," and the same I may say of some part of Wellington-street. Brydges-street, and Bow-street on one side, and Henrietta-street on the other; and I turn for the Flower-market, and wander down an avenue of peonies and lilies of the valley.   Then I come to yards square of blue nemophila, plots of nasturtiums, masses of large and choice pansies in pots or balls—the latter, as yet, undrooping from removal—and all at once I find myself in a parterre of scarlet geraniums, their flashy flowers relieved by whole banks of fresh green ferns and rich mosses, which mingle with blue hydrangeas, mignonette, musk in full bloom, and exotic heath, all blossoming and scenting the air.

I see that Londoners do not despise the flowers we scorn in our country walks; for here is a cartload of buttercups, and further on a donkey-cart is loaded with groundsel, forming about a hundredth part of a bale of that bird's provender which blocks a neighbouring street.

I go through knots of squalid women who are bargaining for oranges and nuts, and in the heat of the argument one of them has deposited, or I might almost say *thrown*, her child into a vast round basket of filberts or " cobs," and it is disappearing as in a quick-sand beneath my eyes.   Now I am on my way to the fruit market, and I pass a main avenue, where sharp youths with gold pins, and rings too sometimes, are dressing windows.

Hitherto I have passed unmolested ; but one of this pert fraternity, perhaps thinking I observe his wares too keenly, asks me in a flippant manner, " What's up ?"   In his window, dressed as it is with great taste and neatness, are gooseberries, straw-berries, cherries, tomatoes, apricots, cucumbers, apples, large round black grapes, and new potatoes. Messrs. Pankhurst have as good a show as anyone, and further on are groves of fancy grasses, petunias, geraniums, and yellow roses. Calceolarias, mushrooms, pines, immortelles, horse-radish, peas, mint, and various herbs are mingled with baskets of peaches, nectarines, apricots, and various fruits, done up singly, or cozily reclining in coloured tissue paper

Here are young girls making up "wedding orders;" the bride's bouquet is just completed, and six of those allotted to the bridesmaids are " waiting for the forget-me-not," which the master of the establishment had ordered, as he impatiently observed, three weeks ago—" *Three weeks ago I ordered 'em!*" Leaving my purple-faced friend in this fix, I thread my way to Drury-lane, and hail yellow Hansom 6257, who is breakfasting on salad and hard-boiled eggs, his tea-can held for him by his little daughter, as I suppose, and I request to be driven to what he repeats after me as "Ledunall."

We thread Brydges-street with difficulty, and are in the stillness and solitude of the Strand. The sun is well up now ; it shines full into the hood of my orange Hansom, and sparkles on the hame rings and terrets of the big, ragged-hipped bay that bowls us along towards "Ledunall." Every shutter is up in these desert places ; but now and then we come upon a lone cab and crippled horse. As far as Temple Bar we meet no vehicles, or scarcely any, and I speculate upon the admirable scene this part of the Strand would form for football, with Temple Bar for a goal.

In Fleet-street there is somewhat of life. Two or three vans heaped with newspapers in large bales are hastening to impart the latest news to the uttermost corners of the earth. Porters sway from side to side with vast masses of *Times* and *Telegraphs, Stars* and *Standards*, with other publications, and there is a stream of costermongers' barrows and trucks trickling down towards Covent Garden.

Cheapside, the Royal Exchange, Cornhill, are all solitudes ; but in Leadenhall-street there is a smell of salt and hides, and I find a bustle in the midst of the beef of that celebrated market.

There I wander from beef to mutton, thence to veal, and so on to a vast acreage of plucked fowls, ducks, and pigeons, flanked by little avenues of bulldogs, inferior terriers and spaniels ; hedgehogs, mottled mice, young magpies, tortoises, a prime young raven of it may be threescore and ten, and Aylesbury or Rouen ducks, all for sale, dead or alive. Rabbits, yellow, mottled, white with pink eyes, black, grey, dun, and wild, are crowded in coops, together with a vicious monkey, a rare singing lark, and a blackbird who considers five a.m. midday, and makes the avenues of the market ring again. Here are parrots, paroquets, and, as I live, two tame kingfishers. Opposite are crates of live "hoopers" and other swans ; close by a peacock and his mate, two Cornish choughs with their bills and legs looking like Roake and Varty's office sealing-wax. I can have any bird, beast, or reptile for my money, and a pert shopboy with a tin botanising case under his arm asks me if I " can do anything in snakes."

Here I see a "store cage" full of quails, with their sudden fate before them ; for a journeyman poulterer is killing and plucking them one by one, just as the poor French victims were drawn for slaughter in the Reign of Terror. As I brush past him, his large coarse hand is grappling for a fresh victim amongst the fluttering group ; before I am out of sight, it is selected, dead, and half-naked, liked those trussed and vine-leaved on the shelf beside the living birds.

Here I see tame squirrels, dormice, a solemn horned owl, two jackdaws, and a half-callow nest of young thrushes gaping and showing their yellow throats. Here are two storks from Holland, and long-coated white kittens drinking " London milk ;" further on, a bowl of gold and silver fish, with little portable globes, each furnished with an indiarubber covering, for convenience of transit. And here, in the main street, I come upon the yellow Hansom waiting me, and, to his surprise, I give him his next order—" Billingsgate !"

We trot down empty Gracechurch-street and I catch a glimpse of Lombard-street, which is a silent waste, save that in one place a knot of artizans, with their inseparable saws and flag baskets, are grouped round a bank under repairs ; and now and then we come upon various operatives walking briskly to their work.

King William-street is pretty well filled with costermongers, and around the base of the Monument they swarm like bees. I am now sensible of a smell of dried fish, and, in the street of that name, I mentally eschew fish for ever.

Here the cab is blocked, and I walk on as well as I may through " fellowship porters," bales of shrimps, and vast covered and open vans, all ready to start north, south, east, and west, to feed the provinces. I turn to my right, and I am in the roar and confusion of Billingsgate.

I pass heaps upon heaps of dried fish, shrimps shot up in stacks like barley in a barn, and a vast rockwork of black lobsters and sea weed. Here are ships on the Thames discharging whiting, cod, soles, turbot, and long boxes of salmon, which I shortly after see unpacked, frozen hard in ice. One part of the market is set apart for flat fish—another for monsters in shell armour. Steamers from Ireland and Scotland, Norway, and various "foreign parts" are lying off; and here a gentleman in a white hat and waterproof (the latter resembling armour, so covered is it with scales) is holding a rapid auction.

"Now then," I hear him say, "Now then, you mackerel-buyers, come on ; and you that don't want 'em, don't block the way—you're stopping business."

Then the crates of boiled crabs and lobsters came along the corridors, filling the air with steam ; and as I neared the main avenue there was more crowding and crushing and confusion over again ; the porters shouting, or I should say singing, as they carried and balanced four or five boxes on their heads, "Hoi! Hoi! can't you *hear?*"

At seven a.m. I left London Bridge, in an atmosphere as clear as Italy ; but the silence of morning was over, and already the streets swarmed with people, and chiefly brewers' drays or water-carts. By the time I had reached Oxford-street the servants were beating the mats against the lamp-posts, and horses were exercising in their clothing. The unhappy "companions" (ladies of small means) were out airing their mistresses' pugs and spaniels ; fat animals they seemed, and troubled with the vapours. The chaffcutters were going their rounds, and hay, grass, and vetches were coming in.

7.45. The early risers are on their hacks, and making for Rotten-row ; and I pass open windows and witness early break-fasts as I near the suburbs.

Twice I observe a cluster, even thus early, around Punch and Judy, and in the last case I stop to see the favourite "dog scene," which proves a complete success. Yet the man who comes to me with the red decanter-stand tells me "He ain't been long at it ; but then," he adds, with a confidential wink, "ain't he cunning, that's all ! We calls him Gladstone—all he wants is temper !"

As I turn round I see a crowd gathering round a large iron girder, which, in turning a street-corner, had broken a window in the High-street of Notting-hill. What a flock of people gather together in a few seconds, where four hours ago all was desolate! I with difficulty thread my way through them, and passing the street of villas, (poached eggs and spinach), reach home in time for breakfast.

"Hullo! I say! where's my handkerchief ?"—Gone.

PAPER X.

THE EARTHSTOPPER.

I WAS brought up with my brother in Leicestershire (there were but two of us) to a thorough practical acquaintance with every country pursuit. Ours formed the centre of four estates, and my father and his neighbours were on the best of terms. We all preserved our foxes, and we shot the outsides of our manors no harder than the best coverts.

The second son always entered the army, and I was to form no exception to the rule; so I had my seven years of it, got my troop, and sold out. I passed a few years on the Continent, and finished with a few months' shooting in Algeria, when I made up my mind to try the United States; and after some good sport in pursuit of ruffed grouse in the Eastern States, I had even the luck, before setting sale for England, to have a very pretty hand-to-hand encounter with a bear.

I landed in Liverpool early in July, and reached our Leicestershire home the following morning, to find my poor old father almost at the point of death. As I entered the room he turned his head languidly on his pillow, and scanned me for some minutes with a puzzled look. His mind had been wandering for some days, and before the partial paralysis of his brain had affected his reason, he had expressed himself most anxiously as to my future prospects.

"I should have left him," he said, as they explained to me, "the property I bought since his mother's death, but he will be too heavy to ride in a grass country. He is three stone heavier than his brother, and he can go very respectably in a vale country with any of them; so I shall leave him my money in the Funds, and when I am gone he can buy a place for himself."

Having satisfied himself apparently as to my identity, he opened his hand, which lay languidly on the pillow, and fixed his eyes upon my face. As I took his hand in mine, he moved his lips as though to give me some recognition or to express some wish, but I could not make out his meaning. However, I understood from

G

the physician who put his ear to my father's lips, that it had
some reference to my weight. He did not live long after this.

A few months after his death my brother and I went up to
London to inquire among the estate agents for a property likely
to meet my wishes. It was in consequence of an interview with
the very blandest estate agent, I should say, in the whole metropolis, that I ran down to a western county to inspect an estate,
within reach, he told me, of four packs of " 'ouns ;" and it was
whilst I made my mental notes of Ersewater that I formed an
acquaintance with the old Earthstopper.

I had satisfied myself that the place, though retired, was pretty
much to my liking, and that the old residence, although anything
but large enough, was comfortable in the main. The stables and
loose boxes were airy, roomy, well-drained and ventilated, and
I was especially taken with a room adjoining the stables, used by
the former occupant as a lathe-room, gunroom, and study all
combined. It had one especial recommendation to me. It was
nearly all windows, and consequently very light, and it looked
down one of the most charming valleys I think I ever saw. I
therefore sent for a couple of hunters which had been my father's,
and which were left me in a codicil expressing his satisfaction
that they " had plenty of bone below the knee, and good backs,
and were therefore equal to my weight," and determined to see
what one of the four packs of hounds was like, and whether I
could go respectably in this western county.

I had about seven miles to ride to the meet from my hotel, the
Red Lion, on a dry and rather dusty day, and I had completed
about five of them, when I could observe the huntsman and his
pack and whips jogging along at a leisurely pace about a mile
ahead, and I was able to keep them well in view almost all the
way until we reached the covert side. Perhaps fifty or sixty
were assembled when I reached it, and the master, on his blood
chesnut, came up just behind me. He was just the weight to
have pleased my father—about nine stone ; but I think my
parent would, for his failing in that respect, have cut off the
huntsman with a shilling.

Several of the nondescript pedestrians usually present at every
meet were smoking or lounging about the fence of the covert, but
one only attracted my attention. This was a thin, active, white-
haired man of perhaps sixty or more, in height about 5ft. 10in.
He had a thin aquiline nose, a keen pair of grey eyes, a pro-
minent chin and thin lips, and a most shrewd, intelligent

expression. He was dressed in what evidently had been a forest-green long skirted keeper's coat of plush or velveteen, but it had faded in a general way to a dull olive. His waistcoat, evidently a cast-off from the servants' hall, was of red cloth or kerseymere, and he wore leggings up to his thighs. He carried a light strong spade upon his shoulder, and was, I observed, noticed by the master as he rode past me, with a smile and some good-natured observation.

A few late men, including a pink exquisite of the first water and a very long melancholy farmer, were the only additions as the hounds were sent into covert and we drew it blank. We drew three coverts, one a large one, with the same result.

I then observed a short conference between the master and my friend with the spade, ending in our making for a middling-sized gorse on the side of a hill, from which, on the other side of a narrow lane, we looked into a valley of grass land, with a brook about eight feet wide dividing two estates. I saw the old Earth-stopper (for such he was) making for a knoll about a quarter of a mile to my left, and keenly observing the hounds, which began drawing with increased activity, and occasionally plunging over the gorse, and then showing nothing but their sterns. As they neared the further corner one or two gave tongue, when I observed my old acquaintance crouched down to a level with a bush which obscured him from view. At the same moment the whole pack opened, and the Earthstopper, taking off his hat, gave such a view holloa as I think I never heard before.

The pack flew the bank that inclosed the gorse, in scattered order, and scrambled down the steep incline for the valley as best they could ; but, once over the lane, they raced sterns down for their fox, literally like a flock of pigeons.

I got down the bank and dropped into the lane as gently as I could, and had scarcely time to do so when the master's rough rider, on a brown thorough-bred, took the lane in his stride, and before I could follow him into the field beyond, he was gathering himself together for the water jump, which the master's chestnut and he cleared abreast. I should say we had about ten minutes at a slapping pace (which tailed off the boys and trousers, but could not shake off the pink exquisite and the long farmer), when the fox turned to the right, and made for a fir plantation, and very soon after the hounds threw up.

As I knew it was a case of open earth or a drain, I was in no hurry, and observed the Earthstopper close at my girths.

"Just what I told the Squire," he observed, touching his hat ;
" these keepers never will stop 'em out anything like workmen."
And as we had reached the earth by this time, I could see the
huntsman dismounted and the master coming up.

"Oh, yes, dig him, Bertie." said the master as the Earthstopper threw off his olive plush and went on his knees to
scrutinise the earth.

"Not very far in, master," was his quiet observation, as a
smooth white terrier, which had been barking in there out of
sight, came out for a little fresh air, and was seized by the old
Earthstopper before he could honourably inter himself again.

Fifteen or twenty years ago a game, active, handsome, willing
fox-terrier was by no means a common thing. In the south of
England you might meet with one occasionally just as you might
drop upon a light airy hack. or a strong, handsome, elastic pony ;
but it was almost impossible to get possession of such a dog as
the old man had with him. A black-nosed, black-eyed and foxy-
faced varmint-looking fellow, perhaps little over a dozen pounds
in weight, with a hard, impenetrable coat, straight legs, a
famous loin, and ears small, round, and dropping close to his
head, and nearly as thin as bank-notes. A few blue-black mottles
on his cheeks, and black ears, were the only exceptions to his
white colour, and he was smooth enough until he was excited by
being sent to ground, and even now, at a word from his master,
he was content ; and although he still kept up his hackles, he sat
down moderately patient, venting his curiosity by listening
intently with his head on one side, for any evidence of a move in
the earth below him. The old man called him "Denny," I
remember, and said he was given to him by a gentleman at
Dennington. near Barnstaple, which accounted for his form and
quality, both of which would have satisfied even the fastidious
taste of the fox-terrier breeder of the day—I may as well say
at once of Mr. Wootton.

"A good thing he passed that breeding earth above, by the
little vale, or we should have had a night's work," said Bertie ;
" but he isn't more than six feet in this time." And without more
words he set himself to shovel away the steep bank, and in
about twenty minutes we were handy to our fox.

The huntsman then took the spade and opened the mouth a
good deal, and we could see just the tip of his brush. A little
more digging and he seized the brush firmly with his left hand,
and ran his right hand up the fox's back, then took him firmly by

the poll, let go the brush, had him by the hind legs, and drew him from his hiding-place in an instant.

All this time the hounds were kept away some considerable distance by the master and his whips, and, although they were perfectly acquainted with the whole matter, their discipline, which was excellent, prevented their attempting to interfere.

The old Earthstopper, I observed, had taken a small billhook from his pocket, and quickly made a small fagot with two bonds. This he pushed into the earth with his foot, observing at the same time. "It isn't that it's *wanted* there ; but if these keepers *do* look round between this and Christmas, they will see how earths *should* be stopped next time."

The huntsman gave the fox some law, hoping he would take to the water meadows again ; but he made for the same covert, and nearly reached the breeding earth by the oak tree when they pulled him down.

When his head was hung to the huntsman's saddle, and his pads and brush were distributed, and the hounds had broken him up, I saw the master and several who had now come up, giving their small silver to my friend the Earthstopper ; and, as I never liked a two o'clock fox, I determined to turn towards home.

I never was good at finding my way in a strange country, and so I did as the others did to old Bertie, and asked him to show me the way. This he did cheerfully, and after a few minutes conversation it came out that he lived in one of the cottages belonging to the estate, which (to make a long story short) I eventually purchased.

As my horse was rather out of condition, and a slow pace best suited both of us that pleasant evening, I gathered as much information from this intelligent old man as I could, and so present it to my readers.

"An earthstopper ? Well," he said, "I have been doing it about ten years. I was a keeper before that, and," he added, with a sly twinkle of his eye, "a poacher and all sorts." He told me that he had six children. "And eight shillings a week isn't much," he said, "when you have a shilling a week for rent, and shoes to buy ; though I can't deny," he continued, "I had a good garden, and turf for the cutting it; but then I had to take a bushel of wheat (tailing or chicken wheat) all the year round at a certain price. So I used now and then to knock a rabbit out of his form ; and then I took to wiring them. I generally had a net in my pocket which I used to clap over the

bolthole in a furzebush ; then I used to tap the other end with
my hand, and bang, in goes the rabbit. I let the pheasants
alone for perhaps a twelvemonth, because I couldn't get a gun,
and I did pretty well at them, when I got one. I used to watch
them up at roost, you know, and I generally knew where the
keepers were. I never sent them knocking round the pot. I
used to sell them to the carrier. I got 2*s.* for a good cock
pheasant, or 1*s.* 6*d.* But I got caught at last. I was coming
home with my gun in my pocket and a fagot on my back—but
the fagot was only a blind—when I saw in a bare larch tree on
the road side three pheasants all just got up. I let fly at the
one lowest down, and not one moved ; but an old pied bird flew
out of a Scotch fir where the shots rattled in ; and I, innocent
like, had put my gun down and was feeling for my bottle of
gunpowder and pipe to load again, when out pounced the keeper
and his watcher, and I see it was all a plant. Bless you ! the
birds was only *idols*" (the name given by poachers to imitation
pheasants). "They took me to the Squire, and I up and told
him I couldn't live. Well, he's a rough way with him ; but he
says : ' If I forgive you shooting at *my pheasants* '—' I beg your
pardon, sir,' I says, ' they was *idols.*' 'Well,' he says, ' idols if
you like. If I forgive you and take you on at twelve shillings
and a cottage, will you let the game alone ? ' ' Yes. sir,' I said ;
and I did it. I was there under-keeper the last ten years, and
then the manor was let, and now I go hedge-trimming ; and I
make these heath brooms, and I cut turf for firing, and I mow
in harvest, and I work in the woods—make hurdles and so on—
and I do the earthstopping over this manor and the next. But
Lord," he said, "half the keepers know nothing of a fox. You
know you ought to stop foxes out of their earths *altogether* from
cub-hunting until March. It's no use stopping them with clods.
You should make a little fagot and put in the hole. If you stop
a fox in, he will dig himself out. There's no fear of that ; but
I generally take my little terrier. He's very clever, and if there's
a fox in he will bark. Generally I have a line on him, because
then he can't stop in, for once he kept barking (in a breeding
earth he was) for four whole hours. I know every earth round
here. The breeding earths have been used for hundreds of
years. I believe the badgers make them. There's a chamber at
the end, and a larder, and all sorts ; and if you were to bring a
fox from a hundred miles away, when he got to the covert, he
would go to the earths as natural as if he was born there, and

knew his way to them. If you stop them out, you will always find a fox will lay in some place where the wind can't get to him nor leaves fall on him, such as a pit, or on the top of a dry hedge. If he has been travelling all night, and there comes a storm at three or four in the morning, he won't go to earth if there are twenty earths open, not till he is clean, any more than you would go into a room with dirty boots. I have dug many a fox," he said. " Did you see the huntsman draw that one? Well, I can't draw one like that, though that's the proper way. I gives him a stick to bite, and pulls it from him, then I dab on his poll; but the right way is as the huntsman did it. I do all sorts of things for a living, and this is one. All the best time of the year for it I catch goldfinches, linnets, bullfinches, and sometimes woodlarks, for the London markets; and I trap the moles, and I keep about four or five ferrets and some terriers, and go rat-catching for the farmers. *I does it the right way. My dogs watches the boltholes.*"

By this time we reached the main road leading to my village inn, so, after receiving very minute directions as to my road and filling his pipe for him, I turned to trot on, but he had one word more to say.

" I beg your pardon, sir," he said, " but if you should like to *have* a good goldfinch—quite *a star*," he added—" he does the *whittle so blink*, and *choulmy, choulmy, chay*; and now and then does *suck, suck, chay*, all in one run!" I thanked him for his courtesy, but declined to accept " the star."

Subsequently, when I left the inn for the new manor, I took him on as a trapper, and he was the very best I ever saw. The way he caught an old otter quite surprised me by its cleverness and simplicity; but of this another time.

PAPER XI.

THE SHOOTING PONY.

I RECOLLECT, many years ago, that I saw in a print shop at
Oxford an engraving of the Waterloo Marquis of Anglesea shoot-
grouse from the back of his pony on the moors. He is represented in that work of art as having turned nearly round in his
saddle, and dropping his second bird, whilst his clean, well-bred
pony stands motionless, with the single rein of a thick snaffle
bridle hanging on his neck.

Though the old nobleman left his leg behind him a little beyond
Brussels, he never gave up his inbred love for English sports ;
and I am told, by those who have seen him do it, that it was
worth something to see him handle his yacht in a stiff gale of
wind, and to witness his activity and pluck, though one of his
legs was made of cork.

Where there is a true feeling for sport, nothing extinguishes,
and few things can deaden it. They used to tell me that I should
think less of a good setter team, a patient and 'cute retriever,
and a fine scenting morning, when I had come to years of discretion ; but the feeling for sport is as strong in me now as ever,
although the snows of winter are gathering upon my head, and
the grey hairs are pushing aside the brown ones.

Nothing checks a true sportsman so long as he can move about,
either on his own legs or borrowed ones. Near sight can be got
over by the aid of glasses, unless the fates send mist and drizzling
rain ; and some of the best shots that I have seen get on their
bird, and drop him, by the assistance of what are irreverently
called " gig-lamps."

Heavy professional engagements, "lots of work," eminence in
law, physic, or div—stop ! I am going a little too far—eminence in
law or physic, none of these things stamp out the love of sport ;
and if you could throw a net over the Highlands in August, you
would catch nine-tenths of the genius and glory of Great Britain.

Time tells it tale with many a would-be sportsman, however,
before he can throw care to the winds and do his work by deputy,

or dare the criticism of clients who would grant no rest—certainly no sport—to a wearied mind. And, as Anno Domini is no respecter of persons, old squires fall under his influence at last, and limp along painfully over the swedes and rape and clover seed, which they see coming again young, green, and fresh as ever, whilst they are growing old and feeble.

I don't like to see young men with a shooting pony in the field behind the guns, unless there is a very wide stretch of "the enemy's country" intersecting the morning's beat; but a genuine good safe walker, which you can shoot from if need be, is a great acquisition under certain circumstances, and especially in the Highlands, where you may leave off sport (or have it cut off for you by atmospheric interference—fog, mist, and so on) when you are perhaps many miles from home.

The ponies and gillies, with the afternoon setters in couples—especially the thick-set cob which carries the luncheon pannier and the flagon—form a very interesting tableau indeed at half-past one, and you experience a decided feeling of animation as the indistinct group, standing sharp against the sky line on that heathery knoll, resolves itself into a little clan of adherents as you approach them, and you speculate as to what viands they are placing in order on the ground, and whether there is a *really* cold spring close by.

After doing the Turkish bath upon some trying ground (especially without quite enough sport to satisfy you)—when there is but half a mile between the muzzle of your gun and the game pie and cold tongue—when the dogs are called in to heel, and you hand over your gun to an attendant until after luncheon—the excitement gone, and nothing for it but to reach the rendezvous under a scorching sun, you don't lift and free your foot quite so gingerly; and, if I mistake not, provided a Scotch shelty rubbed his nose against you, you would pat his neck and climb into the saddle.

As a man gets old and stiff about the knees, when after a trying walk through high swedes his legs feel like two posts, he inclines more and more to put his hand in his pocket and purchase a shooting pony. He is acted upon by the same impulse which prompts a Liverpool merchant to give a stinging price for good dogs. Let him have the luxury, and he does not care to remember what it cost him ; and, as the supply is never in this case equal to the demand, cobs and ponies fit by nature and art for the shooting ground have realised outrageous prices.

It is hardly necessary to say that such an animal must be the most perfect of its kind, possessing *mens sana in corpore sano.* There must be no vice nor lameness, the constitution must be hardy, the eyes good, the temper docile, or it is useless. Then you must have strength and activity. One that warps and twists under the saddle—that can't walk without effort through deep or (as they call it in Oxfordshire) a "loving" ground—that can't carry you up a bank, and creep down on the opposite side, or push through a quickset and jump off—is not the animal for a heavy man.

I have had animals suited for the gun in every respect save *nerve.* I never tried so hard as with one I got out of Wiltshire, a grey, up to twenty stone if you liked so to weight him, and with that light, corky action which makes your seat on him easy as sitting in an arm-chair; but he never would get over the terror of firearms, although I tried everything but Rarey's dodge, which at that time was not known. If I got off his back and tied him up, as I took a morning shot at the ducks, when I returned to the fir tree to which he was fastened I found him in a lather, and the ground scraped and trampled as far as the chain permitted. Getting on his back with the offensive weapon in my hand was out of the question, and as long as I had him I was compelled to lay my Westley Richards on the branches of the Scotch firs, and take it off them as I rode him by. And then, when thus cajoled into carrying it, we had a a fine caper or two for the first hundred yards, and a sideways dance on unpleasant ground, with the prospect of a little rearing, which he could do as well as any brute I ever bought too dear.

I tried a bit of powder and a pistol for some weeks, but all in vain. They tell me cavalry horses are thus brought to bear the report, the pistol being fired at feeding time. With him it was an economical arrangement, as after hearing it he would not touch his corn for hours.

I have dropped upon two in my lifetime which gave no trouble at all, but submitted to the gun at once. In both cases I got on them, and after riding a mile or so I snapped off the gun, loaded with a little powder, and they took no notice. I then got bolder and shot off a few times with a full charge; and in the evening the first (a grey) was made.

An old gentleman, who advertised for such a quadruped in the *Field,* gave me fifty pounds for him, and liked him so well that two or three years after he wrote to me for another; but he might as well have ordered a sonnet, for it was the merest chance I had him.

Another I got by a fluke. It was a brown one, which at five years old had been taken in off the common by one of our farmers, and hawked about at a neighbouring fair. He brought him to me in desperation because " the keep was short," and begged me to " ride him a trial, and buy him at a bad price." Eleven pounds he cost me—not dear for a five-year-old that trotted and cantered five miles to a friend's manor without faltering, with nothing to support nature but what he got on a heath, and at night came home over the dips and ruts and fallows without making a blunder ; and that in a week was carrying 10,000l. a year amongst his deer and " buffaloes," and standing still enough for the double rifle to good service and not " spoil the haunch."

The first thing you want in a shooting pony is docility. A narrow, hammer-headed, calf-kneed, flat-sided brute, whose tail springs about a foot above his hocks, will answer the purpose if he has the disposition required ; and from such a wretch, if he has a gallop in him, a keeper might shoot a Chillingham bull. It is surprising what some half-kept, rough, lean keepers' ponies will do, and how they can go and carry their masters, in defiance of all *our* rules for make and shape. Upright shoulders, short back ribs, cow hocks, short necks, weak withers—I have seen all these defects *admirably* (?) combined in a keeper's pony, which, if he had form and substance, would have been cheap at " three figures ;" and this anatomical specimen would carry sixteen stone from morning until night, his master said, with ease. I don't suppose his owner ever gave the matter consideration, or reflected whether his nag was good-looking or not. He took the saddle and bridle off him when he returned from a hard day, and he could go to the barley straw and help himself. The next morning his old grey would probably be looking over the garden wicket, ready to salute the old keeper with a loud neigh as he came out to bridle him ; and I have seen venerable Jones send his rusty retriever to herd him back when he had strayed beyond the confines of that old homestead on the moor.

Of course a man of taste likes beauty to be combined with excellence, and of all things a shooting pony—confessedly the pet of the country house—should be a model of symmetry, and the pattern of cheerfulness and good humour. You like to see him stretching his neck over the wire fencing that keeps him in the paddock and out of the flower garden, and walking side by side with your wife or daughter, only separated by that slight barrier, and to be certain that he will take that delicate fragment of breakfast roll from those taper fingers with quiet, and I might say almost gentlemanly, grace. All the better if the children can hang to his tail or examine his hind feet without danger, and if the eldest boy of eight and three-quarters can ride him bridleless, with that precious piece of daily and nightly vexation in long clothes carried in front of him like a patent waterproof.

I have seen good Irish, Scotch, Exmoor, New Forest, and Norwegian ponies; but certainly there are not the number, nor do they possess the quality, which prevailed thirty years ago. At that date you hardly went into the yard of a flourishing agriculturist but he asked you first "what you would take?" and next whether you would like to see a good pony; and from out of some rough stable came such an one as now you scarce find out of London—nor in it.

But supposing that you light on "the very thing," with an Arab head—the most graceful of all forms of head to my mind, especially when surmounted with large or moderately large ears, well carried—a long-necked one, with legs like a cart-horse, and open feet large enough to prevent difficulties in spongy ground ; with deep shoulders, sloping backwards, and a round barrel and quarters ; broad across the hips, muscular in the thigh, long from his hip to his hock, with pasterns long and strong, and *moderately* oblique ; with the disposition of a Newfoundland dog, hardy enough to lie out all weathers, as he ought, and with that safe action which gives you confidence in him before you have ridden him twenty yards ; ready to draw the basket carriage or bear the luncheon panniers, or convey an invalid son or daughter for an hour's airing in the October sun ; and that from indisposition or idleness, or want of health and power, your shooting depends upon this conveyance, it is as well to be provided with the "et-cetera" necessary for the work. If a man wants a very easy seat, he must have one of those padded abominations called "a somerset;" but, from the redundancy of padding, they do not enable you to *turn* quite so easily as the plain saddle, provided it is roomy and large enough in the seat.

If a man wants a shooting saddle in the south, he requires it ten times more in the north, and so it should be fitted, if need be, for carrying a deer.

Therefore behind, on each side of the saddle, and seven inches apart, are two *dees* (each one inch wide), and to these may be attached a strap on each side about eight feet long ; then there should be a strong dee in front of the saddle on each side of the breastplate staples in the skirt of the saddle, for a carbine bucket and strap ; and a small bag should hang on each side of the saddle behind the flaps, which will carry a flask or a sandwich case if need be.

As the ground is often steep, this saddle should be provided with a crupper. If it is desired to carry hobbles they may be attached to a ring behind the saddle croup, and they should be well padded.

The breastplate (generally used where deer are expected) should be strong, and furnished with a large dee, to which one of the straps may be connected in case the big game has to be hauled out of a ravine or river.

If a pony cannot be trusted, he may be tethered by a spike something like an elongated mangold wurzel, which is easily driven into the ground ; but I think hobbles answer best, and are the easiest to carry. Of course all this reads like a complicated equipment, and for general purposes little of it is needed ; but I think I can produce a shooting bridle which is perfection.

It is made of brown double webbing, woven, as I imagine, on purpose, and the head is constructed like a headstall, so that the most artful pony cannot slip his head out of it. A dee in front of the noseband enables the gillie to lead the animal without hauling at the bit, and he has a long rein at hand by simply un-fastening the spring hooks by which the reins are attached to the ring snaffle. There is also a sliding dee on the hand-piece of the bridle, and a spring hook on the bridle head (off side), by which means the bridle can be looped out of the way when the pony is hobbled. The fittings are of leather, and the holes for the tongues of the buckles are very substantial eyelet holes, neatly put in with collars. I shall be happy to send the pattern to any-one who desires to see it, or to supply them with the address of the maker.

PAPER XII.

WHISTLE AND WHIP.

SOME years ago I would drive any number of miles to see a good fiddle, especially if it was " in the market "—let it be " Amati's," " Strad.'s," " Joseph's," or even " Peter's " make. The wretched wonders I have seen on some of these occasions, wrapped by their infatuated possessors in flannel shrouds and cased in birds-eye maple coffins, with seven-guinea locks and ten-guinea bows, and yet no tone !

Well, let that pass. I would go a good distance to get a good dog-whistle now, provided I had not got one ; and without further preface I plunge into my subject, which once on a time, (nay, more than once), by way of apology I may add, inspired the spirit of Burns.

There are plenty of men who will tell you any whistle would do, and that you might get one for sixpence at the first gun-maker's you passed in every little provincial town ; and I am not going to argue with these wiseacres. We (the enlightened British public who read our *Field*) know better. I never graduated at the rough and ready school ; the best is always just good enough for me, and, what is more, it is cheapest in the end.

I don't know anything more perplexing than a weak, thin, sharp whistle on a very windy day, or one that gets choked up, or in which the " pea " (as it is called both in this instrument and when under one or more of three thimbles, though it never is a pea) gets blocked and won't rattle ; whilst your dog, a trifle wild and uncontrollable, and which never saw you till yesterday evening since last season, scours after the old shepherd in the distance, who is waving with both arms to his 'cute colley, and looks more like a telegraph post than a Highland herdsman as he is.

More than once, shooting with a man who liked his own way and his own whistle, and persisted in giving impotent blasts with his toy, I have rejoiced to know that its wheezing note never reached my setters, and that it amused him and did not interfere

with me; but when, in accordance with human infirmities, I have
put on a fresh coat and found myself ten miles from home
without this ivory dependent from my buttonhole, I have wished
that my servant's, which he handed me as a substitute, were as
good as mine for that day only—*but it never is.*

Contrary to the assurances of men who speak at random, and
who are positive in proportion, I repeat the assertion that to get
a good instrument is not an easy thing.

I never saw a boatswain's whistle but once. It was, if I
remember aright, a silver thing, between a surgical instrument
and a cigar-tube, with two or three holes flutewise in the centre,
and, when blown, it emitted most dismal and unmelodious sounds.
The fault may have been in the performer (myself); for the
shopkeeper, in whose window I saw it suspended at Portsmouth,
affected total ignorance of its capabilities, and seemed to think
that in my hands a little of it went a great way, for he said
something about having a sick wife upstairs ; so I declined the
bargain, and most likely it hangs by the ticket in his window
still.

I was led to look at it from having read in some work on dog-
breaking that the author had got his dogs to range when he blew
one note, and to come in when he sounded another; and, whilst
with all submission I don't think this feasible, it occured to me
that one of the notes the boatswain used might, and probably
would, be very shrill and piercing, and that it would be worth
while to try. To my surprise, the notes were poor and husky—
and, in short, it wouldn't do.

I tried the Burlington Arcade. There I saw tassels of whistles
of all kinds—gold, silver, torquoised, gemmed, double-tongued,
single-tongued, ivory, pewter, brass, and wood. One of the most
obliging shopmen I ever saw handed them to me by the gross,
whilst a dark-eyed partner, with his back to me and his face
towards a resplendent mirror, was able to see clearly that none of
them went astray.

For cab calls or ladies' favourites they were excellent, no doubt,
but no dog of mine could have heard them on the moor, as he
went lashing his stern and his feather blowing in the breeze of
an exposed and wild Scotch hill ; and I extended my pilgrimage
towards the Strand.

As I walked that way and gave a cursory glance at the shop-
windows, proclaiming myself deeply imbued with rusticism, the
drivers of Hansoms naturally thought I had lost my way, and

seemed to fish for me with their whips. I had nearly made up my mind to commit myself to one of them who followed me pertinaciously, when I saw a range of something like whistles in an optician's window. I could hardly believe it possible, for there was an "electricity" look about them, and I should have as soon expected to see the whistle, pure and simple, hanging amongst the gloves at Houbigant's, or lying on the marble slab with the fish at Groves's.

It was a fat brass instrument, with an ivory mouthpiece and a sort of bell attachment, acting, I suppose, on the principle of the old pulpit sounding board, which, after the lapse of centuries, some one pronounced useless, when people tried without it and gave it up. I fully expected that the sound of it would collect the police and fire engines, but on trial it was by no means powerful ; its din would be more likely to scare a dog away than bring him to me ; and, for aught I know, the optician is still able to see his whistle without using one of his telescopes.

I could find nothing new—no improvement upon the old form, provided you fell in with a good one—and my whistle-beating in London streets was time thrown away.

There were many gunmakers who exhibited them in their shops ; but I did not care to go into their plate-glass repositories for so trifling an errand as a sixpenny whistle, when they would scarce open the door for my exit if I bought less than a pair of breech-loaders and gave my cheque (and reference) for three figures.

I might have braved their coolness and disappointment—all of which, remember, may be my pure imagination—had I seen anything very new or very promising ; but I did not, so I came away as I went. And then it occurred to me that I would get the best whistle I could at as many shops as possible, keeping to the old-fashioned shapes and style. I would get good, rattling, loud whistles—the best I could anywhere—and try them with a dog that turned well, on wild moor, in woodland and covert, and under all varieties of the atmosphere. I would see what a dog answered to best—I mean what musical note, and of what size, pitch, and material the whistle should be.

No sooner said than done, and I purchased half a dozen accordingly. I try a few experiments myself with a piece or two of elephant's tusk and my lathe ; but I find as yet the professional ivory turner beats me, though I hope to make something as good as his.

The note I find best adapted for the purpose is *D in the treble ;* next to that G, but D in the treble is the best.

With a round bit of cork in it (the best are absolutely round, and very slightly greased or oiled) this is the most piercing, shrill, and audible pitch of any that I have tried ; and whilst we must not forget, according to scientific " patter," that " some ears perceive sounds emanating from vibrations a little beyond the extremes to which the perception of other ears is confined," if we get that instrument which the generality of dogs *and men* hear best, we shall not be far wrong.

Generally the dog has to contend with the wind when you whistle for him, and this is to him a great disadvantage. You must have a note so distinct, shrill, and yet of such body or volume, that it will meet this disadvantage, and the rush of such covert as he may be beating over or through.

In a calm, and without either of these disadvantages, you can best at a distance distinguish the bass notes of a band, the stroke (not the roll) of the drum best of all ; but I have, from trial, concluded that you would against the wind, and with the rustle of leaf and heather, or stubble or swede, rape or clover, best distinguish the shrill whistle in D.

The note will be clear in proportion to the excellence of the material and the thickness of it, just as in an orchestra the leading fiddle is intelligible and clear above the cloud of instruments, because of its structure and the quality of its wood.

When we reflect that many an unlucky dog has had his ears pulled, been subject to a lot of rating, and that rating supplemented with a brutal flogging, because he did not turn to a whistle which he could not hear, I think we must all conclude that, in common fairness to him, we should be careful to give him every advantage by using the best procurable instrument.

Lead, pewter, or whatever it may be—at any rate, I can cut it with my knife—is too dull of sound, and too liable to be bruised or bent out of shape ; and, again, it is very heavy, and occasionally, in jumping a hedge and so on, dangerous. Ivory, I am nearly certain, is the best material, because it admits of precision in the manufacture, while, from the fine grain, we get the best sound and the most ringing clearness. The best whistle I could get, the best I ever had, is made of it, and it is light, portable, and durable.

The simple possession of this call in perfection leads me to make a few remarks upon its use.

Much depends upon the dog and his breaking. Some well-trained dogs, either used for the open as setters or the covert as Clumbers, are always attentive and on the alert for a signal; whilst dogs of high spirit, or young, scatter-brained, and thought-less, look upon their work as " a lark," and simply gratify their passion for the chase.

This feeling comes over them when they have ranged a little wide. They often forget the consequences of rebellion, and *won't* hear. This error ought to be corrected by a servant, not a master. The former should go round the dog and drive him to the whistle. He may even correct the dog for his wilfulness when he is in hand; and if he is difficult to catch, he should carry not less than twenty-five feet of line upon his collar, or in the open, except in rape or turnips, three times that length or more.

After correction, the master should whistle to the dog, *not loudly, but low*, so that the whistle should sound as at the distance when it was disregarded; and the sound should be thoroughly impressed upon the dog, who may then be forgiven and hunted on.

It requires patience, temper, and experience to use a whistle well. I have, perhaps, none of these—decidedly not all of them; but I have attained my end very often without any whip at all, watching for my dog to turn, giving him one touch of the whistle as he did so, and turning my shoulder from him, when the worst dog is more likely to " come" than if you used any other means.

Above all things, not too much music, nor that wearisome " Hold up ! " " Hold away ! " and that woodpecker-like mouth whistle which is only fit for the eight-stalled stable. You may whistle until the dog is weary of it and you, and will pay no attention. A little of it, and take care it is always obeyed and followed. If you are always " noising " (as they call it in War-wickshire) to the dog, very soon you may as well whistle to a hare. With some keepers it seems a relief to their feelings, and nothing more—like the sibillations of a strapper to a post-horse.

I have generally found the top buttonhole of the shooting jacket the best place to carry it, and that a loop of strong elastic is the best material. My breaker, I observe, has his fastened to his waistcoat buttonhole, and, I suppose on Conservative prin-ciples, uses the " four-in-hand point " which was the favourite " whistle cable " of his great grandfather, and which the grandson assures n.e will never break. Buckle, the jockey, said this of his old stirrup leather, and when. after forty years' service, it gave way at last, lost Buckle's employers the stakes, and nearly broke the rider's neck, " he couldn't believe it, as it had carried him so long."

This is a digression ; and as I never did like " harking back," but prefer, like the foxhound pack, casting forward rather than the harrier's tactics, I will go on to " whips."

A brutal keeper may tease a dog with a whistle, but he may be a monster with the whip. Many a time have I with difficulty restrained myself from thrashing a stubborn, ignorant fellow belabouring his dog for some blunder of his own. Keepers and breakers, as a class, don't do this. They know that the use of the whip with young dogs requires the keenest judgment and observation, and that once overdo it and the dog is done for. If a retriever, he won't fetch ; and once let him see he can do this with impunity, and all your blandishments or your barbarity have no effect. So with a pointer, " blinking " is a sure sign of injudicious punishment. It results from the superior power of man over a poor wretch he holds in a vice. Any man who knows how to handle a dog can, with very little effort, put the poor thing at his mercy, and after a very few days' acquaintance few dogs will use their teeth, if they are ever so unfairly beaten.

Jim, or young Adams (the head keeper of Wardour Castle, and, let me add, quite as good a breaker as his father, which is saying a great deal, though I regret to say he has not time nor inclination to undertake the dogs of the public)—both these men, who are eminent as dog-breakers, can tell you that there is no part of a dog's breaking which requires so much calmness, quiet well-bred firmness, or self-control as the use of the lash. It must be the last resource. It must be always a *preventive.* Sometimes it must fall lightly, producing no pain, and be an admonitory signal only. It must never be administered without that remonstrance which at school we found so irksome, and which always preceded the cuts ; to which my nearest relative alluded, in the year 18—(well, never mind the fractions)—in a letter which cost 10d. postage, and began, as letters at that age always will. I suppose, with "I hope you are quite well; in which document he relieved his feelings by saying he didn't mind " taking his gruel," but he " hated the jaw."

The dog, like the idle schoolboy, has a peculiar distaste for the preliminary remonstrance. See how he shivers, and observe the nausea of his countenance. I have known dogs limp when they saw they had arrived at that *très mauvais quart d'heure*; or, in the midst of their master's reproaches, affect to find a thorn in their foot, or a flea in some inaccessible part of the back or loin.

How this has called to my remembrance the exquisite torture inflicted upon me by a dwarfish master, who, with that calmness which mocked my fears, rejoiced to utterly terrify a little urchin in linen trousers, dallying with his cane as he looked for what he called the ripest parts, where it could descend in a shower of blows. I thought I recognised his skeleton the other day in an anatomical collection, it was that of so small a man! and I felt almost inclined to put out my hand, that he might "spat" it as in days of yore.

As I have already said, for it will bear repetition, *don't be too hard upon a dog*. Far better let a fault go by now and then than meet every peccadillo red-handed. You can always give the flogging—you can't undo it. As often as not—especially when it is a matter of *scent*—the dog is right, the man is wrong, and more dogs are ruined with the lash than without it.

Like Jem Shave and all reflective dog-breakers, *flog by deputy*, if possible. Your executioner flogs without temper— possibly with a good deal of compunction.

I am aware that these remarks are about as useful as hints to people on fire to roll themselves in a rug, which they never do ; or to people when a horse runs away, who generally act like the old woman who trusted to Providence until the breeching broke, when she jumped out and broke her neck. I risk their not being appreciated or followed, and I go on.

Don't give a lot of blows, but one smart one—*not that, if you can help it*.

Take care, if it is a thin-skinned, light-coated dog, that your whip is light. Have one on purpose for such animals ; for rough retrievers or heavily plumed setters you want one heavier.

In some cases you may be more merciful by using a thong $3\frac{1}{2}$in. in circumference at the larger end and 18in. long, than by using a very light one : with other dogs it would be monstrous. The stick should be at least 12in., so that upraised the dog should see it at a distance ; and if the thong be longer than I describe, you only hit yourself.

Knotted thongs don't do : they break (without wear) and become rotten. The lash should consist of three thongs, woven one round the other cablewise, and woven into one at the point and eye.

The keepers on the stick should be short; one of them may be left two and a half inches longer than the other, and a large buttonhole cut in it will enable you to carry it suspended to your button *at the double,* which is far better than hanging it at the end of the handle. I fear I have exhausted my space. At a future time I may add " *a few more last words.*"

PAPER XIII.

OLD TRAPS AND SPRING GUNS.

SINCE I wrote an article on "Traps and Calls," I have received numerous letters of inquiry through the office of the *Field*, desiring information on various points connected with the subject, which must be my excuse for compiling an unusually dry paper.

I have always felt a mania for collecting, from the time that I was a boy in skeletons, escorted to a day school by an old groom. There, in spite of thwacks on the head with lignum vitæ rulers, and "spats" (as they were called) upon the palm of the hand, which sometimes produced festers, and left stripes and weals of the colour of mahogany, I could not give up my inclination.

I began with a collection of birds' eggs, of course, and traded principally in those of the house sparrow. I then went into pens —they were mostly quill pens then—and I had a nice arrangement of the various shapes and forms, from the masterpiece of art fashioned by the writing master, and nibbed on the tip of cowhorn always worn in readiness upon his left thumb, to the coarse article—much preferred, by the way, in one form—which a now eminent barrister used to fashion with a pair of scissors. As time went on I ran the gamut of old keys, spoons, cracked china, coins, buckles and buttons, pins and brooches, according to my age and pocket money. Although the antiquarian business is by no means profitable, I still incline that way, and hence my collection (not large, it is true, but choice) of old traps fashioned for the taking of man and beast. Let it be known that you are on the look-out for any "rubbish," and plenty of men will bring it to you. At the next market town to the village from which I write I have seen a wonderful collection of old Roman weapons. of bronze and other "torques," armour, flint and metal celts and axe heads, cinerary urns, surgical instruments of old days— gathered together these by the old-established custom common with the higher grade of "chiffonniers," to let nothing go back, but worthless or priceless to purchase at a liberal price, in the hope something some day may turn up.

In all matters of collecting I believe I " know the ropes." I
had but to hold up my hand, and my friends came forward with
kindness, as I hereby acknowledge with many thanks ; whilst day
by day I saw some lounger meet me in my stable yard offering
me an old trap in a handkerchief, or perchance a part of one
which he had dug up or dredged from the river's floor, and for
which he " hoped I shouldn't think sixpence out of the way."

I had spread a goodly array of these old toils over the floor of
my den one day, and " set " them all, so that you must have
picked your way to get at my writing table, like a poor victim
amongst the red-hot ploughshares. There they were—man traps
six feet long and more ; fox traps (woe betide the makers of
them !) large enough to hold a wolf ; and then otter traps,
hawk traps, and little gins for mice—when poor old Bertie
looked in, as he walked by the open door, with that expression
painters give the fox who is about to enter a hen roost, but is
uncertain whether it will do or not ; and, putting on an air of
innocence, he asked me what those large traps with the crooked
teeth were for.

" Man traps, Bertie." I answered, scarce looking up, for I
was running over my banking book, and the balance was the wrong
way.

" Oh," he said, walking off, still regarding them with surprise, and speaking to himself ; " and those smaller ones are, I
expect, *to catch the children*."

I have perplexed myself a good deal with the inquiry when
these traps were first made. I incline to the opinion that they
are almost coeval with the pitfall. Man was spoken of as
" walking upon a snare," and the gin was said to " take him
by the heel," fifteen hundred years before the Christian era.
I admit that the Hebrew word used may signify, and does signify, a noose, snare, or springe ; but, although the lasso may
be meant, I do not forget that a painting was discovered at
Thebes of a hyæna caught by the feet *in a metal trap*, and
carried on a pole by two men. Certainly a trap which would
hold a hyæna would hold a man, and, though he might release
himself (which I doubt), he would be too much disabled to
escape. Indeed, I don't think any man caught in one of my man
traps could possibly get out. His strength would be destroyed
by the shock, and his muscular power would fail him, just as a
dog's power goes, supposing that I squeeze his foot.

I have spun such a barrister-like preamble or "recital," that I must now proceed to business, and introduce my first trap upon the stage. Here it is, sixty pounds of iron according to my German scale. It measures 6ft. 7in. from end to end, and each spring is 2ft. 7in. long. As you always find in old traps, the maker was not content with a trigger and trigger plate ; he surrounded the jaws with a substantial iron frame. There are abundant reasons for doing away with this unnecessary addition, but I need give none, having merely stated that it is useless, or I may be accused of following the example of the Irishman who desired to give old Crockford a hundred reasons for not gambling, " Go on, sir," said " old Crock." " First," said the would-be lecturer, " I have no money." " Oh !" said old C., " never mind the other ninety-nine."

This useless frame of substantial wrought iron is nineteen inches square. The jaws work in two double studs, each of which would, as Shave, the trapmaker, tells me, take a quarter of a day to make. The closed jaws reach ten inches above the trigger plate, which is nearly a foot square, and each jaw is armed with seven spike teeth, an inch and a half long, and so set as to tear the flesh of any unhappy struggler. The combined strength of the two springs—for there is one at each side of the jaws—pulls at least 560lb., enough to almost sever an ordinary birch-wood broom-handle at a blow.

I have two of these formidable engines, but only one of them belongs to me. They were obtained many miles apart—one of them from the close proximity of Wardour Castle—and both were marked " J. V." The workmanship is first-rate, and each trap must have cost the first owner three or four pounds.

A few days ago a very large, powerful "frame trap," made doubtless for wild and martin cats, was brought to me, bearing the same monogram as this pair of man traps. It might have served as the model for these barbarous toils, and on the spring I found the name " J. Veal"—a Dorset maker, I believe, who lived before Hall, and one or two Dorset trapmakers who were famous in their day before the " Shave period," to use the language of the scientific world.

From young Adams (now head keeper at Wardour Castle) I borrowed another trap, also with double springs and circular jaws. The spike teeth are on the *outside;* there are nine of them, flat and wedge-shaped. This trap weighs nearly 40lb., and is 4ft. 6in. long. It has a peculiar trigger plate 9in. by 11in., furnished with six large points, like small dog spears, for holding on a bait. An experienced master of foxhounds, who saw it a few days since, pronounced it a fox trap, and told me, as a boy, he had seen many of them in Kent.

Unlike Veal's traps (the springs of which have all the life and activity of new steel), those on this trap have lost all their vigour, and it would not hold a rat. The jaws are suspended in single studs, and the whole thing is coarsely made. I should judge, from its rough-make and certain peculiarities in its form, that it is of foreign manufacture—possibly a wolf trap imported from the Continent quite as much out of curiosity as for use.

Another man trap which lies before me dates from the same old castle—*a humane trap*, weighing something less than 20lb. It consists of a light yet strong iron frame of about eighteen inches, and two active but not strong springs; the jaws are of the same size as the frame, and run upon an iron jointed rod notched at one end, and self-locking at each side. The jaws close to the size of the leg, and there hold the delinquent until the keeper releases him in the morning. I have seen the rusted parts of such a trap in the park at Charbro', minus the trigger and locks.

In a treatise on the game laws, written by Professor Christian (1817), the author speaks of " the man trap as an engine of horror. If life is not destroyed by it, it can only be ransomed by the loss of a limb. . . . . If these are so placed that the person killed by them must have been in the commission of a felony, or have come to the spot with that intent, the person placing them might perhaps be in law justified ; but they are generally placed to prevent injuries in gardens or in preserves for game, where, if a person was killed by a gun fired from the hand, the person firing the gun would certainly be guilty of murder."

The learned author goes on to state at length that where they are not set for the prevention of felonies, *the act of setting* them is an "indictable offence, as a misdemeanor ;" but I can find no proof that the setting man traps and spring guns was forbidden until the 24 & 25 Vict. c. 100, s. 31.

Not many years ago there was hardly a village which was not well supplied with these barbarous things. It was common enough to see them placarded in gardens and orchards, and they generally were combined with spring guns (for humanity sake), that the man caught and maimed might be shot and put out of his misery.

I have ascertained that four or five have been beaten into

horseshoes by the village Vulcans within a radius of ten miles, as have many pieces of iron of rare antiquity, no doubt.

The present iron trap would be perfect but for two things—its cruelty and its liability to catch and maim foxes. They must be very portable, or they cannot be carried in sufficient numbers, and unless they have teeth they are liable to let vermin escape, Thirty years ago (I am told) the Kentish trap, like the present hawk trap, had no teeth ; directly the Dorset trap was introduced, the toothless-gum trap was displaced. I should be glad to hear how the "rasp-lip trap" has answered, and why "the indiarubber gum" is a failure, as I have heard it reported, though I know not upon what grounds.

I am very much inclined to think that the original "gin" had no teeth at all. Decidedly the first application of teeth was in the form of *spikes*. which folded over each other *underneath* the jaws. All the old frame traps are thus formed—at any rate, all that I have seen—whilst the spring, instead of being bent over in a loop, is simply bolted with one large stud and eye. I am inclined to think this the best manner of attaching the spring after all, though not so pleasing to the eye.

I have a beautifully made trap of Veal's thus constructed. working in double studs, and, after years of exposure to all weathers, quite as good as new. The spring, resembling half of a carriage spring, except that it is one piece, is as quick and tenacious as the day it left the forge. This frame trap weighs $5\frac{3}{4}$lb., without the chain and swivel, and is spiked underneath, even down the angle of the further jaw. It covers eight inches square of ground, and it would seize dog or cat $5\frac{1}{2}$ inches above the trigger plate. The usual Dorset trap made by Shave is 4 inches square, and when closed the jaws are $2\frac{1}{4}$ inches above the plate ; and yet this large trap first described can be covered with $2\frac{1}{2}$ inches of earth on the trigger plate, which is the deepest part.

With one of these large traps a keeper caught a cunning rabbit, which "tormented" his cabbages. As the tale is told to me, he had trapped for this 'cute old buck for a good many weeks, but the traps were always "thrown." It mattered little how many traps were tiled, or in what places. In the "jumps" or out of them, he sprung all in his way, and ate the keeper's greens to his heart's content. It occurred to him to see if he could get one of these large traps. which I fear are intended for vulpecide ; at any rate, I should look with much suspicion on any keeper who set them. He borrowed one of Shave, the trap maker, who keeps a sort of museum of these engines, and set it in the most likely place. Occupying, as those cruel jaws did, twice the ordinary space of ground, poor bunny was taken the first night, and found dead in the morning.

This feat in trapping was performed with (as I understand) an old otter trap, fished up from the Stour after years of immersion, as good as the day it left the forge; the S.—the "monogram" as we call it nowadays, of Shave's grandfather—being still distinguishable, and the springs as sharp as the day he tempered them.

It will do the poor old smith little harm if I expatiate upon the barbarity of this instrument, $4\frac{1}{2}$ inches deep in the jaws when closed, and bristling with thickly-set spike teeth, not only along the surface, but at the angle of the jaws. There is no occasion to use such severity, even to hold an otter, confessedly the most difficult of all British animals to catch and keep. Give him plenty of chain (six feet), and he will drown himself; and this old Shave well knew, for he has attached a strong six-feet chain to his old trap, with a well-made and still acting swivel. To my mind, only let the spring be good, and teeth are not requisite; at any rate, *spike* teeth should be exploded, and the rasp lip or even smooth lip will, I trust, eventually be the description of trap commonly adopted.

And, whilst I write of otters, I will mention a clever piece of trapping which occurred to me some ten or twelve years ago, when I was renting a decoy to which an otter travelled from another "outside decoy pond," also in my occupation, and marvellously disturbed the fowl. He used to come generally along the old brick causeway which led from the decoyman's house, and my old servant twice or three times pointed out his "spraints" with manifest irritation.

"*Theere* he is again, sir," he said. "I've heerd un when I couldn't see un, and so have my boys; and, indeed, one of 'em see him about four o'clock coming up, and blowing and diving, and all the teal and ducks flying round in clouds; and we can't catch un, they be such *warry birds!*"

This went on for some weeks, and I began to think the otter was an excuse for laziness or something worse, especially as the bill for barley and the douceurs for weed seed to "toll the widgeon in" waxed heavier and heavier, and the decoyman's good-looking daughter, who could trap vermin and break a

retriever as well as any man in England, about the same time
came out in a new and exceedingly becoming flaming yellow dress
with a chocolate sprig, and a white bonnet with cherry-coloured
streamers *en suite.*

" Oh," I said to myself, " this is the otter with a vengeance ! "
But I did the old man wrong, for one morning, as I came down
before breakfast to look round the kennels, I saw him radiant
with smiles, his white hair glistening in the rays of a bright
December sun, and, having touched his hat with reverence, he
swung from his back the otter which had caused us so much
vexation, and had turned my heart to gall when I met his smart
daughter in her new costume.

"Here he is, sir!" the old decoyman exclaimed, as he threw
down the otter with a thump ; " I thought you'd like the ' pelt '
(skin) of un. My son caught him, not me, and I'll tell you how he
did it. He got a lot of round pebbles and covered his track just
where he used to go over the little bridge where them blue
flowers (the gentian) grows in the bog there, and put the trap on
the side close to the watercourse. When he felt the round stones
roll under his feet he turned out of his track, and went straight
into the trap."

Of course I was anxious to see the trap. and, leaving old Bertie
to skin the otter, I rode down that afternoon. The trap was
simply an old rabbit trap, nearly worn out. but it had got the
poor brute by both fore feet, and she was positively uninjured
until the old man killed her with his paddle. I was all the more
vexed, as there were evidences that she suckled young ones ; and,
if I had been fortunate enough to keep her alive, I would have
done my best to secure the " cubs," and have devoted all my
energies to train and rear them for fishing. as the Chinese use
the trained green-eyed cormorant. As it was I made the
best of it, and had the skin dressed in such a way that it
was nearly as smooth as velvet, quite as pliable, and much
more enduring.

I need not run through the various old traps of other forms,
which, as I write, are arranged symmetrically upon the floor :
suffice it to say they all have faults sufficient to condemn them in
the eyes of any practical man. Some have limp springs ; others
badly formed jaws which would let vermin escape, because not
so constructed as to hold their grip ; and a few so severe that I
think they would guillotine the leg of the oldest bull-headed
Jack hare at Ashdown. But I must refer in a few words to the

improved hawk trap which lies before me, and which I have
little doubt will answer.   I have forwarded one or two of them
to friends of mine for trial, and they are a great success.
   The old hawk trap has a narrow trigger plate.   This new one
has simply a notch at the end of this *perch* or narrow plate,
which holds down one of the toothless jaws, and acts beautifully;
for if one jaw is held flat, of course both are.   The largest is a
circle of 6in. in diameter, the jaws (closed) $3\frac{1}{2}$in. deep.   This is
a very serviceable trap, and would take any hawk (even the
largest peregrine) *by the leg ;* whilst the usual trap, 4in. in the
jaws, although seldom failing to secure the bird, almost always
catches them by the toe.   This little trap is used by keepers to
place in the nests, for which the larger one is too cumbrous.   I
need hardly add that these traps are used without bait, and placed
on the top of a post in some bleak and barren spot.
   Spring guns or alarm guns may be used still, supposing that
they merely make a report, and are not dangerous.   The old
spring gun was a murderous weapon, and was prohibited at the
same time and by the same Act as the man trap.   They are still
set in India for the destruction of wild beasts, and the son of a
friend of mine, going down the river, was killed by one on landing
from his boat.
   Alarm guns were made by the celebrated sword cutter Wilkinson.   He sold a metal plate with a gun-metal hammer worked by
one strong spring.   This could be screwed to a post or tree, and
the trigger could be made as sensitive as the keeper desired ;
whilst the strings or wires could be arranged in all directions,
and at any height from the ground.   The explosive substance
was secured in a " maroon " of varnished string, absolutely imper-
vious to weather, and the hammer fell upon a tube of detonating
powder.
   Lately I have seen a far better alarm gun, made by W. Wigg,
of Barnby Foundry, near Beccles.   It consists of a rough, cast-
iron, short barrel, with such a spring and hammer as that I have
described of Wilkinson's metal ; a metal projection or shed protects
the percussion cap from rain, and it can be lightly or heavily
charged, as the situation may require.   When the muzzle is
placed upwards, the report is much louder then when it is turned
downwards.
   The Russians seem to have carefully studied " infernal ma-
chines," which are spring guns of more elaborate construction ;
and I remember that one, cone-shaped, and at its widest part

three feet across, also ignited by pressure upon wires, was found in the dockyard at Kertch in the late Crimean war. I have a notion that one of those exploded also at sea, and injured one of our ships. Probably the time will come when we shall trust to these submerged explosives for protection against invasion rather than to iron ships or forts.

PAPER XIV.

TOM FRERE THE HARD-RIDING FARMER.

You couldn't be long in our neighbourhood—that is to say, if you are a hunting man—without seeing, or hearing of, or making the acquaintance of Tom Frere; and if you didn't make his acquaintance, he would make yours. There was no shyness or *mauvaise honte* about Tom ; he might have heard of such things, but he despised them as " outlandish," and he was as imperturbable, impassive, and incapable of blushing as a plaster cast.

I had not been long in these parts when he introduced himself to me. I was a guest—the only *disinterested* guest—at a rent dinner, where some thirty well-to-do agriculturists had assembled to meet their landlord at quarter-day, and to dine with him afterwards. The dinner waited whilst the last two or three bored the squire and kept the groom from galloping to the National and Provincial with the coin and cheques. Meanwhile the emancipated tenants were at liberty to inspect the old masters and sculpture in the picture gallery, and they could amuse themselves as they liked. The gallery was pretty full, and the fine old steward, whose work was over—and a hard day he had had of it —had just come in with his dress coat on, quite ready for the soup and haunch.

We were all on our best behaviour when Tom came in, bringing with him a rummer of brandy and water—" cold without " he called it. As he was a peg too low, and as there were only a few carved oak benches, he seated himself on a sleeping Venus, and placed his brimming goblet on her right temple, ready to his hand. He was rather below the middle height, with small features, keen eyes, a largish mouth and good teeth—which he was fond of showing, or which naturally drew your attention—and a bull neck.

There was that about him which intimated a want of imagination—a state of mind which frequently accompanies hard riding—and his dress and bearing were of the exceedingly sporting farmer order.

He might be five-and-twenty in age, but he was threescore and
ten in confidence ; or, maybe, I should be better understood if I
said that in this matter he was seventeen ; and as to his being
wrong or mistaken, he was as self-opinionated as the Delphic
oracle, and about as much to be believed. " Mornin'," he said to
me, with as much familiarity as if we had married two sisters,
and perhaps a touch of condescension—it was about seven o'clock
p.m., by the way—" I don't think your nag would see much of it
if we met down in the vale." I had come to grief over one of our
rotten banks, well honeycombed with rabbits, a few days before,
and Tom, who came with a rush on a young Irish horse he was
riding for a friend, had all but landed in the small of my back.
He would have proceeded to enlighten us on the subject of
hounds and horses there and then, but that the last tenants
had subsided, and the squire was waiting for his guests to
assemble.

I saw little of him during dinner ; but afterwards I heard him
vouchsafe some unpalatable truths about missing snipes, and
describing some neighbouring squire (not present, of course) as
" a regular duffer," quite at his ease, though his landlord was
observing him with a cool stare, for the duffer was one of our
host's particular friends.

He was not exactly a tenant, but a tenant's son, and came as
the old man's representative, and as being the eldest son. The
younger ones looked after the business, but Tom never went over
the land without his greyhounds, and seldom came home without
a hare or two. He was also one of the best snipe shots in the
county; for he was born and bred amongst them, and the little
green terrace at the back of the old farmhouse had been redeemed
from bog and quagmire by means of a deep ditch and wall. He
had but to cross this ha-ha and walk ahead for miles. He was a good
flyfisher too ; for all the rapid streams about here were preserved,
and none interrupted him, so his rod and tackle were always kept
at full length, and he could whip the streams for an hour or a
day all the season. But all these sports Tom despised compared
with hunting, and in that sport he shone in his own way.

His " people " hadn't much money—some said that they had
none ; but sometimes people with none get on the best, and this
want of the needful was Tom's excuse for not riding expensive
horses. " I can't get them," he used to say, " and I shouldn't
enjoy them if I could."

When hounds were going he never valued his horse, and his

system as to fencing was, "Over, if you can; through, if you
can't; or down and up again on the right side."

So Tom became known as a bruiser across country, and, being
of an obliging disposition perhaps, or fond of danger and excite
ment, or preferring to ride a brute to staying at home or shooting
snipes, he was "game" to make a horse for anyone; and if they
would send plenty of oats and beans, let who would find horse-
flesh, Mr. Frere would find neck.

On these wretched youngsters, a month up from grass, or just
over their physic, he would "get on" fourteen miles to covert, keep
away from the rest, get a good place and keep it, fall and get up
again, turn up when everyone expected he had been carried off
on a hurdle, pound half the field by his resolute riding, go at
timber forty miles an hour, or ride a horse that wouldn't rise a
foot, at a hog-backed stile.

I don't say that he had a pretty seat—far from it; but if
he had been sewn on to his saddle-flaps he couldn't have been
firmer. He sat very far back in his saddle, kept his hands
down, rode without gloves, and was over-liberal with his spurs
—that is, if he was riding a horse that wanted rousing,—for
with a hot horse he was as quiet as a Quaker, and almost as
silent.

He had a peculiar fancy for turnpike gates, and has many
and many a time ridden over them for a trifling bet. His
black mare, about 14.3 high, would go over them like a bird,
and it was Tom's theory that "any horse could do it." He
was quite sincere in this belief, and declared that the first time
he tried it he was actuated by kind feelings towards the gate
man, and didn't want to call him up; and as it was moonlight,
and he knew the mare had jumped higher, he rode at it, and
landed all right. Some of his neighbours twitted him about
it next day; so he did it again, and subsequently repeated the
performance with a broken-kneed mare, which he bought in the
street after a horse-fair, and with which he cut down the field
when she was about half fit, and eventually won a steeple-
chase in excellent company.

Tom had no groom, and hardly any stable. His black mare
went in the market cart or the hay rake, and took her turn at
plough: and after the hardest run she was shut in the stable
undressed, with her corn in the manger, if she chose to eat it.
As for his bridle, it was about the colour of a copper kettle
with rust, and exactly matched his stirrup irons; and he rode

I

with one girth and a crupper. A stranger might perhaps cut
a joke at him as he came on to covert ; but he must be well
mounted and have the right stuff inside his waistcoat who
could give Tom a lead, let the pace be ever so good.

He could give a good account of himself on a pony, too, if the
hounds ran on the heath, and he had a vixenish bay forest mare
which went on her hind legs, and never was shod, and exas-
perated half the " three-figure " men.

She wasn't more than thirteen hands, was as thick and wedgy
as a cart horse, could get along under any weight, and was the
best hack and trotter. or rather runner, in these parts. I ought
to know, for I bought her out in the hunting field, and she
was delivered next day. Tom rode her over full swing without
a saddle, racing his brother cross country to my house for a
glass of brandy and water, and beating him at the run in,
which is a severe "gradient." Of course she was in a white
foam, and as I paid him the money he observed, " She's nasty
in the stable with a stranger," vaulted behind his brother, and
went up the hill for home at slapping pace. I am describing
these things just as they occurred, and if they are uninteresting
I am sorry for it.

I found Tom had not exaggerated, for she would cleave the
skull of anyone she disliked ; and we fed her for some days (at
least my man did), with a long-handled saucepan, clambering over
the stall, when I insisted on his saddling her and bringing her to
the door in fear and trembling. But she soon got over these
vagaries, and from first to last was gentle with me, and many a
good day's sport I had on her ; for, though we were mutually
afraid of big places, she would lead over anything, (including gates), and soon followed like a dog, or waited to be
caught. In the spring she proved in foal, and I was obliged to
part with her ; which accounted for my getting her such a bargain, though Tom came over and wished he might have many
things happen to him if he knew it.

I don't think that I have said that Tom was a bachelor. He
was never known but once to show any symptoms of having what
he called " a soft place " in him, and this was how it came
about.

The huntsman—his only confidant—and he were jogging home
together, and the conversation was confined, of course, to the
events of the day, and more especially they exchanged opinions
as to the merits of those who had shown themselves in the front.

"That there young lady on the fleabitten thoroughbred went well, Mister Freere," said Davis, turning round jauntily in his saddle to see that his pack was close at the heels of old Jacob (his black hunter), and thus failing to notice a sort of confused look in Tom's face, and a heightened colour which was as near an approach to a blush as he ever made—and very well for a first attempt. "How she did creep along over the plough ; and when we got to the grass lands she *sailed* away like"—the huntsman never heard of confusing metaphors,—so he said "like a bird."

The said Davis had got past the age of romance, and preferred what he called "his little comforts" to a very angel in the shape of a woman ; and these "comforts" aforesaid were the cause of some differences between him and Mrs. Davis at times, as they were made up of spirits and a bar parlour.

Well, Tom gave vent to his feelings in a sort of bucolic hiccough, which he meant for a sigh, and confided to Davis that when he saw her fly Bradford Farm "double"—"*What me and my mare done at twice, Davis*"—he was struck all of a heap ; "and what's more, Davis," he went on, "she fair *grinned* when her flunkey went round to the gate." For, you see, Tom was unused to ladies' society, and he called a spade a spade.

"I wonder who she is, Mr. Freere," said Davis ; "she never was out with us before." But here the conversation was ended by Tom's horse "lumpering," and a suggestion to pull up and get some gruel, which generally means entertainment for man as well as beast ; and both Tom and the huntsman accordingly pulled up, for they were close to a public when the old mare hit the stone.

The object of their admiration was there before them, and she had dismounted to see that the flour and water was mixed properly, when Tom in a bewildered way offered to do it for her ; for no one was at home but the landlady—a coarse old woman in a shawl—and the only daughter, who was a deal too fine to wait on what she called "*h*animals." "Thank you very much," she said in a frank manner ; "my servant has missed me ; be so kind as to mix the meal with a little cold water first, get it quite smooth, and then stir in the boiling water—excuse my giving you directions—now please cool it down." Tom was enchanted to wait upon her, and when she requested him to get her a chair, but on second thoughts she put one hand on his shoulder, another on the pommel, and leapt into the saddle without an effort, and was off down the road. Tom turned round to Davis and gave vent to his admiration in language and with a blank expression which I won't attempt to describe.

Tom was smitten, and had serious thoughts of " settling." " She's exactly my handwriting, Davis," he went on, when a surly-looking groom, with a face like a pug dog, rode up and asked if a lady on a grey was ahead. Tom was very willing to show the way, but the surly groom was not sociably inclined, and all Tom's offers of beer, or even something better, could not prevail ; nor was he going to tell " they roughs," as he called them, who " *missus and me was,*" and so on.

Tom went home and thought about it. He broke his short pipe, gave over smoking, bought a teacaddy with a moulded glass sugar basin in the middle, got his mother to cover the front of his bridle with blue velvet, and set up for a respectable man. But he didn't see her again (as he described it) till " barley sowing ;" and I will give his own simple description of the scene.

" I was in our market, when who should I see but that pug-dog-faced chap driving a yellow chariot thing, with crowns on the doors, and two great ramping brown carriage horses, seventeen hands high, with gilt harness and crests all over it ; and she was inside, dressed first-rate, quite like a lady, with a little boy in a velvet coat and a hat and feather—about two or three years old, he was. I nodded to the groom as was on the box, but he took no notice, nor she neither, though they pulled up close to me ; and the footman with his hair powdered pushed me a-one-side, and told the shopman to bring out some toys for My Lady's little boy. I was rather low about it for a bit, but of course arter this *I give her up !*"

And " arter this" Tom, who was not poetic enough to hang himself or take poison, found excitement in the hunting field, and speculated, deeply for him, in horses. " Next Cadbury Hill Fair," Tom told Davis when he met him at exercise—" Next Cadbury Hill Fair, Davis, I'll spec'late in the Irish drove." " That will suit you better, Master Frere," said Davis, " than having to ride second oss with a countess ; and I'll come and help you deal. Let's see, it's next Toosday."

There were a lot of rough Irish colts, and men as rough who owned them ; but Tom never got beyond looking, and at last the men wouldn't pull any more out for him, and told him to go on and look at the next lot, and so on. At last the whole mob began to move off, and there was scarce a horse left upon the place. The van men, actors, dwarfs, and monstrosities lit their

fires for the night. It was the latter end of September, and Tom
was strolling down hill to his father's, not a mile off, when he
came upon a little knot of gipsies sharing their gains and losses,
and "knocking out," that is, selling by auction to their gang, a
three-parts bred, or perhaps a thorough-bred, six-year-old bay
mare. She had a broken knee and was shin sore, wearing
carpet boots on her fetlocks, and there was little of her but the
bones. However, she caught Tom's eye, and Tom caught the
gipsy's, and Tom had "a run." From sixteen guineas they got
to ten, and from ten to something like half sixteen ; and all the
time a gipsy lad, with half boots and a fur cap, and little more
in the way of dress, was galloping her backwards and forwards,
pulling up short, and turning her round as though she were on a
pivot—the surest way to show a spavin if there is one. "Heads
or tails?" said Tom to the brownest gipsy, whose skin was the
colour and complexion of a pancake ; "I'll have her:" and,
amidst the united gipsy chorus of "Sold again," Tom led her to
his paternal stables.

What became of her and of Tom I must leave until another
day.

PAPER XV.

EXPECTING BROWN.

IF you live in the country as I do, and rarely see anything passing along on the other side of the invisible fencing, except a drove of sheep or a herd of bullocks—if you are five miles from the nearest house whose inmates have any idea of more than one language, and that a most corrupt one, spoken in a harsh key— you will have learnt that you depend a good deal upon your home visitors for a cheerful autumn and a merry winter.

As the mellow tints come upon the forest leaves, and by the time your gay dahlias are cut down there will be fewer and fewer wheel tracks on the gravel ring, and presently the morning calls will have come to an end. A few of your neighbours who are blessed with wives and daughters free from delicate constitutions will turn out on a cheery clear day and pull up in the open phaeton, the lady occupants well protected in thirty-guinea sealskin jackets and bear-skin rugs ; or, perchance, when the snow lies thick upon the ground, the new-married couple, who don't know the price of a basinette or the best emporium for baby-linen *yet,* will skim along your entrance in a sledge—the only notice of their approach being the peal of bells upon the leader, until you hear a rich mellow voice from beneath a shawl and moustaches suggesting that "it's good weather to try that Morello cherry brandy you were talking of."

In a week or two there is the first advertised meet of the hounds, and, as you finish a rather early breakfast, you can see a smart groom or two taking your neighbour's horses on to covert at a walk. As you leave your own gate, you fall in with him and " the house party " in the break, the collars of their " pinks " just betraying their business to the approving yokels as they trot through the village and scatter the water at the brook ferry by the ruined water mill, doing twelves miles an hour, and able to get up to fifteen if required. For that pair of own brothers by Hotspur, who ran the Dutchman to a head, are in hard condition, and, although they have come six miles in a little under thirty

minutes, they have hardly got their coats down, and the near-side
one is ready to break away into a canter if he were not driven as
quietly and with as much judgment as you can get into any head
at five-and-twenty years—twelve and a half in the stable, and
the other half in the kennel adjoining, except when the body was
at Eton, where the mind never was.

If they had not been driven by a middling hand, they wouldn't
have got well round the turn, when the old milldam was passed;
but I could see the young one on the box draw the reins through
his hand, and take them into the middle of the road. And well
he did so! for here comes the miller's van, the man driving with
rope reins to the wheelers only, and of course he is on his wrong
side, hidden by the high hedge until the phaeton is close upon
him. Then he pulls *up* instead of pulling *in*, and cracks his
whip, which resounds like a pistol, and unsettles the going of the
Hotspurs; by this time they are just inclined to back a bit, and,
feeling the influence of this bracing, sunny, crisp-aired November
morning, are bridling well, and stepping up and out as only blood
ones can.

Here, by the wrought iron gates, which admit of a fine view of
the old beech avenue—the trunks of these same beeches admirably contrasted with their carpet of russet leaves—I come
upon a knot of beaters, "waiting for the Squire," and lose sight
and sound of the phaeton and pair simultaneously. The keeper,
in his best bran new suit of autumn-tinted velveteen, waits at a
little distance with "master's retriever," his face displaying, in
spite of a good humoured expression, a little anxiety lest the fox
should make for his home coverts and scatter his tame birds to
the winds (and, what is worse, the poachers). He makes me his
confidant as I trot by him, " hoping that I shall be able to come
to master's next Saturday with the London gentleman, for master
is depending upon us, and he knows the woodcocks were pitching
in last night."

" All right, Evans; I shall be there!" and this puts me in
mind of Brown, who always comes once a year, and more frequently twice.

Brown is fifty, but so wonderfully coopered up that he would
pass for thirty-five. There are secrets between him and his
valet concerning his teeth, hair, and padding, which defy detec-
tion, and which will never be revealed. He always will have a
fire in his room to heat a little saucepan or pipkin, which Mr.
Marsden (his valet) locks up as soon as it is done with; and my

little boy, who took his letters to him one morning, is the only mortal who ever saw it. The imp couldn't see Brown well, but he *thought* he had his hair in papers, and that he didn't look so young in bed as he did at breakfast. Brown is "something in the City," but I don't know what, and a good deal at Acton, where he is called "the Squire": and two or three unmarried ladies admire him and go to him for charitable contributions, which they always get.

He was captain of the eleven when I first went to school, and I was his wretched little valet. No fag ever had a better master, though ; and the way he put up with my bad toasting of muffins, and the patience he manifested at my awkwardness at football or cricket, are past belief.

Only those who have passed some years of their lives at a public school know the advantage of having a big fellow on your side until you are a big fellow yourself. I was head boy at a tutor's who *prepared* boys for public schools, and my word was law there. I wrote the best verses, and had more hampers than any of them, and I expected to carry this importance with me when my father put my little portmanteau into his phaeton and chucked me after it.

The last few stages we were driven by a stage coachman who drove the coach in my father's time, and he and "Old Jack" met as old acquaintances. It rained during the last mile or two, and the school gates did not look cheerful. There was that sober expression about the head master's butler, which I have seen worn by the keepers of a private madhouse ; and the school might have been a lunatic asylum, or a gaol, or both. The barred windows were not encouraging, and the dining room (into which we were ushered as though both of us were going to enter as disciples) was severely classical. The prints, half circular, and of austere copper-plate design, were all from pictures of martyrs and angels, and the latter seemed as gloomy as those they came to succour! There were preparations going on for a large dinner, and the sober domestics (sober as yet) kept bringing in little clusters of wine glasses and tumblers as we waited.

"Holloa!" my father exclaimed, "hock for dinner! I wonder if these are the old green glasses they had in my day, when this head master was a little child in petticoats."

Presently more fathers and more little boys, and we soon looked like a group of patients in a dentist's waiting room. I could have looked upon the jug of hot water, clean tumbler, and towels as a matter of course, when the head master himself called us into his long, rather narrow, but handsome study.

There were few questions to ask and few words to write, and my father took me out to dine with him, the master promising, when I came in at six p.m., to introduce me to Brown, whose father and mine were old schoolfellows. Here my acquaintance began with "the London gentleman," who (like the old general's butler, that robbed his employer himself, but accorded that privilege to no other) kept a tight hand upon me in my schooldays, but protected me from all petty tyranny—initiating me into the mysteries and slang of school life, and putting me in the way of taking my own part, by occasional scientific lessons in the art of self-defence.

I suppose that he was sixteen at this time, and we were about a year together. I recollect his father coming to see him once, that he gave him a five-pound note and tipped me with two pounds (one of them all in silver), and that he seemed to me an old man on the verge of the grave (he was about forty-four), and very like the present Brown, whom I look upon as in the prime of life. Soon after my schoolfellow left for Oxford, and when I went up to reside I found him the junior fellow of my college, with London chambers and a moor in Scotland.

I believe it was at his father's urgent request that he held his fellowship, and submitted to the martyrdom of good rooms, good living, good hunting, and plenty of money at a moment's notice, until he saw me safe through my first year, when he resigned his preferment, and became junior partner, or "co.," or whatever it is, with his father in the City. I was very much inclined for business when I saw the state of things, only I had no father to join ; for this "junior partner" always had time to fish or shoot in Norway or Scotland, and was chiefly employed in his morning ride, his afternoon drive, going to his club, and smoking the most choice cigars. Then his chambers! What a luxurious home for Young England! (He was one of that body then, and his waist was barely twenty inches !)

What a row of Wellingtons, and what presses of coats, waistcoats, and unwhisperables! Here, over the fireplace, behind plate glass, are his Purdeys, guns and rifles for all sorts of game ; and on either side his pet tandem and pair-horse whips—straight, taper, and with the crops well quilled. Here is one he shows me —a blackthorn with the bark on, which has upwards of a hundred and fifty treble knots. He presses it, as he says this, upon the thick Axminster carpet, to show me it is as it ought to be, as stiff as an iron bar to within two feet of the top, and as straight as a gun barrel, with a beautiful " fall." His sitting room has a bed room opening into it on each side, so that he and his visitor can dress by easy stages over the fire in winter ; and on the floor of each dormitory there is a large bath, with a sliding lid, a waste pipe, and water hot or cold laid on. There is a speaking tube to the servants' rooms, and every possible convenience, at the modest rental of, say, three hundred pounds a year—for which he told me they took care of his pictures (Copley Fielding's, Tayler's, and the great Turner's), and kept at arm's length all bores, whom the porter knows as well as a huntsman knows his hounds.

Notwithstanding all this luxury and comfort, nothing pleased " the London gentleman" better than to leave it all, and put up with the rough living and hard walking of a country shooting box ; and, alike in my father's time or now that I can find him a bedroom, for the last five-and-twenty years I have visited Brown, or he has once or twice a year been to stay with me. His valet, like his master, with whom he has lived full five-and-twenty years, delights to escape from a cook, whom he married in an evil hour, and to seek for the solace of his long winter evenings amongst our less polished servants, by whom is regarded as an oracle of wisdom and a model of polished manners. Even our keeper, who has been to Norway, is silent when he speaks, and approves the *theory* he propagates as to shooting, though it jars with his *practice*, which is deficient—*very*. They tell me he is allowed a silver fork at dinner ; and my own man, a village wit and a confirmed boaster, levels no shafts of ridicule at him, and always calls him " Sir."

What a blessed influence he sheds over my rough, unpolished household ? for this well-bred domestic takes no holiday when he comes here. He tried it once, but became insufferably " bored," and begged to be allowed to " wait." In a couple of days he had done wonders with the stable-boy impressed when we have a house full, and had so redeemed that youngster from savage life that I regarded the reformation in his head with wonder and admiration. His hair, in his happiest moments, used to resemble those brushes of brass wire which gunmakers sell with cleaning rods ; but now it is glossy and well parted, " fore and aft," as a sailor would say. He has learnt not to

slam the door or leave it open ; he does not blow down my neck
as he holds a guest's plate on the "off side," in spite of the
coachman's rough whisper of "near side, Jim"; and he puts on
the wood or coal gently and without noise. Were my friend's
London valet single, he would turn all the servant's heads—I
mean the women servants, of course.—The cook, who owns to
forty-five, wears during the evenings that he is here a chignon,
which is about the size of a half-quartern loaf, and my neat
Phillis mounts cherry-coloured ribbons in his honour.

Imperturbable, quiet, self-possessed, Brown's "gentleman" goes
about his business as though he saw them not, and between the
courses appears unconscious of any presence save that of the
demon at his home, who has most likely written to him that
very morning to remind him the Christmas rent is due.

Old Horace tells us that black Care sits behind the horseman.
I see a shadowy outline of some such grim adherent in the box
of Brown's "fly," as, master inside and servant on the box, they
pull up at my cottage door ! What a contrast between master and
man ! The former blithe and cheery ; tinkered up by the greatest of
London artists in their walk, he might be one of those truthful
portraits, so confessedly the transcripts of boredom, which occupy
the space of the Royal Academy year by year ! His luggage,
double gun case, and cartridge pannier are of the best, and tell
you in broad branded letters that they are "warranted of solid
leather." His own name, figured in enormous capitals, could not
be more "pronounced," even if he were an Indian Viceroy !
What a dressing case that must be, judging from its leathern
envelope and straps ; and a snob would form a high estimate of
Brown, as he beheld that morocco courier bag garnished with its
gold clasp and buckles. Then his umbrella—attenuated as a
parasol, with a stick so bedizened, so decked with gold shield
and crest, that its proper place would be some cabinet with
Watteau panels, and its associates articles of vertu and buhl ink-
stands.

As he descends, the valet, streaming with water, offers Mr.
Brown his elbow, and gently repudiates the flyman, who has his
hand upon the door, and whispers him some inaudible message—
concerning fare and gratuity no doubt for the driver—touches
his hat, and transfers his simulated endearments to the "osses,"
which, as their name implies, are merely a collection of bones.

There is a flutter amongst my household. and I infer that the
chimney in Brown's room is "smoking." He has one half hour

before dinner, and he will make the best of it, though I impress
upon him he need not dress. For all that, as I have a gossip
with him whilst his valet is laying out his change of garments, I
observe that he is determined to have his own way, and that he
will come out in that new dress coat by Poole, which preceded
him yesterday in a deal box, and which my youngsters longed to
open.

Now, if the fish hasn't missed the train, all will go on pros-
perously, and Brown's advent may be marked with a white stone.
I don't care although the cook gave warning a week ago ; for
haven't I bought another for two shillings at the register office,
and offered eighteenpence for a housemaid ? The present *chef*
will outlive Brown's stay, and, let her do her best, my old friend
won't grumble, though the sauces are inferior to those which are
furnished at his club. His valet approves the claret, and has
superintended the icing of the dry champagne. Early as it is,
we have arranged a snipe pudding, and *terrine de foie gras* is the
same in clubs and out of them. I only wait the light tread of
my old acquaintance as he emerges from his room, and a knot of
us are grouped round the hall stove, wondering where he is.

A tub and a wet hairbrush are all a youngster wants, unless
he condescends to rondeletia, the Jockey Club scent, and bando-
line—such fripperies take time ; but at fifty odd, if you are
determined to look boyish in patches, you can't be hurried.
There are various little deceits which you have to practise, first
upon yourself and then upon your friends. It takes longer to
arrange a little hair " thin on the top " than a thick crop of it ;
and, as Brown has barely a curl left, the arranging that one wisp,
which is in the same situation as the forelock of " Father Time,"
necessitates the wasting of moments which at last weigh heavily
upon the cook. Around the logs of beech we are fast drifting
into politics, as a last resource, for we have gone through the
merits of my kennel, reviewed Lexicon, Lucifer, and Labourer of
the Poltimore kennel, and abjured big hounds to a man ; there
is scarce a gunmaker or his gun which has not been approved,
criticised, or condemned ; and the battues and future " bags " at
well-known manors have been prophesied of, and declared to be
great or small according to the fancy of the speaker. Horses
have been mentally inspected, too, and the number of foxes would
seem to be prodigious—I earnestly hope it may ; and whilst one
of the company, his legs wide apart, is extolling the new huntsman just imported from the Shires, I am conscious of a slight

smell of Truefitt's and the Burlington Arcade as I hear Brown's step upon the stairs.

He joins our group of what he playfully calls "rustics," whose coats are provincial; and they (old friends of his) appear not to notice his silk facings and white waistcoat, which looks better on him than the common herd because he doesn't (as a London schneider told me I did) " want the chest." That suit presumes a good dinner, and enfolds the most easy-going, prosperous man in England, the *beau idéal* of a sleeping partner—sleeping pretty soundly, too, until the day of reckoning, when he receives his "bit of grey paper," puts it carelessly into his waistcoat pocket, and bowls off in his cab for Coutts and Co., or Barclay, Bevan, &c. I wish I had an account with either of them—but I haven't!

PAPER XVI.

BROWN IN THE COUNTRY.

ONE finds out rustic inconveniences when the house is full. In my case that means when my few spare bedrooms are occupied.

Perhaps I felt it the more when I had one of my very oldest friends with me—the "London gentleman" accompanied by his imperturbable valet.

If you lie awake three or four nights before your visitor arrives, thinking of what there is the house won't furnish, still at last there will be some omission a "club" man will feel. I live twelve miles from the nearest lobster, fourteen and a half from ice, and five from pickles or Durham mustard. I believe there is no real pale ale nearer than Burton—that is, about one hundred and forty-seven miles as the crow flies. If these things are not "in stock," you can't have them ; and if you have a fit of indigestion, you must fight it out till morning, or rely upon my medical resources and my not having mislaid my copy of "Domestic Medicine." Generally this volume of common sense, and science made intelligible to any educated mind, is on the same shelf as the Cookery Book, that the one may be at hand to remedy the effects of the other. If it is not, the search may be prolonged, possibly until Nature has righted herself, for there is no doctor to be had under three hours.

And, being on the subject of cookery books, let me say you are sure to run on shore if you attempt too much or aim too high in country dinners. A little novelty is well enough, but try anything for which London is famous, and you are wrecked ! Soup is frequently a breakdown, and my cook—promoted now to 25*l.* per annum and "all found "—used to think that you couldn't boil a turbot too much. I believe she once boiled it all night with the plum pudding. Saddle of mutton is safe to be all right ; so are those white fowls, and the sauce so like gruel under ordinary treatment, both in appearance, taste, and smell.

Breakfast is a village difficulty, except the sideboard dishes, where by means of a good deal of parsley and a little cold meat, you can get on moderately ; but don't risk beefsteaks. *Take my word for it, they are indigenous to London, and tough everywhere else.*

Every meal in a village is an embarrassment, more or less, owing to the childish thoughtlessness of your domestics, who, when they are "shunted" from the ordinary groove, instantly lose their heads.

At the last moment always expect some catastrophe ; the probability is that you won't be disappointed. No oil for the lamps, or oil but no wicks—that's a common thing ; but the kitchen "chimbley" on fire at the last hour is by no means an uncommon, nor indeed an uninteresting, thing. Sometimes these annoyances begin at the dawn of day, when you have to borrow butter because the cream has gone to sleep, and the churn has been going incessantly for six hours, and is going now. We had no milk one morning, nor cream either, for a mouse was found drowned in the milkpan, and the cows had strayed in the night, and were probably half a dozen miles away. On another occasion, when we wanted two or three extra horses, and were the last party to start—four in my Whitechapel, one the great gun of the party—my horse hopped off like a frog; for the day before the blacksmith had "pricked" him, and said nothing about it, nor did my man see that he was lame until I called his attention to it, when he declared that he "often went like that"—of course !

On the occasion of *this* visit—for I must give up grumbling—all went *moderately* well. Someone asked for Vichy water, which we hadn't got (we are twelve miles from Vichy water), and I think Brown asked for a shalot, but compromised for a pickled onion, which was exactly twelve minutes in coming. I also observed that he turned up the whites of his eyes at the soup, when his attentive valet removed his plate, probably at this preconcerted signal.

Country dinners, complimentary banquets, and even Lord Mayors' dinners, come to an end at last, and so did ours. We also got over the evening after a fashion, and I believe that we did not destroy one neighbour's reputation. I think even whist is more Christianlike than that ; some people don't. We had contrived to exceed our usual number of house visitors, for the bachelor portion put up with the schoolboy's beds, except Brown, who always has the same room, and bestrews it with clothes of every description. These are never put into shape without great energy and consideration by his valet, and then only to be stirred together again—resembling, in the mixture he makes of dress clothes, shirts, boots, and cartridges, a sort of Irish stew on a large scale.

We generally have a sort of " camp-fire " meeting when the civilised portion of the household have gone to rest, held in the tiled kitchen, with potash, soda, and the spirit cruets for those that like it ; and the copper kettle (" A 1," three parts of it kept bright and a porcelain handle) is expected to be boiling on the hob.   The only thing that puts us out is that nearly all of them want their clothes aired, and that it is difficult to make room for half a dozen fellows and a clothes-horse heavy with coats, knickerbockers, and flannel shirts.

I remember hearing of one old fellow who used on these visits to be very particular not to keep his powder dry, but to dry it when he was on a visit to his friends, and that on one occasion he had, unobserved by his host, taken this usual precaution, most likely feeling pretty sure that his usual plan would not meet with the approbation of his friends.   They had a very pleasant evening indeed ; it was a frosty night, and they had a roaring, blazing fire of wood and coal, and towards morning they all retired of course.

At breakfast next day the footman brought in on a tray what looked like a very large copper gluepot, stating that the kitchen-maid had just found it in the oven, and had sent it in, imagining no doubt that it was something designed for breakfast, instead of being the old gentleman's powder magazine, containing about six pounds of Curtis and Harvey, which he had forgotten to remove after the evening's diversions.   Rather a pleasant visitor this, who, when you did all you could for him, instead of thanking you, did his best to blow you up!

You can't get " the London gentleman " to understand that you have not an unlimited supply of horses and wheels.   Brown, for instance greets me as he comes downstairs at eleven a.m., " dressed the character " to a nicety, and irreproachable as to knickerbockers, shooting jacket, and all the rest of it—" I say, old fellow, would it be troubling you too much to send to your railway station for a little parcel from Purdey's ?   The fact is, it's my cartridge extractor.   I called at their place, but came away and left it on the counter ; and depend on it, he has sent it down. I may not want it, you know, but it's as well to have it, if it's not troubling you too much."   You see Brown can't get it out of his head that we have a cabstand close by.   If there is anything wrong with his London groom or the horses (in fact, if his men or beasts are indisposed to work), he lifts up his finger ; a smart Hansom driver responds with that nod of the fraternity which is a mixture of condescension and acquiescence, and, pulling up short by the kerb stone, leans forward as he lifts the reins, and touching his hat brim, says in sharp accents, " What part ? " The shabby driver of the four wheeler, on the other hand, puts on an injured look when you hail him, and asks in dudgeon and a hoarse voice from behind his huge cotton necktie, " Vere to ? " Probably he has just taken a sixpenny fare to the small-pox hospital, and is sorry for you !

Often in a village one horse is a bore for weeks together, and your man, tired with the monotony of doing nothing, sleeps half his time; but when you have three or four friends with you, four or five can't do it, and all of them begin to " go a little feeling," or have what our veterinary surgeon calls " a favourite leg."

Numbers of humane people, believe that the amount of work you can get out of a horse depends on the amount of whip ; and many a man does not know a lame horse when he sees one, or rides behind or on—I might better say *over*—him. Jullien didn't; he almost lived in cabs, and every cabman knew him. He hadn't a very good *eye* for anything, they say ; and one day, as he stepped out of a Hansom, an intimate friend observed, "What a lame horse you've got, Jullien ! " " I never *saw* a lame horse in my life," he replied ; " but I noticed that this one *didn't move his feet in correct time.*" Many *drivers* are quite as ignorant as this great *conductor*, and few town visitors make allowances for the difficulties of country locomotion.

One of the banes of country life is your friends' luggage. Doesn't it " work up " your patent leather dashing irons ? Are not ladies' boxes—those with ragged iron corners—nice things on the top of your pet brougham ? Did your ever pull up to give an agricultural parishioner a lift as you saw him toiling back from the doctor's with a hedge stake for a stick ? If you did, didn't it set your teeth on edge to observe his efforts to ascend your Whitechapel ? and didn't he to a dead certainly put his hobnails on the shaft of it, and leave an impression on the paint and varnish reminding you of a crumpet, until you next paid seven pounds fourteen for painting and leather washers ?

Horses and carriages are the great bores of country life, always excepting that extinct animal the cook, and that rare animal the obliging groom, who (before he gets his livery) will turn his hand

K

to anything, but after he has got it doesn't get up till eight, and
then grumbles at his breakfast, and thinks the gardener, who is
worked to death, ought to clean his boots.

I was deluded into the country by the common error that
everthing is so cheap. It's the same price for everything as in
most places, buy what you will, only your *must* keep a horse to
fetch it; and if you get a store the probability is that it becomes
mouldy or is lost. "Such a pleasure, your metropolitan visitors
say, to grow your own cabbages!" Why, they cost you half-a-
crown apiece, and you must grow them or have none. Just as you
want eggs the fowls are on strike, and won't lay, or the fox
clears you out. I wish he would do that to me, but I fear the
atmosphere of pheasants is "too mighty" for him, as they say
here.

"Bagmen" are the consequences of large "bags;" and what a
poor subterfuge it is at last, when the hounds won't break him
up, and his brush is full of chaff and barley husks! Wove wire
is cheap enough; why don't those who go in for their five
hundred a day rear their long-tailed poultry in an inclosure of it,
clip their wings, and let them out as they want them? Or
pheasant shooting from the trap would be a novelty, and a resource for blank days; let's try it!

But to go back to Brown, who, good fellow as he is, knows
nothing of the difficulties of my situation—that the drawing-
room party want to go out; that Purdey will certainly send his
extractor to the post town, which is nine miles the other way
from the station, and that probably it is now on its way in the
letter bag; that we have four miles to drive to the covert my
friend shoots this morning, and that we are late now, and only
waiting for the mail—whose horn (the cart driver's) I hear now,
and in five minutes I gladden Brown by the sight of a little
parcel tied and sealed as though it contained diamonds, but
which *does* contain the extractor, as I expected.

We are off now. I hear the wheels of the waggonette, and
the near-side horse, who is a bad starter, my man says—and well
he may be, with a collar two sizes too small, and curbed and
bearing-reined, and gagged with a nose martingale—won't leave
home at any price. To put all these things to rights and
change for a ring snaffle takes time; but at last he comes
round to the front. Then Brown, always fussy and "most
particular," wants a soda and brandy, telling us one of those
confounded dogs kept him awake all night. But I know better;

it was the crowing of our invalid rose-combed, feather-legged, pedigree Cochin China cockerel, not yet arrived at puberty and afflicted with the gapes and rickets, whose spasmodic attempts at articulation I can compare to nothing but the chorus of geese at the brook yonder and the donkey on the green when they vociferate—I was going to say in unison! Well, that valuable bird—whose parents have occupied what fanciers call a "prize pen," and to whose merits my pen certainly can't do justice—that rare specimen never begins until 8 a.m.: a poor excuse for soda and brandy certainly! But. now it *is* suggested, the rest of my party vote it "not a bad thing," and a quarter of an hour goes in that way.

We start at last, have just cleared the gates, and I congratulate myself on a good start, too, when Brown says, "Wey! I say, do you think your friend would object to my taking my retriever? You know one of your fellows can lead him, and he will follow us capitally."

I don't like to hurt Brown's feelings, so my man runs back. I didn't know that Brown had brought a dog. He said nothing to me about it ; but I soon saw him now. He had been tied up in the stable, but with a length of chain allowing him to so effectually gnaw the stable door, that in the morning my groom saw half his head protruding—as far, in fact, as his lynx eyes— and, as he told me afterwards, he really thought it was some wild beast out of a show.

The man ran back and released this monster—a knock-kneed, bitter-beer-coloured one, and, having done so, not looking to see where he went, ran to resume his place with us ; but no dog appeared. We tried the usual plan. Every one called "Rock" —that was the brute's name ; and the stable-boy whistled, standing exactly in the wrong place, of course. Five minutes gone and a long hill to climb, with a very fair load too ! At last Brown went himself, and found his retriever with his head in the hog-tub foraging for scraps. He condescended to notice Brown at last, and for about a mile he followed moderately well ; then he began to flag, and we had occasionally to wait for him, generally on the steepest part of the road ; and after rolling over and over upon a dead rook, or something worse, and that too when he had just refreshed himself with a horsepond bath. Brown suggested that "we should lose him if we didn't take him up."

I thought such a contingency possible, and I regret to add that I rejoiced at it. What could be better than to escape the responsibility of such a sinister-eyed, bat-eared, shambling, flat-sided street dog ? And then I didn't care about the responsibility of introducing a friend's dog as well as a friend.

There was not much time lost in deliberation, for when we stopped he eyed us suspiciously, and turned for home. Brown's hurried descent from the vehicle was his signal to mend his pace (he didn't know Brown well), and with a look over his shoulder, he broke into a sort of long wolf's gallop until he came to four cross roads, when he took the wrong turn of course, and was immediately out of sight.

A man of Brown's temperament, who has no domestic cares, no school bills or doctors' bills either, *makes* troubles when he can ; and I needn't say my friend was inconsolable. There was nothing for it but to follow him. " Never mind the shooting," he said ; " I would not lose that dog for fifty pounds. Turn round sharp, old fellow ; here, let me drive ; you can gallop this bottom and spring the little hill in no time." But, as the changing seats took time, we got over that difficulty, and I expressed my willingness to do the best I could for him.

There is something ridiculous in the pursuit of a dog. It is more humiliating than a hat chase in a high wind. In fact, you are following an animal which is supposed to follow you, and at a manifest disadvantage. In this case the dog was not worth following—nor, indeed, worth catching—which deprived the catastrophe of all excitement. The truant didn't awake any feeling but fear.

Two young ladies and a governess behind a gate told us a mad dog with his tongue out was just gone on ; and a clodhopper, with hedging gloves and a billhook, who listened to their remarks with grave interest from the opposite hedge, corroborated their statement, and showed us by arm-measurement in pantomime that the animal's tongue hung out about a foot and a half. We nearly reached the dog in about a mile, when some labourer, evidently badly impressed by his appearance, gave him a cut with his prong to help him on, and merely regarded Brown's clenched fist and objurgations with a look of stolid indifference as we drove by.

We are up with him again now ! for we have been doing twelve miles good in the hour, and every stride makes us proportionately late for our engagement ; but this time I feel sure we have him. He seems to recognise Brown's endearments just as we approach a mended piece of road ; but the rattle of the wheels on the loose stones starts him, and I suggest giving up the chase. Brown agrees, and I am afraid that he consigned the dog to a very indifferent master—" Let him go to the ———." I didn't catch the last word, owing to those freshly-broken flints ; and with that Brown lit a fresh cigar, and dropped his cigar-case.

" Woa one minute, old fellow ; now we are right again. Thank you" (to my groom, who had got down to recover it, and now handed it back to him). " A dog," Brown moralised as we went on, " a dog, especially when he doesn't know you, is the most inf—" but here we got to some rough road again, and I lost what I have heard old people call " the thread" of his discourse. I don't know what the thread was, but he certainly applied such a string of epithets to Rock as I never heard rivalled, except by a Scotch keeper, who used to reason with his dogs in Gaelic, and expect the dogs to understand him.

" I only hope, Brown," I said, for I wanted to give him a crumb of comfort—" I only hope your dog won't do what those two pointers did that my friends got at Salisbury." And, as I found Brown not indisposed to listen, I went on to tell him.

" It was in the old coaching days, you know, Brown, and these two men were going off on leave together. They were in some heavy regiment, and it was about the beginning of August. They got to Salisbury about midday, and ' the coach' lunched there ; if they wanted an extra half hour they could have it, as Bob, who used to drive it, sympathised with a man who wouldn't be hurried over his dinner, and could always keep his time, getting there a few minutes before and leaving a few minutes late, and galloping the bottoms, and all that."

" Go on," Brown muttered ; " I know Bob well enough ; tall fellow—played the bugle—wore his hat on one side."

" Well," I continued, " they were just come out from luncheon, or dinner, or whatever it was, when a fellow came up dressed like a keeper, with a brace of uncommonly nice-looking pointers—whip sterns, you know."

" Go on," said Brown ; " I know what the story is. They were prigged from old Alec Wyndham's, and———"

" I beg your pardon," I went on. " They gave the fellow five or six pounds for them, and arranged to take them on inside the coach, ' with the proviso, mind,' as Bob told them—' with the proviso, that if a lady wants to get in those dogs must come out.'

"There was no need of the proviso, and they and their new masters reached their destination. The dogs seemed to know their work, and the two friends nearly came to words as to which should have the brace, it seemed such a pity to part them. At last the biggest one with the most money became the owner; and do you know, Brown, I always have thought that the little one smelt a rat.

"They were staying together all the 'leave,' and they had some rented shooting and a sort of villa. Well, one day they neglected to tie up these dogs (there were no kennels), and for three or four days the dogs were missing.

"'Ah, well,' the little one said, 'it's all right; they've got names on their collars, and I dare say they'll turn up.' And so they did, for one day, a wet rainy one, as the two friends were rubbing their noses against the windows waiting for it to clear up, an old shepherd came to the backdoor leading these two pointers, which seemed positively in better condition than when they absconded; and this was accounted for when the messenger handed in a note, a dirty crumpled one, from a farmer about fifteen miles away, stating that these dogs had been caught in the act of worrying his ewes, and that off and on they had killed over two score, eating only the kidney fat, and sending also a very pretty bill indeed, with deductions for the skins. The story got to the regiment somehow, and when they wanted to rile the proprietor of these sporting dogs, they had only to order mashed potatoes and kidneys for breakfast, I can tell you.

"Holloa, Brown!" for I see that he has not heard a word; "wasn't that a gun?"

"Yes, and there is another. They've begun without us."

"I shall put all the blame on you. You Londoners are always getting us into trouble in the country!"

Brown isn't in a joking humour, and, as we pull up at the old wrought-iron gates and he touches his hat to the under keeper left to pilot us, he eyes a tough ash plant that functionary carries in his hand, and I believe that he would like to give it us all round; but he is a "prefect" no longer, and I am not his fag. So he hands me a big "regalia," and remarks—"Make some allowance for me, old fellow; I wasn't brought up in the country, and unless there happened to be plenty of society, and good society too, I shouldn't care to live in it for more than a month or two at a time." I think any sensible man will agree with him, unless he has a park, a groom of the chambers, and, what is better

than these even, a contented mind and a gift for country occupa-
tions and amusements.

The shooting—it was a battue, with "stops," "beaters," a
"bouquet" at the end of the principal covert, and a luncheon
brought out in a Norway kitchen (which may be improvised with
railway wrappers and a saucepan)—was just like other battues,
and need not be described. I may observe, though, that at the
very last, just as we were coming to the end of a covert singularly
short of birds, a large fox broke away, and that there was a chorus
of "Tally-hoes"—ending in a laugh ; for it was Brown's bitter-
beer-coloured dog pointing for the carriages, the white tag at the
end of his tail streaming in the wind. He was captured by one
of the servants, whom he bit through the hand immediately, and
Brown ordered his execution next morning.

He now fertilises the soil round our Ribston pippin, and since
his burial we have had an excellent crop yearly. We always
contrive to place this dish opposite to Brown, and we call them
"Rock" pippins, for each apple hung on a "cordon," and so did
Rock.

PAPER XVII.

THE EARTHSTOPPERS' FEAST.

IF I see my saddle room in very precise order—the spare bits
and curb-chains with an extra burnish; the saddles "sumple"
and polished like an old-fashioned mahogany; every collar, spare
trace, kicking strap, knee cap, and "foot swab" looked over and
fit for the exhibition case of a west-end saddler; when a new
straw plait is down in the stable, the buckets have been scrubbed
and filled with fair water, and the nags look extra well—I know
one of two things is imminent: my man either wants "a day
out," or, "if it's convenient, he would like to settle."

This was the state of things one morning in the middle of
May, and less than half a score of years ago, when I came down
about an hour before breakfast, and took a turn round the premises in that excellent humour which proceeds from a capital
appetite with no immediate prospect of satisfying it.

I was not in the best of tempers; and my men, who are true
disciples of Lavater, were not long in recognising it. The first I
met gave "the office" to No. 2; and I knew as well as if they
had spoken to me when one said to the other, "Little cloudy
this morning, Bill; shouldn't wonder if we has a storm before
night." To this William (with a wink which I saw through the
privet hedge), "Shouldn't wonder, *Mr. Smith* (this was irony);
it *do* look black, sure enough." Now I thought I would disap-
point their expectations; so I called "Mr. Smith" and suggested
a look through the kennels.

Mr. Smith was all alacrity, and when he had fetched his keys
we looked over the setters together. Everything was as it should
be—gravel without a soil, floors untainted, drains clear, troughs
clean scoured and put out to air, plenty of water in the cast-iron
pans, chains and couples all hung up in the little spare yard;
dogs glossy, bright-eyed, with coats like satin; feeding house a
pattern of neatness—no waste; all utensils scoured and bright;
and the few dog boxes we use had been lime-washed and sprinkled
with carbolic acid and water for fear of ticks. The beds had

new red-deal shavings, and, to use Smith's words, he didn't
believe there was a "vlea" about the place ; "and as for rats,"
he went on, " why, no rat in his senses would bide where there
are such ferrets as these"—and so saying, he took up a goodish
handful of them, polecat and white together, all active, clean,
and with thick pile all over them standing straight on end, like
those long-bodied, straight-tailed terriers which take their name
from the Isle of Skye, and move mysteriously, for they seem to
have no legs.

There is no admittance to these kennels except on business,
and a knock at the outer door roused my stud setter, who set his
hackles up, and rushed at the panels open-mouthed.

My housekeeper (Mrs. Brownrigg we call her, for she is just
the sort of woman to all appearance as that worthy was, or
should have been, who tortured her apprentices ; but a better
sort of dragon, or one more expert at managing, never ate my
bread)—my housekeeper brought a letter which she told me had
been conveyed by *a boy*. She is no physiognomist, and she
judged of his years by his proportions ; for that boy was Harry,
the second whip, aged—what shall I say ? well, about two score,
and weighing after a hearty breakfast about eight stone. He
was sitting, when I went out to him, in an easy attitude, on
what he told me was "a young Irish oss, as master chopped
for ; " but before this information was given to me, in a grating
voice strongly impregnated with Yorkshire dialect, he touched
his low-crowned hat, and, having stuck his whip under his thigh,
was diving into the breast pocket of his old stained red coat for
"a bit of a note" he had brought, and which he said he expected
would require an answer.

As the "dog pack" was outside, he then left us to look after
the straggling hounds which were basking in the road, and I
went in to answer the master's letter. It was but a few lines,
asking me to accompany him to the earthstoppers' feast " on
Tuesday next," as I had expressed a wish in the beginning of the
season to be present at this annual gathering. I write to
"accept," and from my window I see Harry place my envelope
carefully beneath the lining of his hat, and in the interval of his
long pulls at the pewter tankard he rates and remonstrates with
a few vagrant hounds which have picked up a lamb's foot and
quarrel over it, Now I gather why all about the premises is so
spick and span, the kennels all white and trim, and the jug of
lilacs and wisterias is set out upon the saddle-room table. The

men want half a day to go to the dinner, which is one of
their rare and valuable holidays. Smith (Mr. Smith) gets his
"reg'lar" invitation ; and the groom *must go*, and dines afterwards with the two or three other gentlemen in livery and the
waiter on joints "kep' back a purpose."

An earthstopper's dinner nowadays is an assemblage of gamekeepers, whippers-in, kennel men, grooms, helpers, working
bailiffs, with here and there a farmer who patronises the festivity,
and perchance has made a "whip" for the benefit of those who
in their humble way are friendly to the hunt. The old earthstopper, with his horn lantern, spade, billhook, rough pony, and
rougher terrier, whom Cooper loved to paint, in his worn,
huntsman's coat, stained leathers, and scarlet waistcoat, is seldom
met. In the last generation such an old crony existed, and might
be seen the first at the covert side or near it, with his spade on
his shoulder, and a hard-bitten, scarred-faced terrier coiled up, and
shivering in his sleep—the man was a sort of hanger-on to every
hunt, drawing many a shilling for his shrewd guesses as to a likely
find ; and when the fox broke making his way from point to
point, cutting corners, opening gates, now and then making gaps
for the "middle-aged," the nervous, or the men in trousers—
services to be requited surreptitiously "some other time" by old
clothes, broken meat, a long pint at the nearest public, the change
at the turnpike, or a lift to or from the next assembly of hounds
and horses in the back seat of the dogcart.

A faithful henchman, too, he was. I have one in my eye,
always in his place ready to dig a fox, keen as a hound at the
sport, and with a rare eye and voice, but prepared at a moment's
notice to help catch a horse, scrape a "field officer," lead a child's
pony, or go back with a lame hound a score of miles without
waiting for a gratuity ; civil to soured huntsman or misanthropical
second whip, left behind to get the rest of the pack out of covert ;
and all at—what shall I say ? Well, 10s. per week "reglar,"
and the odd money. His class has passed away. Occasionally
you find a labourer or two who will incur any amount of brow-
beating but *they will see the hounds ;* and the sound of a horn, or
the sun glinting upon a scarlet coat or two—contrasted, let us
say, with the squire's flake-white hunter or the hill yonder—will
draw half a village to see the sport. 'Tis bred in an Englishman,
whether he be peer or pauper, and, unless he is all but a fool, he
will be there. The only human beings I have ever discovered
who are indifferent to sport are schoolmasters, and occasionally

Bish—oh, I forgot, foxhunting is a pomp or a vanity, or both, and forbidden to the church!

But, though the earthstopper is extinct as an individual, earths must be stopped before daylight, by keepers or their subordinates, and many a good day's sport is spoiled by their neglect, or from M.F.H.'s forgetting to remind them of their duty.

At two or three o'clock of a winter's morning he has to go round the earths, to face the raw air, sleet, rain, or snow, and secure the entrance of Pug's earth, whilst he is travelling for love or food ; or it forms part of his night's work as he goes his rounds with his brindled night dog, and, in his fur cap, big top-coat, and mufflers, resembles Herne the Hunter or the ghost of a German courier, or any outlandish man or animal you will. Years ago a donkey hide, with the hair outside and holes for the arms, was gravely recommended for the purpose ; and I know one or more night watchmen who are clad from head to foot in red deerskins, and thus attired are safe from cold or wet or vigilance!

But it is not only the earthstopping that you want a keeper to attend to—he ought to be the natural guardian of the cubs. It only costs him a charge of powder and shot to kill a few rabbits for the breeding vixen ; or to save the rats, especially the young ones, for her larder, and to generally look out for her at that trying time when she has so many mouths to feed, and so little power or energy to provide for them ; and if he is a good-hearted fellow, he will do this for his own sake, as well as his master's — for nothing is so likely to damage his reputation for pheasants as two or three hungry "mother foxes," or his master's, when the time comes, as to have his coverts drawn blank. A few young rooks, a jackdaw or two, and now and then a jay, or even a hawk, are better left where they fall than nailed upon his vermin board : a thing well enough in its way, but sometimes offering a strange contradiction to the manor itself—frequently full of hawks and weasels, but barren of game indeed!

It is true enough that merely giving fees to keepers won't insure their being friendly to the fox ; but it will secure the honest ones ; as none of them would take the sovereigns at an annual dinner and strychnine the foxes on his beat. If he did, he would deserve any punishment these modern days permit ; and he might be put on a par with the garotter, and share his stripes, I think, with perfect fairness.

But enough of this digression. The day came ; Smith walked on, and I followed some hours after, with my groom. I just caught sight of Mr. Smith as he started full-blown for "The Royal Oak," about ten miles from us, where this feast had been held for two or three score of years. A new olive velveteen coat he wore, with the sleeves turned back to display the linings, which were serge or twilled cotton, known as " swansdown," or perhaps to let the public see the wristbands of his scarlet shirt. 'Twas a decidedly *baggy* garment, cut to pieces with vast pockets, and skirts that overlapped behind, and formed a sort of fish tail, or a kite's ; waistcoat the same, and a crimson cotton scarf ; corduroy breeches, and deer-skin gaiters ; lace boots, bran new, suggestive of galled feet and corns prospectively ; and the whole surmounted by a felt hat, so hard and heavy to all appearance that your head reeled to look at it. In his hand he carried an " ash plant," a foot too long, and also new that day. I subsequently discovered this to be the popular full-dress, excepting always helpers and ostlers, who appeared in stable suits of tweed, and in trousers which must have been miraculously put on, and appeared so tight that they could only be removed by supernatural powers, or piecemeal.

The " banquet " commenced at three o'clock nominally, but we were told it would not be punctual, as several of the guests came from a distance ; and, besides, there was some business to be transacted before they sat down, which would perhaps give a zest to the men's appetites. It was, therefore, full twenty minutes after two before I ordered my cart round to the door. It had been drawn out of the coach house half an hour before, and I never saw my grey put to with such alacrity. My man jumped in as we walked off, folded his arms, and seemed not only in a vehicle, but in Elysium.

As we passed the keeper's, I missed his dark chesnut forest pony in the paddock, and I could track his " trap" directly I passed his cottage, by the "wobbling" of its off-wheel and its deeper impression on the wet road ; for he was not only an important man, but physically weighty, and he was only counterpoised in his equipage by his " boy." As we neared " The Oak," we overtook men in various shades of velveteen, in every sort of conveyance, and one small thick-set pony was dropping down the hill at a smart trot and with a loose rein, impelled by no less than five human beings (if not Christians), whilst an aristocratic glossy black retriever, underneath, was keeping within two inches of the little animal's heels. Now and then we passed an under keeper, or trapper, walking along with his coat over his arm, and his face

red as a peony ; and presently we came alongside of the hound
van, drawn by a pair of rough-and-ready steppers which would
have been at home in a London "bus," or on their master's
"arable." These were tooled by the huntsman, a wiry-looking
man of forty. with very thin legs and a low crowned hat. He
was airing his new stable suit for the first time probably. and was
conveying his two whips, feeder, kennel men, head boiler, and
clansmen to "The Oak." with a very self-satisfied impressive air.

Though forty only, his face was much seamed and furrowed ;
in fact, it seemed to be as rough and seared by care or weather,
or both, as a Savoy cabbage, and wore as sour an expression as
the old white terrier with torn ears that sat on the footboard
between his legs. Indeed, but for their costumes and a few
flowers in their button holes, they might all have been going to a
funeral ; but this solemn expression, accompanied by the want of
front teeth, and high cheek bones, is peculiar to the craft. After
passing this dark-coloured vehicle, which was not unlike a " Shil-
libeer," we came up to " my lord's keeper," in a high dark green
game cart, with a coronet on the backboard, and crowns of brass
on winkers, loin straps, collar, hood, pad. and the cheeks of the
bit itself. Quite a remarkable person I assure you, was this
"keeper to my lord," and wearing trousers and coat *en suite*, of
that tint distinguished as "donkey brown." The second coachman drove, and these two might be described as " attending "
under protest, and leaving their mark upon the meeting. The
head keeper, I remember, wore a white high-crowned hat, with a
black band round it, known as " butchers' mourning," and what
are ordinarily known as " mutton chop " whiskers.

A little further on, and we are at the Royal Oak, which stands
on a down, with a garden inclosed by clipped yew hedges, an old
bowling green in front. and a skittle alley ; two score of yards off
are fir trees in a clump. with settles and benches round them, and
groups of keepers and servants to the number of thirty, forty, or
perhaps more. The house itself must have been a substantial
one when fifteen or sixteen coaches passed and repassed daily ;
for the high road between two large cities runs parallel with its
old bow windows ; the long range of low stables still remains, and
they are pretty full to-day.

Inside, the house is all abuzz with business, and the waiters are
running about in their shirt sleeves with cans of beer and porter,
and clumps of " grogs " on trays. A brace of foxhound puppies
out at walk here—for the landlord is a hunting man—are wan-

dering from one group to another, and are subjected to the
severest scrutiny as to loins, shoulders, heads, legs, gaskins, thighs,
and resemblance to old Lancelot by Lexicon out of Lady Blush,
by the Belvoir Guider. These criticisms are not finished until a
mail phaeton is seen coming along the flat, and containing the
master and a friend or two ; he dismounts presently with a heavy
leather bag of moderate size, and a shoulder-strap fixed to it, like
those the betting men carry at the small provincial meetings ; and
better replenished this one is than some of theirs !

It must take a middling good horse to carry him, for he must
be over fourteen stone ; about five feet eight inches, or thereabouts, with a good deal of waistcoat ; but below he falls off
suddenly, and if he were a horse we should say that he was
over-topped. A man of fifty, hale, and with good teeth ; but
his hair is white, so he looks older. He has keen grey eyes, a
good profile, and a smile and good word for everybody. He just
glances at the long old parlour, where the tables are spread for
dinner—where, as of yore, there are trophies formed of hunting
whips, horns with the ends corked up and utilised as flower vases,
and scrolls of painted calico with appropriate mottoes and
devices. He will empty that bag presently amongst the keepers,
three guineas to one, two to another, and so on ; and the smiling
landlady, whose face is parboiled with looking after the puddings
and peering through the steam, ushers him into the bar parlour
to that end.

My lord's keeper and one more, a very stout, florid one
indeed, whose black velveteen is heavily braided with broad
worsted, introduce the recipients, who are awkward and bashful
before company, and wipe their shoes from sheer embarrassment,
ere they cross the threshold ; but, as paying money doesn't take
long, they are soon settled with, and the waiters begin to clamber
upstairs with the joints, enveloped in a fragrant steam.

'Twas a regular dinner à la rustic, but a sight worth seeing.
There was no scrambling for precedence, however, and bashful-
ness seemed the great feature of the assembled company. The
M.F.M. took the chair of course, for he was the host—paying, I
think, five shillings per head for the entertainment, including a
certain amount of beer ; the rest the men paid for themselves,
but, as each pocket had been well replenished from the Squire's
capacious "portemonnaie," this didn't matter. As I was a
stranger, and not professionally included, I was at the right
hand of the chair, whence I could see a long double line of

stalwart forms resolving themselves into their appointed places preparatory to the short but simple grace.

At the bottom the vice-chairman—a brewer, a welter weight, but a genuine foxhunter, with a genial, intelligent, and uncommonly good-looking face—was preparing for the onslaught on the viands ; but my friend knew better, and got his butler to carve for *him*. There were no soups or fish or *entrées*, of course, but plain roast and boiled, with salads, cucumbers, and vegetables, fresh and wholesome looking. The old room with its three bay windows overlooking the wide expanse of down and the highway, had seen many a goodly company assembled in it ; and through the green glass, overshadowed now with blooming lilacs and " golden chain," which made the air heavy with its perfume, a little knot of highwaymen years ago had watched the inside and outside passengers completing their supper, and as they rose from table galloped on to intercept them and rob the mail.

The old pictures, telling of the sports now happily passed away, were obliterated by the smoke of years, but I could make out a series of *tableaux* depicting the " noble sport," engraved after Reinagle—at any rate, that of Byron's Jack Musters on his grey, cheering his hounds—and some coloured prints of cocking, in one of which a black victor is dragging his adversary across the pit.

I had all the noted characters graphically described to me one by one by the host, who would *really* dine at eight, with explanatory notes occasionally rendered in a deep bass by my *left*-hand neighbour, a goggle-eyed, red-faced keeper of perhaps twenty stone or more, and whose small-eyed, razor-backed, foxy-faced terrier was a remarkable contrast to her master. " That big Hercules with the red hair and high shoulders is the feeder ; the first whip, with the pork bone in his fingers, is opposite to him, you see ; and the man sticking his fork into a potato is the rough rider. That fellow in the white tie with the little gold brooch is the second horseman. He came from William Day's."

" And that," said the goggle-eyed keeper, cutting into the conversation, " is Bill Bishop the saddler, who has more tongue than brains, and takes care of every man's business except his own ;" for the keeper—whose eyes were like the patent white castors on Gillow's best sofas in form, and unlike them in only one respect, that they were never still—looked suspiciously on everyone, not excepting his own wife, who was a good-looking though bad-tempered young woman of fifty-eight, with angular eyebrows and sharp finger nails to boot.

It was a long business, and the universal taste seemed to be to have a cut at everything. The plum puddings, however, went like lightning, and one keeper opposite to me, who had what I mistook for a brown crust at his left hand, but which I subsequently discovered to be his fist, devoured a whole "boiling" in a twinkling. "Night watching," my left-hand neighbour told me, "gives a man a terrible appetite, and sometimes I've been pretty nigh ready to eat my night dog; the sourer you are, the more you eats!" At the last moment a waiter handed round in a bowl what I in my innocence believed to be yellow soap, but it proved to be very waxy cheese. which was received with much relish, though apparently as indigestible as the "night dog" already alluded to; and as the five shillings per head had now been consumed, the entertainment became, I supposed, a personal affair. But first there appeared—and it seemed a solecism in the entertainment—half a dozen tureens, as I imagined, of mock turtle, clear gravy, and other soups, which proved to be "punch," contributed by the vice; and then came the chairman's hammer (lent by a hard-riding auctioneer), sundry long faggots of pipes, and cigars for the "high table." Next came "the usual loyal and patriotic toasts," followed by the vice-chairman's requesting permission, which was granted, and the M. F. H. was so bespattered with compliments that a helper opposite my ox-eyed neighbour declared he never saw any one better dressed over in all his life. Of course the chairman replied, and well buttered his *vis-à-vis*. Then Goggle-eyes sang a song about "William and Mary" in a wood; but, as he sang Mary's modest replies in a deep bass and inexpressibly loud voice, the illusion was imperfect.

Such was the entertainment for about two hours, when two keepers at the further end came to loggerheads about a dog and a badger. The dispute soon ranged from dog and badger to personalities; thence they came to arguments as to strength, comeliness, and respectability, not forgetting certain delinquencies on the part of their female olive branches; and the last I saw of this friendly meeting I can only describe as a *mélée* and *tableau vivant* of Babylon, which the chairman vainly strove to quell; but I believe that the dispute was ultimately settled on the lawn, the aggressor being, as usual, the man who had volunteered to his neighbour that he "would never see him hurted," and followed up this assurance with an assault.

My man, I am happy to say, was sober, except his eyes, which hung out of his head like a lobster's; and as he prepared to start me without fastening the pad girth, perhaps his disease extended to the brain. Be that as it may, he begged to call my attention to his legs, which, he assured me, "drink what he would, never got limp." More extraordinary than all, he had only drunk two glasses of table beer; and the master's butler "guv" him one "*small drop*" of sherry.

I don't think that I should care to go to another entertainment of the sort.

PAPER XVIII.

THE WHITE SNIPE.

IT was about Christmas time, and before any enterprising gun-maker had thought of breech-loaders, that I got an invitation, badly spelt, though written by an Oxford man, to start for his father's " place " and have a bit of skating (he spelt it " skate-ing ") on the flood ice, and to shoot wild fowl.

As he is still " to the fore " (though rather bald, a trifle florid, and taking such a lot of stuff to make a waistcoat that he may be said to " carry all before him," not only as county member of Parliament deputy lieutenant), I shall not say where he lives. Times have altered him since he rode Brown Stout, Old Plenipo, Victoria mare, Aërated, and drove Vanish, or " King Dairius," as the stable men called him. to Chapel House, or what Jem Hill called "Braddle Grove," and with a seat almost as good as Mason's sent his horse along with the best of them, and generally landed safely.

He had been well entered as a boy, and rejoiced to see "hunt-ing " pure and simple. The first day he rode with the Heythrop, Jem and the "Flying Captain" (whom heaven preserve!) pro-nounced him " quite a sort ;" and when Jem, as he got forward, saw him taking his line a bit wide to the right of the hounds, and going straight for some pollard willows which looked ominous, he was heard to say "it was a shame them small knees of his'n should ever be hid in trousers, even to go to chapel."

Hereditary gout has done its worst for him now, and he could write his name on the door with the chalk that forms in his knuckles. He had symptoms of this gentlemanly disorder at the time I landed at his door, and his father was then, waistcoat and all, the counterpart of what the son is now.

'Twas an old-fashioned Christmas, " frosty, but kindly "—not such a one as we have lately put up with, fog, mist, drizzle, mud, and water—or that sort of Australian Christmas when you put the fire out and wear a spring coat and summer waistcoat, or shoot the coverts in a straw hat and alpaca jacket. It was a hard frost—a *very* hard one—and a clear sky all blue, without a cloud. Snow had fallen in the night, and where the sun had melted it had frozen into "ice candles," as they call them here ; while the turnpike roads were sometimes a sheet of ice for miles together. A hilly road with the skid worse than useless, is not a pleasant thing for four horses and a heavy load of holiday people, who have to journey thus twenty or thirty miles to reach a station : but Old Will—Black Will he used to be called—drew the leaders' reins through his hand, went slowly off the top of the worst "pitch," and got down well. More than that, in spite of delay and sleepy horsekeepers, we caught the train with about two minutes in hand ; for when we heard the whistle, a quarter of a mile from home, Will hit his leaders under the bars, and galloped the run in, though the old lady on the backgammon board, as it was called, clutched the outside rail of her seat, and apostrophised Will, whom she called "driver."

If I had been telling this story thirty years ago, I might have described the railway journey and the tunnels ; but they are now well-beaten ground. At that time it was a sort of heroism to travel on the rails, and Black Will, as I gave him his fee, touched his hat, and behind his milk-white shawl with the blue spots wished me safe through the bridges. That was a favourite vale-dictory remark with the old stagers, who believed in nothing but cattle and leather, and wished the iron pot and its belongings anywhere. somewhere, or nowhere.

I think a vague idea of risk and uncertainty always floats upon the mind even now, as we rattle over viaducts, crash over those tremulous girder bridges. dash through junctions, meet express trains, or glide down inclines at sixty miles an hour with the steam shut off ; and that even commercial travellers, whose lives are spent in rapid flights across the country. and who may be said to be used to it, must breathe more freely when they reach their destination and are at rest for *that* night. Such was my feeling, at any rate, when I gave up my ticket at the coldest little station in broad England, which. standing some twenty or thirty feet above the level, commands an extensive view of a flat plateau, all dykes, reeds, black bog-water, and dun-grey withered grass.

Here and there, along the track we are to follow in the broug-ham, are white posts to mark the way in times of flood ; and now and then we come upon a tree. struggling to live, but growing all aside, bent over by the prevailing wind. which blows generally south-west across the wold, and are guided by that purple and gold

hill in the distance, behind which, and the old minster on the top
of it, the sun is setting in a bank of clouds.

"Woa!" says the close-shaved saturnine London coachman;
for his horses, cold with waiting, are all abroad and restless at
the shrill whistle of the starting train, which soon shows us its
red light at its rear as the last guard's van leaves us in the
gloomy station as though we were outcasts. The ducks,
pochards, widgeon, teal, and a heron or two from the large railway reservoir of ten or a dozen acres, roused by the train, swing
across the telegraph wires and are getting well up to be off to
sea. There are but two passengers left behind; my fellow
traveller has a pony-cart waiting for him, with a rough-and-ready
white pony that can go, I warrant; but, as I have a brougham
in readiness, and probably am good for a shilling, the porter is all
alive for *me*, and won't allow the footman with the "smoke-
jack" in his hat to touch anything but the gun case, so "them
'ot 'osses" of the squire's have little time to wait. The coachman has smoothed his own feelings by a little objurgation which
I am not supposed to hear, and by a cut or two to the quietest of
the pair, because, being on the off side, he is the easiest to hit;
but he gives a rapid touch to his hat as I appear, and when the
door is slammed he walks them off about four or five yards, and
then trots on.

An outside lamp reflects a good light from the little window
in the back, and here are the cigar case and some lights put
ready to my hand, and a wicker flask of cherry brandy, which
hails from Copenhagen, and with which I shall shake hands
presently, for we have five miles of trotting ground, and a bleak
road too.

Four miles or so, and the sun gone down. I can see the
rabbits crossing the road, and, dazzled by the lamps, running
almost under the horses' feet. And now, suddenly turning to
the right through an old pair of wrought-iron gates, which
would not have disgraced Quentin Matsys, we climb a steep
winding hill, and from the terrace in front of my friend's home
—a large manor house—I look down across the wold, where the
light of the station I have left is glimmering in the distance.

A fine old hall that wide stone porch leads to, with deep bay
windows, and black oak seats in their recesses, and a carved roof,
with thirty or forty foxes' brushes disposed amongst the old
picture frames, peacocks' skins hung up at intervals, and an old
suit of armour, pikes, and beheading knives. The glass case in

the centre being filled with memorials of the ancient Britons and the forays of the Roman legions, together with flint celts and arrow-heads, for the father of my college chum is an antiquarian, archæologist, collector of coins, and always on the look-out for what the earth may give up when a new ditch is dug, or any mass of soil is removed to make way for the improvements of modern days.

I have not time to notice much of this, however ; for the butler, in a superhuman white tie, and a twin brother to *my* footman of the brougham, are divesting me of my blue Witney ; and at the same moment out come father and son to give me a thorough English welcome—one that gets warmer and more genial the higher you go northwards. We don't waste much time before the blazing stove in the hall, the sides of which are almost cherry red and all aglow, but repair by the wide old staircase to my bedroom, passing on the way the large open doors of the saloon —a vast upstairs drawing-room, in fact, with a fire at each end of it, commanding a view of the wide sluggish river which bounds the flower-garden and bowling-green, and from the balcony of which the old man, with his binocular, could watch his son's movements on a moonlight night, as this was (for the moon had risen grandly since I had arrived), when he was working up to ducks and preparing for a shot with his long duck gun. But just now each side of the swollen river was frozen over, and the "launching punt" was as firmly fixed as the Resolute in the Arctic regions.

It made you shiver as you looked behind the curtains from the old oriel window of the saloon, and Fred (that's the name of my friend whose waistcoat is now so large, and whose two eldest daughters are married) called my attention to the dinner bell, which, after ringing a few strokes in measured time, had put on a spurt, or, as we used to say of the chapel bell, had " begun to swear."

Skating was the general topic ; for the ice—" flood ice " it was—was beautiful, and we were half inclined to have an hour's exercise by the help of the moon and torchlight ; but the motion was lost on a show of hands. Billiards and a cigar were carried unanimously, and so to bed and sleep at twelve or thereabouts. Those manor-house clocks are not to be depended on, and the hour hand, as I went to bed, pointed to the smallest hour, and struck it too.

I must not forget, though, that in the interval of play my

friend suggested a campaign against the snipes, which, frozen
out of their swamps, had taken refuge in the warm springs and
ditches which intersect the wold, and, covered with treacherous,
quaking bog earth and half dead vegetation, form rare feeding
ground for both snipes and waders.

"You recollect (he said) Old Fussy." A superannuated keeper
this, who had been attached to the manor for fifty years or more,
and who could find his way over that wild country in the darkest
night with the sagacity of the sleuth hound.

A queer old mortal, who had grown fat with age like a bishop's
cob, and perhaps had some reason to attribute his enlargement to
the good things he was welcome to at the manor buttery. But
such a spluttering, busy talker, so full of noise and excitement,
that, from youth to age, he was, out shooting, the greatest bore
on earth; though for wildfowl or snipe shooting indispensable,
partly from his knowledge of locality, but especially for his
acquaintance with the haunts and lurking places of every bird
that visited those desolate solitudes.

He was rather under the middle height, and of a most mercurial
temperament, but so adroit at all pertaining to his vocation that,
whether trapping for an otter, rearing pheasants, breaking a dog,
or working up to wild fowl, he was sure to do it better than
anyone else, and to be the last man to talk of his exploits afterwards.

But even by himself he talked, and in the punt they used to say
that he put a stone in his mouth to stop his tongue, as an old
historian tells us the geese used to do, lest they should gabble on
their passage, and attract the eagles.

Well, enough of Old Fussy, who in his rambles over the manor
had seen a white snipe. Yes, he was sure of it; he had been
fidgeting about the yard and stables from five o'clock until nine
that morning, to give this information to the young master; and
he had delivered himself of this fact, hoping to be one of the party
to circumvent this rare variety of the *Scolopax*.

"I told him," said Fred, "it was a dunlin he had seen, but he
says he isn't such a flat as not to know a snipe from a dunlin, of
which, as he truly says, he has shot scores some winters; and
you can take your choice, my boy, skating or snipe shooting, with
the chance of bagging Old Fussy's albino."

As I preferred the snipe shooting, which I had experience of in
seasons passed, we arranged for that, to the old man's great
delight, when morning came; and we took one general or useful

dog, and one only, with Old Fussy's assurance that what was wanted he and the dog could do as well as any "other two people" in that moor.

Fussy's spaniel was rather a leggy one ; he had only moderate ears, a pointer-like head, and not overmuch coat, and he was either uncommonly well broken or fond of an easy place—at least so it seemed to me. Old Fussy took his gun too ; and a Norfolk keeper, fresh imported, and rather sulky at the preference given to the old man, brought up the rear, accompanied by his "man"—a sort of untutored hawbuck of perhaps nineteen or thereabouts.

The little rough skewbald and the cart were to make a wide *détour*, and join us with the luncheon at one, at a piece of furze we could see very plainly from the garden ; and, breakfast. over, we started for our sport.

The frost still held, and the day was clear, excepting an occasional slight fall of snow, which was some time before it reached the ground. It was capital ground for every kind of fowl—rushes and grass up to your knees, and now and then bare patches of soft ground where the hard frosts had no effect upon the water—the broad river bounding us on one side with a belt of yellow reeds and bullrushes, and making sudden swerves and bends : and behind this natural screen of vegetation, seven or eight feet high, it needed little generalship to get up to pochards, mallards, sheldrakes, or sandpipers, especially as the ground we beat with moderate caution made no noise, and our water boots were well "sumpled" by the wet and snow. Old Fussy's dog, Bob, he called him, walked close behind his master, sometimes standing still as we tried the fences, and took no notice as at the second or third trial we put up six or seven wild ducks, and three fell close by him, while a fourth, after a flight of a hundred yards or so, clapped its wings above its back, dropped into the stream, and began to swim to shore.

We got three or four widgeon at intervals, and at about the broadest place put up a good skein of teal. As they flew by us and turned on their side, "keel up" as Old Fussy called it, we dropped five or six of them, and when we began to retrieve them I saw Bob was a workman. He got the mallard first, which had come to shore and hidden himself under a hassock of rushes. Just as he stooped to lift him the bird rolled over into the stream, and dived, and Bob with him, coming to the surface with the cripple in his mouth. He roaded one of the teal nearly a quarter of a

mile, never raising his head from the ground, and at last tracking
his bird to a furze bush, where he stood him for a second or two
like a pointer, dashed in, retrieved him, and came to Old Fussy
at a gallop.

In the water he was just as good as on land, working to his
master's signals, and going away from him as straight as a colley
on a Scotch hill—rather a difficult thing to get a dog to do, as
half of them, when they are in the water, are in a great hurry to
get out of it. In the midst of this sport a rough head pushed its way
through the reeds on the opposite bank, and, holding up a teal,
told us in a rough voice that he had picked it up about fifty
yards ahead; so saying, he threw it into the water to Bob, whom
he seemed to recognise as an old acquaintance. This was the
water bailiff, who gave us the information that some of them
"shore men" had been shooting all along the river further on,
and had sheered off on his approach.

We had, however, only time to try the moor, and had beaten
half of it by the time we reached the cart and skewbald pony.
There we found a twilled blanket stuck up as a screen from the
wind, and a couple of furze faggots ready to be set in a blaze as
we lunched; and not a bad notion either, on such a day as
that!

"Two hours," the old keeper said, "would do the rest of it."
But for him, he was very silent, as he had made sure of finding
the white snipe at a point near the river which we had beaten in
vain.

We had one pipe apiece, and then started afresh, but I noticed
that we had missed about an acre of rushes to our right; so at
my suggestion we took it back, and killed three snipes and a
"jack" as we retraced our steps, on ground we had walked just
before. As we were entering the promising bit I have noticed as
left untried, I had to step over a warm spring at the only place
which was trustworthy, and where a stake was driven as a sort
of guide, both to the eye in the distance, and the balance in
crossing over a fir pole half buried in the ooze. Fussy had
crossed first, and I had handed him my gun, when by some mis-
chance I missed my balance and was thigh-deep in the muddy
water. With the splash up rose the white snipe to my right,
and wide of Fred, who was trying the spring with his back
towards us.

It was deeply mortifying; for, though the light was scarcely
deteriorated, enough of the brightness of the day was gone to

make marking the bird a difficulty, as he soared in a large circle, and eventually pitched heaven knows where. There was nothing for it but to beat out the ground, and, if we failed, to try again ; so on we plodded, not in the best of humours, and with varied success. Sometimes we found three or four snipe together ; then we walked piece after piece, and jumped dyke after dyke, to be disappointed ; and we came to our last piece but one—a quaking morass, where only the dog could go, and well he did it. Along the margin of the dyke went Bob, and *beat it to us* steadily, as though his master were behind him, and bent on putting every-thing to the guns. Two or three snipe got up and went over him the wrong way, and of course rose out of shot. Old Bob sat down each time and wagged his tail, watching them out of sight.

Another coming right over my companion! and he drops him —and the next. Down charge, Bob ! and he sits in the wet mud as contented and as quiet as my Lord's hall porter in his beehive chair.

" All right," and the dog is up again, puzzling at a large tuft of bog myrtle, out of which, after he has run round it three or four times, dubiously creeps an old hare. As she canters up to me, I stand still, and when she is within shot I drop her. The old dog looks up from his sitting posture as before, but at his master's signal goes on with his beat. He is at the edge of the pond now, and the shelly ice is cracking under his feet as he tries a piece of brown weed, half floating in the water. It gives way under him, and he goes in head and ears, but he tries it for all that, and up gets the white snipe, flying straight for me. In too great a hurry to secure the prize, I miss him right and left ; but Fred, though far away, takes a long deliberate pull at him, and I think hits him. Ah! he flutters, and sinks slowly to the ground a couple of hundred yards away amongst the rushes. But Fussy quite deliberately tells us he has marked him to an inch, and, says he, " Me and Bob will get him."

As I look for Bob I see him rubbing his head against his master, with my hare in his mouth, and in the twilight they are lost to me as they make for the point where the bird dropped. We light our pipes and wait but two or three minutes, watching the dull red sun sinking in the west, and listening to the sullen wind breaking across the sea. What's that ? " Who-whoop ! " They've got him ! and here's the dog cart ; for, though the lights of the old Manor House are streaming across the river from the high ground before us, we are three miles from home. As we are putting on our coats man and dog come up. "How much for the dog, Fussy," I ask, with one foot on the step. "Ah, sir," says he, with a twinkle in his eye, "though he's ugly, master says handsome is as handsome does—I musn't sell *him* not by no means

PAPER XIX.

SWANS AND EAGLES.

I DON'T profess to be a naturalist, and·I have been waiting from week to week, expecting and hoping that some such observer of nature as Mr. Tegetmeier would have something to say about swans and eagles, which were the subject of conversation, more or less, ever since the Royal Academy threw open their new rooms in May.

It was generally understood that Sir Edwin made the study for his picture at Lord Ilchester's famous Abbotsbury swannery, in Dorsetshire—a "fleet" or "mere" of shallow water shut in by the famous Chesil Beach, which connects Portland with the mainland : a piece of water this fleet or mere, adapted by nature to support a large "herd"—that is the correct old term—of swans ; and at ebb or flow they can easily procure their food in that estuary, without diving like ducks for the fine grass on which they subsist from year to year, and having lived and grown fat possibly from the days of the Norman conquest, or ages beyond that epoch.

It is scarcely necessary to say that this herd consists of the tame or mute swan, by far the most graceful of the group, the hooper or wild swan being rarely seen amongst them, and that only in the hardest weather ; whilst I believe the Bewick's swan, or Polish, whose young are white from the nest, and not dun-coloured like the tame ones' cygnets, has never been seen at all.

In the old accounts of this large preserve, sacred to what someone has called the "monarch of the lake," there is mention made of a smaller swan than those called mute swans, called by the historian *hoppers*, and which he says "went out to feed, and came back in the evening ;" but there are none now, and I have never seen more than half a dozen of them in captivity, and then they were restricted to the bounds of Charborough Park and ornamental water by the old plan of pinioning them—in which condition they were, I believe, purchased from Castang.

Once or twice it has been my good fortune to see the hooper—
a modern authority writes it "whooper"—wild, and both at feed
and in the air. Several have been shot in former days on an
outside decoy pond which I once rented ; but during my occupation of the decoys I was compelled to content myself with a sight
of the group within the range of my "binocular," nor did I feel
at all anxious to get the punt gun on them, or to destroy birds so
graceful in the water and so profitless on land. Thirty years ago
their cumbrous quills cost 3d. each, and were the ambition of
many a scribe. Now they are used chiefly to mount sable
brushes, and are going out of use. Tin mounts are more
generally adopted for the brush, and gold or iron pens have
superseded quills and the customary blunt penknife. So I did
not try to stalk them ; but, as I moved cautiously round on my
cob to get a better view, the sentinal of the group detected the
splash of my retriever's foot in the half-frozen burn, and up went
the lot, sailing away in an undulating line and serried rank—
but, for all that, *not* resting each bird his bill on the tail feathers
of the other, as one or two of the old writers would
pursuade us.

So there went all my hopes of tasting the flesh—which (I
think) Willoughby describes as "like heifer beef"—or the chance
of my having a swan, skinned first, then roasted, and then the
"pelt"—"at any rate the tail feathers"—sewed on again, and
then served at the domestic "banquet." Nor do I believe with
Hearne that it would have been necessary to shoot ten or twelve
yards ahead of them, or that, with the advantage of the very stiffest
nor'-wester, the best flyer of the lot could have made, as he con-
jectures, one hundred miles an hour. That is great going,
Master Hearne ! Some time ago, as I went in the fast train to
Newark, doing—well, forty miles an hour—I once or twice could
measure our speed against the swallows, and we beat them with
several pounds in hand ; and, when these swans were well up,
and making for the sea, with the wind astern—"on the beam,"
I believe, is the nautical term—I had a rare opportunity of timing
them a measured mile from a hill-top to a clump of fir-trees in
the offing ; and if they did twenty miles an hour, it was all they
did, and much more like eighteen. At this rate, I thought, as I
shut up my glass, and went on to confer with my old decoyman—
at this rate you will be a long time "making" Siberia, Russia,
or the swamps of Norway, when you are tired of eating my decoy
ducks' barley ; and I don't believe in your keeping my inner pond

open in this hard frost by beating the water with your wings—
an opinion my vassal corroborates in a hoarse whisper behind the
rood screen of our nor'-west pipe, where the teal are working:
though the ducks, he says, went up at daylight, and never
touched the barley; for they, he believed, could smell the boat in
which he had been breaking the ice all night with a heavy cross-
axe and sledge, and the aid of a brown jar, which he didn't mean
me to see.

"I wish," he said (for his temper was ruffled by the subject),
"I wish them white beggars was at home to be ridden down by
horses and hunted by dogs, as my books says they are when they
moults in August, up there among the ice and snow, where the
blacks lives, and they eat fat dogs and turtles, and what not."
For my old fenman was a reader you see, and had confounded the
colour of the inhabitants of Iceland with South Africa, and confused their *cuisine* with that of the Society Islands and the
various epicures who pay a guinea a quart, perhaps, for the
West Indian "Chelonia Midas" inseparable from the aldermanic
gown.

Perhaps it was somewhat owing to that brown jar—maybe his
morning draught confused him; for he was one of the few men
of his class who kept a diary of his experience, and could tell
you from his rough notes many a fact worth recording in the
"transactions" of those learned societies which keep most of
their wisdom to themselves, or publish their descriptions and in-
vestigations in language "no fella can understand." Some of
these experiences of his jarred with scientific theories, and were
at variance with the accepted facts of profound philosophers. I
was often surprised at the observations of this old decoyman,
stored up for nearly three score of years—for he was "seventy
good," and had been a decoyman "ever since he could break a
duck's neck."

Swans, however, he had seen little of, and he had never heard
of their being, still less had he seen them, attacked by any bird
of prey. "They look well on the water," he went on at the
time I came upon him behind the screen, speaking in a whisper,
and peering with one eye through a hole in the reeds, through
which he had worked a hollow mutton bone, which served as a
rough telescope; but give me birds that will take a pipe, and that you
can catch and catch again. I never caught but one swan, and that
was in an otter trap, and when I went up to him he zet at me like
a dog. I got six shillings for him from a 'stuffer;' but years ago

they were only worth half a crown. He had been splashing and
fluttering all night perhaps, and there was not a bird in the pond
for a week afterwards, so it was a dear six shillings." He had
never seen the white-tailed eagle there, though now and then he
told me the "fish-hawks"—by which he meant the osprey—
would hunt the fens and marshes and scare the fowl; and one
morning a bird soared over him that seemed ten times as big, and
went clean out to sea. "But," he observed, "the birds was
working to the south pipe, and I expected a good ketch and got
it, for I took home twenty-four couple " (or " coople," as he pronounced it), " teal and all. I was using a tame red kitten that
morning, with a rod pegged down and a running ring with four
inch of chain to her neck, and they swum at her wonderful." Here
our conversation ended, for he signalled me that three mallards
and a lot of duck were within " speaking distance " at the wire
pipe opposite, and he sallied off to wave them in, and of course
succeeded.

And this warns me to go back to swanneries, and especially
that famous one of Abbotsbury, which has grown famous since
last May. Until last week I had never seen one, although I had
found out from books of the swans at Whittlesey Mere, where
the father of Lord Burleigh was the bailiff, when Henry VIII.
was king; also of a swannery at Clarendon in Wilts, and another
in that part of Dorsetshire known as the Isle of Purbeck.

Then, too, I was pretty well up in " swan marks,"—" cigni-
nota " Lord Coke called them—that is, devices carved on the
upper mandible, of which there were ninety-seven, being the
hieroglyphics of as many proprietors of swans on the Lincoln
rivers. Devices these, old as armorial bearings—crescents, crosses,
initials, annulets, rough ideas of crests or helmets, which made
the birds private property, and not the Crown's.

I had read of the London Corporation going " swan-hopping "
or " swan-upping "—that is, taking up the cygnets to be marked;
and I had heard that Oxford had " a game of swans " by Oseney
Abbey and Godstow, the burial place of the Fair Rosamond. So
I determined to go and see the largest swannery in Great Britain,
possibly in the world, and, by the courtesy of the Earl of Ilchester,
its owner, I accomplished it.

For the purpose of seeing these in a compact body, May is the
best month ; but I went in July, and there is plenty to be seen
then, though the cygnets are strong and able to roam away by
the sea-board, and seek their food possibly twenty miles from

home. With the glass I could see them ten miles off at least, in groups of ten or twenty, and, as far as that helped me, I could count them by the score.

Abbotsbury, famous for its swannery and decoy combined, is a bleak and desolate tract of land hard by the sea, and closed in by lofty hills. A few trees in clumps, and an old line of elms, take off somewhat from the sterile appearance of the prospect ; and it is a relief to turn from the shingle terrace walk ten miles long and see a large covert to your left, called Uddin's Wood, and the old decoy replete with alders, stunted timber, and rank reeds, in the midst of which the old swans' nests of withered grass and rushes looked like magnified mince pies. At the entrance to the decoy—close to the gates, in fact—is a high pole recording the high tide of 1820, which swept over the Chesil bar, was 20ft. deep at the decoy gates, and carried barley ricks and such like trifles a mile inland.

We passed this beacon post—one of us, I can guarantee, with a sort of wonder as to the present state of the ocean behind that long streak of gravel, though the day was cloudless ; and the journey from Dorchester might have been equalled, scarce surpassed, by the exploits of Dr. Livingstone. We were burnt, but the horses seemed baked as well as basted, and the thermometer was where the Irish girl found it—nowhere ! We had passed the green avenues of the decoy, and the piles of reeds stacked with a view to future repairing of the screens, and at once came upon the open water, backed by the Chesil Beach, which shuts it in from Portland and the sea. A flat grassy terrace of solid ground surrounds the reed ground, and is pleasant walking ; and close to land the birds were sailing in water perhaps two feet deep. They were very tame and sociable, and some, mostly birds of last year, we could have touched as we passed by.

I had time to note thus much when old Bartlett, the keeper, joined us in accordance with his instructions, and showed us the proper route. The " fleet," " mere," or " estuary," is about a mile and a half long, and has a tidal ebb and flow—and a good thing too, for all the breeding places of water birds offend one of the senses terribly. You can't help it, and swans are in this respect the worst of all.

The water was by no means clean or clear, and such it could hardly be, when it formed the feeding ground of 856 *swans, counted in September,* 1868, *to which must be added* 400 *cygnets marked during the year* 1869. Anciently, and when the royalty was in the hands of the abbot, it is said that the herd numbered 7000 or 8000 birds ; but of late the average number has been 800, and, notwithstanding the annual increase of, say 400 cygnets, there is little variation in the " tale." I asked old Bartlett, the keeper, to account for this, but it seemed beyond his powers, though he had been in the earl's service, as I understood him, thirty-five years, and had known more or less of the swans during the whole of that time. He suggested that they were shot when they roamed away, as they do for miles ; but, as they are pretty well known, are all marked in the outside web of the right foot, being thus private property though killed thirty miles away, and are rather cumbrous game to hide away or carry off, his suggestion did not satisfy me.

Perhaps it is a sort of balance of nature, and as many survive as the grass at the bottom of their feeding ground will support ; but then, if the old abbots could rear 7000 or 8000, why not the present earls, who seldom, if ever, fatten a cygnet in the private pond, and rigidly protect them from all enemies ? It seems more probable that, in parties of two or three, they seek fresh feeding grounds and migrate, in spite of hand feeding, which they enjoy only a fortnight or three weeks annually, and which has been the average for many years.

The birds appeared, indeed, in excellent condition, and do not readily feed on anything but their favourite weed. Bread and buns—which the birds in Worcester College Gardens would not refuse, or the beasts of the air (I mean the bears) at the " Zoo " would have eaten, even on a Sunday evening—the Earl of Ilchester's swans turned up their bills at, as Bartlett said they would, though I would not believe him. And I am strengthened in my opinion that the Abbotsbury swans *do* select fresh localities by the fact that strangers come to waters in my own neighbourhood, and there remain ; and that in one or two instance there are swans no one ever sent for or purchased, but which the keepers say " came of themselves." You can't drive them away ; you can't catch them to examine their feet; and you have little chance of doing so, except when they sail, as they often do, with one foot over their back, when the Ilchester "nick" might be recognised with a field glass, the most useful of all pocket companions to those who like to see birds or beasts, and closely observe them, in their fancied privacy.

After we had seen all there was to be seen from the low land of the decoy, we crossed the water, perhaps five hundred yards

wide, to the Chesil Beach, partly covered with the wild pea.
Pisum maritimum (there's science for you !)—which in 1555
supported the people in Oxford and Aldborough in a famine, and
was supposed to have been propagated by the wreck of a vessel
loaded with peas, though this is no doubt a legend—the tree
mallow, *Lavatera arborea*, and the growth of which in this
locality Ray has recorded. There were other plants which were
new to me, and which as yet I have not found out ; but what
pleased me more than these rare bits of vegetation was the
group of sea birds—terns with fish in their bills for their brood
hidden in the pea haulm and seaweed, besides stints and dunlins
—which flew around, as either accustomed to that immunity
from gunpowder which does credit to the noble house of Ilchester,
or conscious of the protection afforded them by the Lords and
Commons.

"And have you ever "—it was a "momentous question "—
"have you ever seen any *eagles* on this beach, or the swans
attacked by any bird at all ?" This was the first question I
asked him of the velveteen coat and conventional leather leggings,
which always call up to remembrance the days of Lincoln College
luncheon and deep-coloured rancid cheese ! 'Tis a moot question
whether the leggings are cheese or the cheese leather!

The keeper rubbed his chin seriously and said, "No, they
haven't no enemies ; leastways none as hurts 'em." And as to
eagles, he never heard of any, nor saw them anywhere, though
he had seen "these here big hawks what they nails on barns," or
words to that effect. I didn't take down his *ipsissima verba*, for
I saw he eyed my very pencil-case suspiciously ; but these were
about his sentiments, and here or hereabouts his experience began
and ended.

But then, looking through my note books, I find the following :
"In the winter of 1803 numbers of wild swans assembled near
Yarmouth in Norfolk ; seventeen were shot by one man in a
week. They were also seen far inland, and many were killed
near London. Near Mitcham, in Surrey, two out of a large
flock were killed with a common fowling piece. *During the
same winter the sea eagles—i.e.,* the white-tailed or cinereous
eagles—*were most abundant,* and several were shot at Yarmouth."

It may be argued that no one has ever seen a white-tailed
eagle attack a swan. Well, it is acknowledged that the white-
tailed eagle feeds on fish, but no one has ever seen one catch

M

a fish, nor is there any record of the manner in which it seizes its prey, Yarrell says, "We have no authority for believing that it plunges."

Then it has been said that the swan could make no fight against an eagle, or *three* eagles, which are depicted as attacking the swans—in order, we will suppose, to prey upon the cygnets.

However, Yarrell tells us that "Mr. Dunn once saw a pair of skua gulls chase and completely beat off a large eagle ; that they struck at him several times ; and that at each stroke he screamed loudly, but never offered to return to the assault."

We have the authority of Temminck for believing that the cinereous eagle follows the flocks of geese which resort to the Arctic Regions ; and, therefore, why not swans or cygnets in Abbotsbury Fleet ?

Now I have summed up the evidence, and I must leave the verdict.

PAPER XX.

THE PHILOSOPHY OF MISSING.

I DON'T write imaginary days' shooting, like "the run of the season," in a three-volume novel; they are insults to common sense, unless they are written by a very first-class M.P.—in other words. master of the pen.

Take what I say at its value. At any rate, I record facts, only putting one man's head upon another's shoulders, that no one may recognise Browne's portrait; except this time. when, at the risk of offending him, here he is—only you see he is now no more.

He put an additional vowel at the end of his name, observe, to separate him from the throng of Browns, and his godfathers and godmothers did a trifle more for him, for they named him "Whyte-Browne," coupling the two names together, and spelling them both incorrectly, that—in the words of his uncle, who hailed from Munster—there might be no mistake about his name.

There were two talents bestowed on Whyte-Browne, for which he was celebrated in his "corps;" for Whyte Browne was, according to his own pronunciation, a "meejor." He could *generally*, not always, eat and drink more *with impunity* than the youngest subaltern in his regiment. When I first knew him he girthed exactly 4ft. at his third button hole, counting from the bottom of his waistcoat. His whiskers were "a sable silvered," and his complexion might be described with equal truth as apoplectic or expensive. He was still capable of considerable exertion, but after his second bottle of claret his head gradually sank, and his breathing became stertorous. He was scarcely in the sere and yellow leaf, and, what with a spurious front tooth or two and a little "coopering," he was by gaslight *almost* a lady's man.

He has been buried two years in the churchyard of Bally-something, close to a famous snipe bog, where, according to common report, he "bagged" (this is something better than *killing*)—where he bagged, I repeat, sixteen snipe out of eighteen, and the two he *killed*, but did not bring to hand, went off with their legs down. And therefore I shall not hurt his feelings, nor would he

M 2

care if he read these lines ; for, though jealous of his reputation
as a shot, and very touchy on the subject of his name, he was
placid and unruffled at any joke you raised at his expense, unless
you supplemented it with his sobriquet of " Whyte-Browne."

I recollect that the first time I met him was at a house in Staffordshire, remarkable for a profusion of good things and the
hospitality of all its occupants.

You must do the thing well in that county to get a name for
breakfasts and dinners. They *live* there, and when master and
mistress are indigenous to the soil I never knew the entertainment
flag or your entertainers look jaded. If there is a clock in the
dining room, it stops that night, and I have known them turn its
face to the wall before the last bell rang ; but a descendant of
the famous potter (Wedgewood) adopted a system of his own. He
had a " dinner pendulum," constructed, which beat so slow that
it took the minute hand eighty-five minutes to perform its round !

A bleak, frosty Christmas time I was staying at one of these
Staffordshire houses, and at dinner they talked of the old major,
who was expected to turn up that night if he could catch the
train at Crewe. We had not sat down more than five minutes
when we heard the wheels upon the gravel, and in he came,
having posted all the way. I had only time to hear, in the short
interval preceding his arrival, that he scarcely ever " missed."

Well, there are, so far as my experience goes, few such men
about. I never saw one myself, except the worst of men, who
always pick their shots, and only shoot when they are certain to
cut the game to pieces. I don't know whether they are worse,
though, than the multitude who take long, or I might better say
impossible, shots at hares, and let them limp away just fast
enough to baffle the retriever, who, when the gun is loaded and
the quarry out of sight, begins the uphill game of footing them,
until he is whistled back.

For a man of his age, expected to be a leading character on the
morrow, I never saw one so "omnivorous"—I think this is the
word—as the major was that evening ! They didn't know him
well, so the soup and fish came on again. Meanwhile, he explained "missing the train and being obliged to post all the way ;"
the rest of us crumbled our bread, and two choleric and desperate
guests, who were always bickering—chiefly, it seemed to me, because their "manors joined"—got up an argument which was
moistened with a deal of sherry.

At last we were all full sail again, for the major had made

up his leeway, and attracted my observation by his encomiums on every *plat*.

It was not at all a difficult entertainment. There were no disguised dishes. It was before the *à la Russe* period ; and part of the "repast" was the old-established plum pudding flaming with burnt brandy, and mince pies baked upon the model of the twopenny piece current in 1797, an inch and a half in diameter, or a trifle more. Perhaps these, which the major ate as an elephant might have tackled little straws, acted with the fatality that attended the camel with the historical broken back. Be that as it may, he had not done yet ; he was rash enough to encounter filberts and port after dinner, played most unsteadily at pool, whilst he puffed a very strong cigar, drank about a gill of strong black coffee, and, after being assured the whiskey was *Irish*, not Scotch, he "indulged"—that was his expression— in a couple of tumblers of punch, or toddy, or whatever else they call it.

No wonder that next morning he was the last at breakfast, and that he "didn't feel quite well." Cold shivers down the back, you know, and no appetite whatever.

"You haven't got such a thing." he said, turning to his host, "as a little essence of ginger in the house ?" "Well then, I'll take a little in a cup of strong tea without milk or sugar ;" and after that "a dash" of brandy, as he called it—and a strongish dash it was.

If he must have fastened his own gaiters, I believe he would have given up at once ; but the valet did that for him, with a strength of finger and adroitness peculiar to that fraternity.

As soon as he was in the fresh air he said he should be all right. The hot room last night and the fellows smoking had done it all ; but the first strip of the covert we drove dispelled his dream. "I aim slap at 'em," he said to me, confidentially, "but I can't touch a feather." What is the matter with the guns ?" And so it was all day. The celebrated shot was below mediocrity, and, but for fear of offending him, I verily believe my host would have put him on a level with the octogenarians, of whom two of them were there—I mean, he would have let him shoot the hens.

Referring to my diary I came upon this day's shooting, and a slight sketch of "Whyte-Brown" turned up.

It set me thinking why do men miss, supposing that they have the use of their eyes and limbs. It ought to be easy enough to kill winged or ground game, especially as it is not like tiger shooting,. or a gorilla hunt—where, in the first case, the animal eats the first-prize tiger hound (class 201, Birmingham), and then runs after you ; and in the second, he snatches the gun out of your hands, severs barrel and stock with one snap of his teeth, and, after striking his breast and rending his garments, beats the "stub twists" about his persecutor until the barrels are as bent and twisted as a gas pipe.

How is it that so many men are talked of at the clubs as. "fellows who can't shoot a rap, bless you"?

Well, a good many things, save the bird. Some of the best men miss, because they are watching their dog. All honour to them for so doing. Their attention is divided ; with them the end of shooting is a good dog, not "the pot."

I have had my day's performance thoroughly upset by many things. I once saw a beater saved from death by his having put on six or seven waistcoats. If ever a man tried to get shot he did, but his time was not come. His narrow escape, however, upset my nerves, although the charge which perforated two or three of his garments did not go from my gun.

I have had the barrels of a very inferior gun level with my head at intervals of five minutes, knowing that it was at full cock, and that the right-hand lock was "queer," and foolishly imperilled my life during the time because I couldn't get out of the way without appearing rude to an utter stranger ; and my shooting has been worse than moderate for the remainder of the day. The sudden unexpected explosion of a barrel, a missfire, a bad cartridge—any of these things will upset a nervous man ; and of course some constitutions and temperaments are more easily disturbed from their equilibrium than others.

On the other hand, you can't shake the coolness and self-reliance of some "fellows." They will claim every bird, check it down in their patent sliding metallic register, run by you into the best places, and, if in the days of muzzle-loaders they missed, "swore" that there was "no shot in the gun." These are the fellows who run forward when they are told to keep with the beaters, and, whilst they pepper *you*, never get shot themselves.

I know one of this fraternity who always wears a high white "chimney pot," which by contrast with his black beard and red face makes it nothing short of manslaughter to shoot him. I believe that I should have killed him once, as he had crept round

a holly bush twenty yards before me because I had got comfortable quarters ; but, as good luck would have it, the wind set from
him to me, and just before I pulled I smelt a whiff of some odour
which reminded me of a leaky gaspipe, and I recognised my
honourable friend's cigar.

You will often hear men say of themselves, or of another, that
if they miss the first shot or two it "puts them out." I quite
believe this, and I feel sure that in billiards, also, missing to score
for half a dozen strokes at the commencement of the game will
unnerve a man for the evening sometimes, let him be ever so
vigorous and strong in a general way.

Well, this shows us that we ought to be careful at the outset
to get (speaking of covert shooting) a good place, and never to
lead off with a random shot. "Flukes" in shooting are the exception, not the rule. Steadiness and repressal of anxiety may be
obtained by resolution. Hurry makes the finger snatch at the
trigger and involuntarily pull before the gun is at the
shoulder.

Not many years ago a London gun maker—a journeyman—
made a good living by teaching shooting in his little back parlour,
his secret being to get the embryo sportsman cool and collected as
he aimed at his tallow candle and blew it out. His pupils, I
need not say, were snap shots. These men might possibly do
respectably with trapped pigeons, starlings, or at the public-
house sparrow club ; but doubtless the whirr of a cock pheasant's
wing as he got up at their feet, or the chuckle of a woodcock's
wing, even without the grunt, or croak, or neighing noise they
talk of now, would disturb the aim which levelled at the lighted
candle proved unerring. And, even if the nerves of these candle
shots were equal to the flush of any bird, supposing he went right
or left, ten to one if they hit him unless they knocked him down
on the rise, to the jeopardy of hats and heads inside them.
Which leads me of course to pace. Aye, here's the rub! See
how birds differ. A partridge well up, going with the wind
almost a gale, flying almost on his side, as a crack swimmer goes
through the water, or a cutter yacht heels over when racing for
the cup, though I believe the latter ought to sail upright—a bird
going at this rate, or a rocketing pheasant, or a snipe in a light
breeze, or a mallard—all these birds require to be shot at with
calculation as well as aim, and when you get the level you must
clap the aim in front of them. The "rocketer" I verily think is
the fastest bird of all. I should shoot six inches before a snipe,

but I would risk *six feet* before the pheasant coming over my head, and I would expect him to throw up his tail and drop almost at my feet, dead before he reached the ground.

If your gun fits you (and old Purdey very justly remarked, you should be measured for a gun just as much as for a coat), if your coat is easy under the arms, and the collar does not rise to your ears every time you raise your gun, you ought to kill twice out of three times ; *but it is a good shot that does it.* What with your foot slipping now and then, your trying to kill that woodcock which gets up under your foot whilst you have a bramble across your face, "bad cartridges" and "lost birds," two out of three is a good average all the year round.

Nor have I enumerated one-tenth of the disturbances which "save enough for breeders" and prevent the extirpation of game upon the manor. You lose a number of chances from thinking of other things. That bill of Doctor Jones, which you estimated at fifteen ten, is exactly double what you calculated. It was considerately forwarded to you this morning, after a middling night's rest. Your lawyer persists in *not* forwarding his bill, which has been running for eight years. You have a leak in your house, or, the dry rot, or what builders call a "sinking" or a "settlement;" some one has shot your "almond tumbler;" you are out of coals ; and scarlatina has broken out at your boy's school, whence all are to be sent home immediately. Any of these things clogging the brain will disturb my aim, I know ; and, most strange of all, sometimes good shooting leaves you in the middle of your work.

There is something as incomprehensible in this as in the manner in which I have seen hounds baffled if in a run a fox is headed. They have, perhaps, been running him breast high before ; they lose him, and the scent dies too. They hit him off for five or six yards, then where is he ? He seems to have sunk into the earth.

Now and then there is some reason for it. One September morning four of us were shooting *well.* We pulled up for luncheon, and one of the party produced a jar of excellent "home-brewed" —not that "thin pea soup" which tastes of everything except malt and hops, but the real thing. We were a very temperate lot, but after very little of it we could do no more. To use the keeper's words, we "warn't a bit of use." At other times twice the quantity, or three times, would not have affected me ; for I am sure I only drank half a pint this time. We gave it up for full two hours, when we went on as before.

Generally, depend on it, missing means indigestion. Your friend prepares you for the day's work with a dinner of Chablis, oysters, turbot and oyster sauce (*caper* sauce if he is a man of taste), patties, croquets, cutlets *à la* this, that, and the other. Next comes the joint and turkey, game, rich gravy toast, fried crumbs and sauces, creams, jellies, whips, trifles, and syllabubs, rich puddings, iced puddings, and what not, to be succeeded by Stilton cheese and the pie of Strasburg ; then dried cherries, tough figs, grapes *ad lib.*, a sponge cake, crystallised fruit, Spanish plums and roasted chesnuts, to say nothing of the hock, champagne (dry), sherry, claret (château something, of course), and that little glass of liqueur, which is supposed to be plenary absolution to the drinker for all his weakness and profane trifling with his liver and digestion.

Who wonders that next morning, like Whyte-Browne, I get up with my "coat staring," that I shoot too quickly with my first barrel, that my aim is oblique, and that Helvellyn, the solicitor, who has been asked to shoot because he does the election work, and never saw a battue till this day, spreads damaging reports of my qualifications as a shot, and whispers to his engrossing clerk, who carries his cartridges in the professional blue bag behind his master, " *that* Hidstone is no great shakes, he'll take his affidavit.'

Although I have, as the little attorney would say, " engrossed the attention " of my readers long enough, I will give them a carte of a dinner, and some of the results, to exemplify what a liberal host will do to entertain his guests, and how they performed next day.

I went to look over the kennels of a country magistrate some time last year, and to share in two days' shooting. I could not spare time to dine the second day, nor could I reach the "Castle" in time to dine the first. The first day I had nothing to complain of, as my repast was simple, and I hope the second was moderate ; but here's the *carte*, which I preserve as a curiosity, and some day I will have it framed :

Soups.—Turtle, Jardinière, clear soup. Sherry and Sauterne.

Fish.—Turbot, lobster sauce. Wines, Chateau Yquem, Hochheimer, sherry.

Removes.—Haunch of venison, braised turkey, truffled, boned, and stuffed with tongue. Wines, St. Julien, La Rose.

Entrees.—Vol-au-vent with oysters, partridges à la Périgord, sweetbreads à la Monarque, cutlets à la Jardinière. Champagne, Cliquot and Moët, sparkling hock. Punch à la Romain (carried round by a six-foot slave).

Second Course.—Roast pheasants, woodcocks. Wines, Burgundy, Chambertin, Clos Vougeot.

Removes.—Paté de foie gras, iced pudding.

Entremets.—Chantilly cake, Charlotte Russe, pineapple jelly, meringue à la Parisienne.

Dessert.—Grapes, pineapples, apples (Golden Pippin), petites pommes d'Assis, pears, oranges, four crystallised fruits, two cakes, cream ice (au café), water ice (lemon).

Wines.—Sherry; Lafitte, '58; Margaux, '58; Latour, '58; Port, '20.

I partook of a selection of these viands, and that but sparingly. Next day, however, I wasn't up to the mark. Here is my score :

Pheasants, 0 0 1 0 0 0 0 1 1 0 0 1 0 1 1 1 1 0 1 1 1.
Woodcocks, 0 1.
Hares, 0 1 1 0 0 0 1 0 0 0 1 1 0 0 1 0 1 1 1 0.
Rabbits, none.

PAPER XXI.

SHOOTING IN ALDERNEY.

A GOOD knowledge of French was not so common twenty-five or thirty years ago as it is now, and to my acquaintance with old General Levasseur, who commanded at Dunkirk, and the pains he took with me. I owed my appointment at Alderney as soon as I took my degree at Oxford. All the Southampton steamers undertook to land their Guernsey passengers at Alderney, "weather permitting," but the weather seldom did permit, and if the captain of the steamer were ever so accommodating, the old Alderney curmudgeon who monopolised the attendance and the boats would not come out to meet the vessel when her flag signalled for a boat, unless the wind and tide allowed him to do this all alone, and, as he called it, to "sweep the lot." I stepped on board the steamer overnight, assured I should breakfast at Alderney next day, but I woke in sight of the "Casket Lights," and was soon the victim of at least a hundred Guernsey porters.

It was early in October, I remember, and towards the middle of the day, when I heard that a cutter and four hands would start for Alderney in an hour, and my portmanteau, gun-case, and official "portfolio"—it was a tin box, by the bye, and not a folio —were forwarded to the pier-head by the very fattest porter I ever saw, appropriately ticketed "No 1." The cutter was, however, no decked vessel, but a long, narrow four-oared boat, with a mast and a lug sail, in case the wind should serve, manned by four hybrids (in blue butcher's frocks) between slaughtermen and labourers, but good sailors for all that, as I know by experience now, and soon found out then. We shipped two landsmen before we pushed out of the quiet harbour, and waited one of the most precious hours I ever lost for a tailor who had a hankering for sailor life, and who—as brave a fellow as ever was afloat—now commands the Alderney steamer that plies from Guernsey.

It was a sudden change for all of us when we left the quiet harbour, shut out rom the restless ocean by high walls, and encountered the broken waves; but the wind was on our quarter, and we took advantage of the lug sail ; the master spirit on board observing in his *patois* as he hauled in the sheet, "we should soon take the creases out of that sail, *he* knew." It blew a little harder, and the sea got up, and off the Russell Rock it ran literally mountains high. Both sky and water became of an angry leaden colour, and occasionally a " bull's eye " (a small rainbow, or rather a short, broad prismatic streak) appeared as we rose on the tossing seas, and swung down into the dark depths again ; the starboard side of the boat showing free of water to her very keel. But the light craft was a good seaboat, and we held on well, and were calm all of us, but one craven-hearted fellow in the bows. who, if he could not pluck up his spirits, drank them, and pointed with his white finger to the large waves " coming," and could with difficulty be persuaded by brave Pierre Gauvain—I give his name truly—to sit still, a matter of some moment, as we ourselves were the only ballast. All at once the Red Linnet (that was the boat's name) trembled from stem to stern, and the sea flew from her bows as she forged through a current running against us twenty knots an hour. " The Swinge tide," said Pierre, " running between Alderney and the island of Burhou, an hour too late, and the tide has turned." The gale, our enemy before, but now our best friend, hurries us through " the Swinge," but we must " gybe," and " down sail ;" we lose our way, and a sea sweeps us from stem to stern. We bale her with our hats, and though she trembles and lies a log, we hoist the sail again and run straight into the old rough harbour of Alderney, crowded with anxious witnesses of our perils.

Well cared for and well housed in the quaint old town of St. Anne's, and none the worse, and occupied with my work, I had it well in hand, and was ready as the winter set in for the little sport there was. The physician of the place had a pack of clever beagles, and knew well how to handle them ; and for knowledge of the science of shooting I never saw his superior. His physic I never tasted, nor did he ; I cared little for his beagles, but I learnt all he could teach me of the snipe-shooting, and waited impatiently for the arrival of the woodcock. I could do all required of me after the lamp was lighted for my employers, and more too, and many a pleasant day the doctor and I had together. First we (in company) visited his patients, because my French tongue was useful, and occasionally I shook up the bottles in the sick rooms, and gave them a scientific look as I held them up to

the light. Then we loosed his old setter Jarlett, and started for
le sport. Sometimes we breakfasted before daybreak, and got to
the fields covered with "vraick" (seaweed manure) before the
sporting community could beat them ; and in hard weather we
generally had good sport. The snipe were scarcely ever to be
found except where the seaweed was spread, but in such situations we could flush them in abundance, and they lay well. We
possessed the only setter in the island—for a spaniel is the
favourite of the islander, and some of them had good ones. I
remember there was an indefatigable old sportsman, who had
fought at Waterloo, possessed of two large liver dogs I never saw
excelled either for snipe or woodcock, and several of the farmers
had leggy, island-bred ones of nearly equal quality to these.
But when "the cocks" began to drop in on the heathery edges
of the cliffs, we chained up the setter and worked a pair of
Clumbers only.

I was dressing one snowy morning late on in December, with
the comfortable feeling that my work there was drawing to a
close, and that I might be home again for an English Christmas,
when I thought I saw a woodcock fly slowly across the stunted
orchard. I looked on from my bedroom, but the flight was too
slow and owl-like, to my mind. I should perhaps have thought
no more of it, when another followed, and another. The last I
plainly saw, and he flew so near my window I could observe his
eye far back in head, as it always is, and, more than that, a leaf
impaled upon his bill, as he had been boring among dead leaves,
perhaps, in the beech woods of Brittany. My first acquaintance
(the doctor) was the man for me to consult, and his experience of
twenty winters told him it was to be a brilliant day. As it
always happens, one of our brace of Clumbers was footsore, but
the other was in rare condition, and we sallied forth. We went
almost the circuit of the island (about nine miles), and found our
expectations realised ; the cocks had "pitched in" that night,
and in the early morning, and though some were wearied from
their flight, and lean, most of them were in fine condition. They
got up much more slowly than a bird which has rested and fed in
one covert perhaps for weeks, and in very few cases we flushed
birds which made that "chuckle" with their wings as they rose,
which an English sportsman knows so well ; but the sport was
continuous and well sustained. The old Clumber knew his
work, and did it. He bustled up to the edge of precipices, and
once or twice flushed birds resting on the turfless ledges ; but,

with only one exception, all flew inland, and, but for my inex-
perience, we should have retrieved every bird we killed. That
one I did not give time to turn, and he fell hundreds of feet down
a perpendicular cliff into the blue sea beneath, striking the water
like a cricket-ball. We got fifteen or sixteen couple of woodcocks
that day, and left off when the light failed ; and, considering we
were not out until half-past eleven, and left off soon after four, it
was not a bad day's work for Alderney. Next day every man
who had a gun turned out, but there were few woodcocks to be
found (about five couple was the outside of the bag made by all
the islanders), for the birds merely stopped to feed, and took
flight for Guernsey or the mother country. It was the best day
we either of us (the doctor or myself) had known, though there
is a rumour that one man (a good shot, too) killed twenty-five
couple on a similar occasion in fewer hours.

Now and then a woodcock, very rarely a quail, a few rabbits,
and, at the outside, four couple of snipes, after a long march,
make a good day for Alderney ; and so must pass the winter,
excepting that we occasionally extemporised a dance. It is a
primitive island, or rather *it was*, for now they have a railroad. I
believe, and certainly a steamer ; but in my time, when we had a
dance, a girl *sung* quadrilles and waltzes, and we had but one
means of communication with the world—a little cutter—a *real*
cutter, whose captain was the best of seamen. When I left, I
grieved to leave two men I never met again—the doctor (" Old
Colocynth " he called himself), and the captain of the Experiment.
The doctor, as he lived, died—well. The captain, on a return
voyage from Guernsey, was caught in a gale of wind and ran
upon a rock—I think Rock Ortac ; at any rate within sight of
home, just in the dusk of evening, and the shallow space was
crowded by the vessel's crew, who that bitter night burnt their
clothing, as a signal to the shore to try to save them ; but no
boat could live. The next tide swept them off, and in the
morning the rock showed bare as ever.

As spring came on my work had ended, and I was not sorry to
see the steamer " lay to " for my boat, in obedience to the red
and blue flag hoisted by the doctor as a signal. I have had many
a brilliant day's shooting since that time, with matchless setters
on the Scottish moors, or among the partridges in clover tops on
English farms ; I have (I confess it with shame) assisted at
battues, where we have netted the whole covert, and counted our
dead by hundreds, whilst wagons were waiting for the slain : but

(it may be because I am not quite so young as when our gracious
Prince was born) I do not remember ever enjoying shooting more
than when there was not much game but a good deal of walking
in the island there, and a pleasant night after it, with two
doctors, the princes of good fellows, one of whom survives.

PAPER XXII.

"SHIRKERS."

EVERY father of sons who have outgrown the preparatory school, as it is called, has certain misgivings as to what he will do with them, unless they show unmistakable signs of coming out as " stars " in the Eton, Harrow, or Winchester firmament. Mediocrity is failure nowadays, when the three professions are overcrowded, and what is ordinarily known as " business " is a sealed book to those who can command neither capital nor interest.

For the eldest son, even if he be a loafer, there may be the refuge of the old house, the rookery, and the large or small estate. The Civil Service and the Engineers or Artillery provide a future for the constellations or the workers ; but what shall become of the drones ; Like the French *condamné*, they must live—though, apart from paternal prejudice, one could almost say with the French judge, " I do not see the necessity."

And by " drones " or " shirkers " I mean the following class : The easy-going, lethargic, well-behaved boys, of whom every school furnishes a considerable proportion ; fellows who get their verses " done " for them, accept punishment as more desirable than work, and only exercise their wits to avoid anything like continued mental exertion. If you " tackle " them, they take refuge in stuttering when called up, or plead sick headache or any excuse that may come into their weak heads, or perhaps that stale one of " not having been able to find the word in the dictionary."

As a class they are given to smoking ; they have very delicate appetites, a love for tough pastry and effervescing drinks ; now and then play the flute ; are enwrapt in the pernicious novels of French literature ; perchance make feeble efforts at backing horses ; are very particular as to the cut and fashion of their coats and other garments ; possess exquisite taste and discernment in satin and other gorgeous ties ; display an aptitude for getting into debt ; and while away the tedium of life, like a Spaniard, basking in the sun.

I am quite willing to believe that in many cases these hopes of
a "long family" are suffering to some extent from constitutional
infirmity; but then, again, I see so much shrewdness in getting
out of work, such adroitness in avoiding anything like exertion,
that I am most unwillingly compelled to suspect the same acumen,
fitly bestowed, might enable these impotents to earn their bread,
and possibly to pay for their scent, pomatum, dentifrice, rings,
chains, pins, and—tobacco.

Let us see. Some years ago it was my good fortune to meet at
a country house a captain in the army, who was one of our shooting party for a few days, and who, besides having possessed one
of the finest works of art in the Exhibition of 1851, and invented
a system of cooking for the army in ovens applicable after dinner
as pontoons—for which he received, I believe, very considerable
acknowledgment from the Government—had founded, and presided over with great ability, an establishment in the New-road
for the reformation and employment of the city "waifs and strays."
This Home was admirably conducted, and the organisation of the
various departments was simply perfect. There were lathes,
filing and carpenters' benches, a French-polishing room, and all
the appliances of a general workshop. Now, would it not be
worth while to start such a department for the Shirkers—the
well-conducted, gentlemanly, respectable, but withal selfish, in-
considerate sons of gentlemen, whose sphere of action at the
present moment is an arm chair or the softest couch in the
drawing room; whose most violent exercise consists in the use of
a camp stool and a fishing rod; whose knowledge of chemistry is
confined to the price of lemonade; and who, given a map of the
world, could not put their bath sponge over it so as to be quite
sure of covering Mexico, or contradict such an assertion as that
the Crimea was in the West Indies.

Many hundreds have been spent upon the sons of families who,
with no fault in the masters, bring home periodical testimonials
of idiotcy—great, lumbering, 'cute, good-natured noodles, who
sprawl about the premises during consecutive vacations, and yawn
until one cannot help feeling it would be justifiable homicide to
knock them on the head.

Put them out in the world, with the complimentary douceur of
six or seven or more hundreds, and you get in a week harrowing
descriptions of the dullness of the place, the narrowness of the
bed, the rough seams in the sheets, and the coarse fibre of the
meat. Perchance you are upset in your day's work, a few weeks

later, by complaints from the opposition benches, and the master
discovers the true value of his disciple, suggesting that he "will
try him a little longer, but he fears"—you don't read the rest!

You talk the matter over with your most intimate friends ; for
you can't shut your eyes to the truth that a pair of patent leather
boots, a gorgeous scarf, the last thing in trousers, even an
evening costume of blue coat with silk facings and gold buttons,
is almost as unendurable as a tame cat ; whilst the habit of these
"lethargics," running up stairs whistling, playing with saloon
pistols, opening your study door and leaving it ajar, with
occasional bars long drawn out upon the flute, are anything but
soothing to your mind when you are in the habit of making brain
work pay long drafts to bakers, butchers, and the various "co-
operative" tradesmen.

The bad lots of families have always had an inkling for agriculture, looking upon it as an idle, peaceful, and pleasant life,
involving a gun, a pony, harvest ale or long draughts of cider,
and every opportunity for self-indulgence. It removes the pupil
from the society of people who know more than he, and the farm
labourer, over whom he hopes to hector calls him " sir ;" so that he
is a "Triton amongst minnows." It is not until he is out of sight
that the bucolic, thrusting his tongue into his cheek, tells his
brother ploughman " that *vool* 'ull never make a farmer, and that
he shall take no notice of 'un." I have watched narrowly the
issue of such a course of education, but I have *universally* found
that boys who left their books to be farmers have turned out
dismal failures.

The next step is Queensland, Australia, or some distant field
for labour, enterprise, and *capital*—the "capital" being some few
hundreds of pounds. The voyage out is all rapture and smoking,
varied by cards and ship billiards ; but the first letter home
probably describes the funds as sinking, whilst the intelligence
that the money is gone will probably be conveyed personally by
the emigrant.

You can kill the fatted calf or storm at him, precisely as you
feel inclined ; or perhaps you will accept as a propitiatory sacrifice
to your feelings a pair of grass parrakeets and a king parrot
which you could purchase in far better plumage of Mr. Hawkins
at a less price by 500 guineas than these noisy and debilitated
specimens. I have known such cases as an outfit and capital
being acknowledged by the gift of an opossum skin, a Birmingham
nugget (brass gilt), or the feathers of an old cock emu.

But you can hardly blame yourself, for your young farmer was simply an incumbrance amongst the colonists ; and so, why won't some enterprising philanthropist start a model workshop for gentlemen's sons, presided over by expert, well-conducted work-men—of the class and manners, let me say, that teach the amateurs at my friend Holtzapffel's in Charing Cross ?

Let the Shirker learn turnery, the use of the file, the farrier's forge work, joining, cabinet work, upholstery, basket making— any useful manual trade by which he is sure to earn his bread —and, as he has not taken advantage of his opportunities, but has given himself up to self-indulgence, give him six months to make himself master of the details of his new profession, and after that let his food in the establishment consist of, or be pro-portionate to what he earns. If he comes to the conclusion during this probation that the society and work of a professional man are to be preferred to that of mechanics—with whom I would let him constantly associate at meals, and to whom I would make him as respectful as to a college tutor—give him another chance of rejoining his compeers of gentle blood and leaving this asylum for the indolent.

What I have endeavoured to place before your readers will be found capitally described in a story to be found in that admirable old boy's book, "Sandford and Merton," under the title of "The Gentleman and the Basketmaker." In all seriousness, and from having met with many cases of the sort I describe, I do think that such a system is most desirable ; for, with a trade, no parent need fear his son was famishing in a distant colony, except from sheer inexcusable idleness. Gentlemen's sons might certainly learn enough to keep their heads above water in, say, two years.

PAPER XXIII.

OUR BLACK HEATH.

A PASSION for speculation often vents itself in the attempt to reclaim or cultivate common land ; and but for the opposition of the owner, I have little doubt an agricultural capitalist would have tried his hand upon our heath.   We do not own all of it ; I am afraid to say how many miles square it is, but the part we shoot over is not less than five or six miles square.   In one part you may see a line of dark green fir trees stretching right away ; and to the left of that (the way I propose to lead you) an estate divides us from our snipe ground ; but with that we will have nothing to do just now, but leave it until the snipes come in, driven from the swamps and reeds by the hard frosts we look for anxiously just now, to rest our hounds and horses.   The estate, bounded on one side by the line of firs, is simply a continuation of the waste ; and bare and sterile as it looks, *and really is,* more than one company has been ruined by it, although the projectors, of course, were anything but losers.   Old records show that most of the land hereabouts was waste when William Rufus hunted in this neighbourhood, and had only been brought into cultivation partially when King John built his hunting-lodge close to us. Since his day we know cultivation has been brought as far as possible in our direction, and stops at the old farm and the ˙ brook and bridge, where the heath begins, and whence the traveller on the old hilly highway will probably see no human being for five good miles.

  As you enter on the heath at this end, you may observe a belt of fir trees ; then, perhaps, an inclosed piece of land in a ruinous and weedy state.   To the right is a long, low, thatched cottage, and an orchard of stunted apple trees.   Here the decoy-man lives, with a view from his door of the " outside decoy-pond," all open to heath and sky, but tenanted by numbers of mallards and teal at all seasons of the year, and in hard weather by swans (hoopers) or wild geese in large numbers.   But when you pass

through the decoy-man's garden you have done with cultivation.
In the summer, looking towards the south, you see a charming
garden of red and purple heather, mixed with the yellow furze,
but it is all brown now, except where there are large sheets of
mud and "ooze," and there the reeds and long grass hillocks are
a pale muddy yellow. Along this waste a narrow causeway
(probably in old times the track of the strings of pack-horses)
leads between two dykes—sometimes through heathland dry and
shingly, sometimes between two bogs, which undulate as you
walk along—and beneath that matted grass or fibre there on
your right or left are fathoms of slime and clay. Many acres of
this flat have been drained without success, and mapped out into
squares ; but they are breast high in grass and reed, and as the
winter comes on they harbour duck and wildfowl of all kinds,
whilst in some of them snipe and starlings drop in at the dusk
of evening literally in clouds.

A mile or so of this unvaried walking (occasionally crossing a
plank bridge or rude brick arch), and the covert thickens. The
bog myrtle and the alder, and a thick maze of underwood with
some low oaks, form the outer screen of the decoy itself. A low
plank leads us over the outside ditch and on to the soft green
turf, free from any stick to crack under the decoy-man's boot.
Here we can gently open the reed screen with one finger and see
the colony of ducks and teal all confident of safety, for no gun
has been shot off within a mile of that decoy for centuries past.
All around there are hassocks of grass and tangled reeds and
briars, where there is good lying for fox or otter in the dry, and
it is a favourite place with foxes after a rough wet night, when
(as we know) they will not go to ground. And well our master
and his huntsman know it ; for after wet and wind, if there
is a chance of drawing the decoy, they do it, and when they
have gone away the old heath seems ten times as desolate as
before.

Well, leaving the decoy, the ground is broken with hills and
valleys, and the soil is dryer. As we rise a line of hills beyond,
we find the basins beneath dry also, and the gorse growing well
and thick. Now and then we come upon a fine old holm or
holly, and perhaps a clump of them. Sometimes an old barrow,
one or more together, marks the scene of a battle in old times ;
and antiquarians have delved and turned up cinerary urns,
bronze celts, glass beads, or torques and armlets. Here the soil
is deeper, and partially reclaimed ; and soon we come to peat

beds, where, in the season (say about October), the borders of
the turf walls are covered with the dark blue gentian, and in the
more moist localities with some yellow flower I cannot put a
name to. Beyond these, there are fox coverts of gorse laid out
in squares, on some table land (where the air is fresh and bracing
even in the heat of summer, and whence you can discern the
ships and fishing-boats), you can look down on many acres of
green pasture, and have a bird's-eye view of a deep but narrow
river, up which come the salmon from the sea ; then some old
Roman ramparts, and a quaint old town, and beyond its " walls "
more heath and desolation.

Here and there, where he could get permission, a cottager has
built a mud cottage on the skirts of this common land, and
broken up the surface and cultivated it—sometimes, as I said
before, by permission, sometimes taking silence on the landlord's
part for his consent. This wild land extends on all sides for
many miles ; and the scattered spots of cultivated land, with
their little homesteads, are just enough in places to feed the
partridges on the stubble in the autumn, and support—which is
more to the purpose—the little heath-farmer and his few rough
cattle and rougher pony. This wild tract of land, which has
been called for ages the " Black Heath " (probably from its
sombre colour under the influence of winter), supplies the
labouring poor with turf (not peat) for their winter fire, and
affords the sportsman with the best (because the most varied)
shooting that I know. It is a rare field for the naturalist too,
abounding in summer with rare birds (such as the Dartford
warbler), and with hawks, which hunt it like so many spaniels ;
and day and night it is haunted by innumerable gaily coloured
flies and moths and creeping things—lizards and vipers in
profusion, and the very finest snakes I ever saw.

When March comes round, it is a rare place for the dog-
breaker, as it abounds in game ; and at that time black game will
lie under the heather, and frequently in the old wheel-ruts, until
you kick them up before the dog. And besides, the breaker
knows, when there is no scent in the young wheat, or no laying for
the paired birds, he shall have a burning scent in the deep ling
and long coarse grass ; and this the whole hunt know also,
although many of them dislike to ride it, fearing its hidden
dangers, which are not trivial, unless the horse understands the
country and goes well on its hind legs ; and his master, too, must
be a good judge whether the land will carry him or swallow him

as he picks his way to catch the hounds amongst the shaking quagmires.

Just when the young pointers or setters are finishing their spring breaking, late in July or early in August—having laid by since May—we find plenty of early broods of partridges, and a good sprinkling of hares and rabbits ; and as soon as they are steady again to the back and point, and can be trusted to drop to the temptation of " fur," it is time to blood them to the young blackcock, or, as they term them here, " heath poults," supposing they are not going to the north for grouse. Early in September, if the day is hot and dry, we know by experience we shall get twenty or thirty brace of birds on this breezy moor, and that it abounds even in the dips of the hills or barrens, with deep cool pools and springs, which are so refreshing to our dogs after their galloping in the deep ling under a hot sun. So we place two or three good markers on the crests of these heights, and can mark the coveys down—sometimes into the osier beds, at other times in the squares of gorse and fox coverts of bog myrtle. In these situations they get up well, and the dogs are rewarded for their staunchness. Often I have seen three good ones (for the third dog makes sense of it, as my old breaker says) find and stand and back, on the crest of these highlands, all of them showing clear against the sky, as we steadily walked up to the point ; and it is a pretty sight to see the black shaggy-coated retriever, close to his master, prick his ears and creep cautiously, with his eyes intent upon the foremost dog that holds the point, and to observe the various attitudes of the backing dogs, all " stiff as biscuits," ready to drop directly the single bird or whole covey whirls into the air, as though they came from beneath the ground. Then the perfection of breaking shows itself : when without a word, or uplifted hand even, all three setters drop, and are hidden in the covert ; when not one of the retrievers moves an inch, and they all drop too, except perhaps the cleverest of them all, who sits upon his haunches and watches a bird hard hit with an inten earnest gaze, prepared to follow it when he has seen it tower eight or nine hundred yards away, and bring it unrumpled, at full gallop, to his master, who has gone on, certain of the dog's finding the bird, and afterwards finding him. Then comes the loading, and the taking the retrievers up to where their masters' birds dropped. But generally only one retriever is allowed to work, or some jealous dog may take one wing, and another dog the other.

Farther on in the season, when the winter has begun to set in
(let us say after the first white frost), the heath shooting is
charming, for you do not know what may get up next. You
may find yourself in the midst of a second brood of partridges,
simple and easy of access as early September birds. Then it
may be a snipe, and before you have time to load, an old mallard
or a widgeon gets up all in a fluster from the reed or sedge.
Perhaps one of the setters is roading an old blackcock, or as
you walk by the holly trees, especially if there is a spring at the
root of it, you flush the first woodcock of the season, and in all
probability his comrade. I have known on some occasions (for I
have shot this heath thirteen years) five or six woodcocks killed
in a November morning, and the golden plover to come over our
heads fifty or sixty in a flight, and three or four guns get a
blaze " into the brown of them." When once the ducks have
come over well, you don't know how to load your gun (I mean
the size of shot to use) ; and I have also found, by twenty years'
experience at least, that No. 6 is the best for this " all sorts
shooting," for hares, pheasants, partridge, snipe, duck, woodcock,
plover, curlew, or anything but geese, which don't come very
many times in a winter near enough for three drachms and
an eighth of powder and an ounce and a quarter of shot.
    The heath affords all kinds of sport very early in the autumn,
or rather at the close of summer, and good sport it is. Just
before they reap the corn, the young ducks (perhaps fifty or sixty
at a time) fly inland from the sea to feed upon it. They always
take the same direction, and appear just as the dusk of evening
sets in. Exactly as the sun sinks below the horizon they come
with rapid flight, over the same fir trees or the same crest of hill
on the moor, in a line for the farm and the brook that runs by it,
forming the borough boundary of the old town and of the
heath, as well as the " cordon " of cultivation. In the cool of a
summer's evening I place a gun or two in favourite spots, about a
quarter of a mile from the farmer's house ; and with a good
heavy 10-gauge double gun, carrying two ounces of shot, slung
in a leather shoulder-strap, I canter along the old causeway
until we pass the decoy, and turn sharply to the right. My
shooting pony knows the firm ground as well as I do, for he
is not only forest-bred (of which forest this sterile swamp is
a continuation), but he has been here with the panniers for
four seasons, carrying luncheon out and the game home. A
quarter of a mile on I turn him loose, for if he strays my

black dog will catch his bridle and bring him, and has done so scores of times. I creep to the crest of the hill, and lie down under a furze bush, and here I can see the ducks long before they come against the light. I get a double shot—perhaps I have time to load and get two more (I have got half a dozen). I then let my dog go on, and pick them up and bring them. If I have many, I tie their heads together, and ride back with the game across the pony's withers. I pick up my companions on the way, and their ducks too, and we light our pipes and get home. either to whist or billiards, by half-past eight or nine—and so the old Black Heath affords us rough sport all the year through.

PAPER XXIV.

TRAPS AND CALLS.

To kill vermin is to breed game ; at any rate, if you don't do the first you cannot do the last. It seems a very simple fact to record, but, like the old school axiom of a verb agreeing with its nominative case, it needs continually to be repeated. All keepers know it, but they don't act up to their convictions—I mean the idlers and sots.

To trap and wire, to be able to detect the presence of vermin, and then to secure them, ought to be drilled into every boy immediately he leaves the plough to serve his apprenticeship and aspire to a velveteen coat and tawny gaiters. Without a taste for the keeper's life, and a sharp eye and nimble fingers, the lad is not worth his salt ; and very frequently the 'cute fellow, exactly suited for a trapper and wirer, is too expert in mischief and meddling to be available.

The keeper who kills most vermin makes the least noise about it. He is not continually shooting about the manor, and yet he keeps it down. I need hardly say he does this with traps, and unless he can trap well he is not worth his wages.

It is said that a bad workman always finds fault with his tools ; I have known a first class one grumble at his. A thorough vermin killer will have good traps ; they are easily obtained, and not much more expensive than bad ones. "Dorset traps" have been celebrated for something like one hundred and thirty years, for their lightness, their durability, the equal elasticity of the spring —I mean its being as firm at the top when the trap is sprung as when it is set—and for the flatness of the trap when open rendering it adapted for shallow or stony ground, and requiring very little earth to cover *spring and jaws*. The admirable temper of the steel is one of the secrets of the trade ; in fact, it is the chief one. The old original trap maker will warrant every trap he sends out, and he can show you some still good as new after twenty years' service.

The secret of tempering was bought by the present maker's

great-grandfather of a travelling tinker, and the "gin" thus
made, rapidly became a favourite. I am not sure that the pattern
itself was not furnished by this itinerant tinman ; but I do know
that the same 'cute hand instructed his pupil in the art of
tempering a "mill bill"—a sort of cutting hammer for roughing
up the surface of mill-stones—and, as I am told (not by the
maker, but by the millers), there are no mill bills like these ;
consequently, like the Dorset traps, they have found their way
into every county of England. Our artist, who does all the
tempering himself, can only throw off a certain amount of work
with one pair of hands, and the supply is limited; nor can he
prepare the springs or bills to his satisfaction under certain
conditions of the atmosphere.

Having said thus much of the Dorset trap, I will go on to
describe it more particularly. With a chain and swivel 12in.
long it weighs 1lb. 11oz. I put what is commonly sold as a
Dorset trap in the other scale, and I find it weighs 6oz. more.
We will say that a man going his rounds carries three dozen
traps, his paddle, and a small hand-sieve for covering his trigger
plates. He has 13lb. less for his back than if he had the
forgeries in his basket ; for the pseudo-Dorset traps are not made
in this county.

The genuine article which I recommend, but which, to speak
more correctly, commends itself, is exactly 12in. long ; the jaws
are 4in. from hinge to hinge, and when closed they are 2½in.
high. At the same time the extreme height of the spring is
2¼in., and 1in. less at its narrowest part. There are eleven teeth
in each jaw, and the trigger plate is about 2¾in. by 2¼in. *The
jaws and trigger plate can be covered with 1in. of earth*, and no
part of the spring exceeds 1½in. in depth when set.

In the worst trapping ground it is comparatively easy to make
a channel with the paddle, in which the spring can lie ; but it is
not so easy to frame a bed of 1½in. deep for a square of 4¼in.
when the trapping extends over a considerable acreage, and has
to be finished in a given time.

The heavier trap requires 1½in. of earth to cover it at the
jaws, and frequently much more, whilst 2in. of earth will barely
cover the spring. The jaws are 5½in. wide, by 4½in. in length.
When open, the trigger plate is 2¾in. by 3in. square. The spring
when at rest is 2½in. at its highest and 2in. at its lowest part.
The springs of both these traps are as nearly as possible 60lb. ;
but, whilst in the Dorsetshire trap I get this power by a depres-

sion of 1in., in the inferior article I have to go 1½in. or nearly 2in., rendering the setting of a Dorset-made one far superior and much more easy.

The genuine trap costs 10d. more than *the best counterfeit* with which I have compared it, or, as I might better explain myself, the best substitute for that which I have found most adapted for the destruction of vermin.

Rabbits should not be trapped, but snared. The bunglers who are not well versed in wiring will tell you otherwise ; but I can give you good reasons for my assertion. A stoat or weasel, a rat or hedgehog, cannot be caught without being killed nine times out of ten ; but not one rabbit out of fifty or a hundred is killed in the trap.

It will maim or destroy pheasants if forgotten or left uncovered, and, what is far worse, imperils cubs and foxes, which are generally so mutilated by the grasp of the jaws and their struggles to escape, as to make it an act of charity to destroy them.

It is true that the hutch-trap and the deadfall will exterminate numbers of rats, but for stoats you want a portable engine of destruction, and there is no better means than the old-fashioned gin. Setting it for rabbits does not require much art, although practice gives an instinctive perception of the right place for the purpose. To destroy vermin you must know their habits. You are pretty safe as you use a trap for these pestilent fellows, for you can do most with them in a tunnel made roughly of four boards about three feet long. It ought to be a little wider than a trap, say four and a half inches, and not less than a foot high, or the weasel may pop over instead of through it. This channel may go along the top of a bank, or along the bottom of a covert gate—in fact, wherever tracks have been observed—and it will answer well without any bait, provided there radiate from each end of the tunnel *which contains the two traps* two dwarf hedges of furze or any rough material to lead them in.

I have seen these contrivances answer to a miracle upon a neighbouring manor, and there is no occasion whatever for bait or lure. The little miscreant, as he comes along the bank, suddenly finds himself confined to one channel. He has a great fancy for the underground means of transit ; he bolts in, off his guard, and is caught, whilst game or foxes pass by unmolested.

Wires are hardly to be described as traps, but in the form of " springes " they are the earliest mode of capture. As I have said before, the keeper trusts to them, or ought to trust to them, for the capture of almost all the rabbits he requires. Instead of having half a hundredweight at his shoulders, he can carry from sixty to a hundred wires in his hand, and the whole number will not exceed a pound. A pound of wire, at 4s. a pound, will make two hundred wires, and the string will not average a shilling per hundred. On wet days or by moonlight he can set from sixty to a hundred with ease, especially if he has a boy to carry and hand them to him, and they can be prepared for setting and afterwards taken about without disturbing their shape and proportions. True, unless a man knows how to make and set them, he has a hopeless task before him, and it would take a lifetime to arrive at the expertness which can be learnt of any experienced hand.

The small wire known as "annealed brass wire" is the best for the purpose, and four strands, or even three if the material is good, will be sufficient. They may be twisted with two pegs, which form the eyes or slip-knots; or the strands, being placed round a nail over a door sill, may be connected to a weight which is whirled round. In either case they are very rapidly constructed. A thick double string connects the wire with the peg at a distance of twelve or fourteen inches, attached by what is known as "the Tom Fool's knot" to a peg nine inches long. The "pricker," a hazel peg with a notch cut to hold the wire, is about the same length.

To prepare these wires for setting, the keeper in the first place puts the peg under his foot, and strains the wire out straight and stiff before he proceeds to make the fatal noose. It is customary with many keepers to make this perfectly round, and six or seven inches in diameter; but this is a great mistake. The noose should be *pear*-shaped, about nine inches in its extreme length, and four and a half at its widest diameter. The loop should be close to the cleft stick which holds the wire, and it should stand above the pricker not less than eight inches, whilst the lower wire should be three and a quarter inches from the ground. If the wires are set in coverts they should be half an inch lower, and the belly of the wire should be depressed a little more.

The snares should be put *in the jumps* of the runs, and not near a hedge or covert; all the better if they are 200 yards away. The first rabbit caught will create a disturbance, and the whole of them will race in helter-skelter. This is the best time for snaring them, and the faster they go the better, as they do not notice what is before them, but, dropping their ears, will take the wire at the top of their speed. I have said that a good deal of nicety is required in preparing the wires. The principal art is to touch up the swell of the noose to a proper shape. Until the eye has acquired this form and proportion, a cardboard cut to the proper pattern may be useful.

In my neighbourhood we have a lad who is one of the best "wirers" I ever encountered in my travels ; an under-grown, crook-kneed, shambling, snub-nosed varlet, whose countenance is only redeemed from idiotcy by the shrewd expression of his small sunk eyes.

I have known this fellow set a line of wires, and before he got to the end of his rank there would be several entangled in the first he had put down. He would run across the field and fill three or four more, and having carried these home, he would go back with his lantern and take out perhaps two score, repeating his visit again before light, and at daybreak removing all his wires and the remainder of his prey.

But then he does nothing else, *and I don't think he could.* Like a good many trappers, he dislikes a dog, and says that with traps and wires—they are only in the way—and so they are.

If the wire is drawn up when it is looked at in the morning. a rabbit has been through it. If it has been beaten down, he has been over it. This last is a rare occurrence. I have watched hares and rabbits in covert, and I have never seen them go *over* a bramble if there was room to go *under ;* this I attribute as the reason for their falling easy victims to the snare.

The best time for setting will be just before dusk. but any time will do. A little wind should be setting to the wood, and it will be well the first night to pitch at every other run ; the second night changing to those omitted the first time. There is no better way of sweeping up rabbits. In the autumn or summer evenings an active man can look over his ground, and take them out at nine o'clock when there is a moon, and he will be able to shift and set his wires again. "Calls"—instruments for inveigling or attracting birds or beasts of chase—have not been used to any great extent by English sportsmen, although our Continental neighbours have adopted them more or less for a considerable time. The gamekeeper has been accustomed to squeal through his tobacco-pipe, and thus call out to their destruction young rabbits which lacked worldly experience : and occasionally I have seen corncrakes decoyed by means of the time-honoured flat blade-bone and notched stick. The Lincoln-shire decoy-men have used their trained tame ducks in former years to lead their wild congeners up the tunnels ; and some few have trained a yellow dog to do the same, and the ducks follow him—to my mind thinking him to be a fox.

I have known a decoy-man's daughter (who was quite as shrewd as her father) allure the ducks up the pipe or into its entrance by running a big dog ferret along the grass edge to a bit of rabbit which she held at the narrow end.

How much or how little they may be attracted by the "call." as yet I am not prepared to say ; but I am just now trying to ascertain, whilst they make their morning and evening flights from the sea to the standing barley, what effect it has upon them.

The birdcatcher uses his call to attract the flocks which pass over his nets ; and I think that Colonel Thornton, somewhere about 1794, at his sale of gerfalcons, Icelanders, gos-hawks. flight falcons, tiercels (called *tercels*), and eyess hawks, sold some *owls* which were staked to decoy birds. Certainly tethered owls were used at one time for this purpose.

Bits of looking-glass, arranged in a pyramid and revolved with a string like a child's toy windmill, have for years been used to attract larks, and may be seen exposed for sale in many of the London shops.

Call birds are still in use on the Continent, and I observed, to my regret, some time since, that at Capri a person possessed 100 "blinded" quails, which were used for decoying the migrating flights.

Some possess to perfection the power of imitating bird or beast ; but it is a talent rare as ventriloquism. I have known bird catchers, who despised "call birds," contented to have an old hen for a "brace" bird, and able to call without any in-strument or device. Others have been able by practice to "do" any bird with a bit of metal between their lips, and have thus "worked" their nets independently of live birds.

In a communication which I made to *The Field* some time ago I mentioned keepers who were gifted with these powers ; and since that time I have been informed on undoubted testimony that a father and son, in Hampshire, will put up a rough hut in the fields, and there "call" and shoot thirty or more wood-pigeons in a day.

The power of attracting birds or animals has been observed by
the French to some purpose, and, through the courtesy of
Mr. Davis, of 72, Piccadilly, I have been enabled to test the
efficacy of several French calls, which he has forwarded to me at
my request. They are very neatly made, not easily damaged or
worn out; indeed, most of them are quite indestructible, and,
above all, they require no art to use them. Some I am unable
to test—such as the quail call, for I have hardly ever seen quail
hereabouts, and then only in September; but my former acquaintance with the bird enables me to pronounce it a very
perfect imitation, and not only preferable to the call bird, but
humane, whilst the blinding of call birds whether quail or chaf-
finch, should entail the loss of both eyes upon the operator.

I am sure the plover call will answer. I decidedly attracted
one of these birds upon the heath, but whether she had young
ones in the long grass near me I cannot say; I think not, and
if not, the merit belongs to the call alone.

With a very neat and convenient "lark call," as I read the
label, I have brought a weasel from his hole, and, what is more
to the purpose, he paid the penalty of his curiosity. I am quite
sure that this would answer for young rabbits, and bring them
into the open as I lay *perdu* under the edge. I have ascertained
that it will do this on a windy night, but I desire to test it on a
quiet one.

The owl call is an unmistakable success; and I have sum-
moned my hoary friend, as he swept noiselessly across my
paddock, until I was so near that I could almost touch him with
my hand.

Then I have the partridge call, male and female, both marvellously like nature; a duck call; and a very fair call for hares.
Besides this, I have a woodpigeon whistle, which is better than
the real thing, and which I need not try now, for I have used it
years ago in Sussex, where a keeper first showed me one which
was made at Tunbridge Wells.

If these calls answer no other purpose, they would form good
signals for keepers and watchers of game. Having determined
upon a code of signals, the head keeper might almost talk to his
subordinates, or they to him, by means of the owl call at night,
or the woodpigeon as morning broke.

In covert beating I could give my keeper intimation of my
whereabouts without scaring every old hare, or apprising each old
cock pheasant that I was about to pay them my annual visit;

and though I could not in the thick of it put the hare call to my
lips, for fear of some young hands letting fly at me through the
jungle, I might be able to give some intimation of my presence
without that halloo which I have seen so fatal more than once to
sport. It is as well to be prepared for some rebuff on these
occasions, and to take it easily if some one demurs at the imitation and sees nothing in it—like those wet blankets at a feast
who first require to have the witticism shouted through an
ear trumpet, and then, shaking their heads, declare they " see
nothing in it. nothing whatever ; you've got the story wrong
somehow."

Such a rebuff befel the former lessee of a northern theatre, in
the days of Van Amburgh. He had engaged the lion tamer to
perform, and being very fond of effect, he suggested to that
celebrity that it would be a wonderful " effect" if the lions could
be made to roar as the curtain drew up. The lessee's name was
Piper. Van Amburgh acquiesced, but he did not relish the idea of
provoking the brutes just before stepping into the den, although he
did not mind giving them the whip when he was amongst them.
" Well," said the lessee, " have you any objection to my roaring ?"
" None whatever," replied the star. Accordingly the manager
stood at the wings, and when the curtain drew up he roared,
as per programme. It would have passed off admirably, had
not some wag in the gallery recognised the human voice, observed
the performer with his trumpet retiring behind the scenes, and
greeted him with " Bravo, Piper !" which convulsed the house.

O

PAPER XXV.

NORTHWARD.

I HAVE frequently been asked for information on the following subjects: 1. What is the best means of conveying dogs to Scotland and other places, as the trains terrify them? 2. What is the best mode of packing grouse to keep the birds, and prevent pilfering?

I have constantly *sent* dogs very long distances—which is, of course, far more hazardous than *taking* them—and of the scores that I have transmitted by railroad only two have suffered from the journey when they were sent in baskets or boxes, and but one retriever was so injured (being sent with chain and collar only) as to die a few days after reaching its destination (Liverpool).

No dog ought to be without water in hot weather for more than six hours under any circumstances, although he can do without food for twenty-four hours without any inconvenience ; and, unless he is to be exhibited, he should be fed at such intervals, and always at night.

I think a dog's comfort is studied best if he is carried either in a dog basket or a dog box. Let either of these cases be large enough, and you effectually prevent your dogs being stifled in one of those black holes which I believe terminated the career of the bulldog Romanie, and which have stifled many a good brace of dogs on their way to Scotland. You secure your setters a place in the guard's van, or a truck ; at any rate, they are certain of air, and probably *in transitu* they will provoke the attention of some good-hearted railway official, who will give them a pan of water.

Whether your dogs travel in box or basket, there ought to be some easy plan for furnishing it. I have both baskets and boxes, which I will describe.

I have wicker cases of various sizes, and provided they are strongly made, and the dog has no inclination to gnaw his way out, they answer very well. They are cheaper than travelling boxes, and cooler also. They should be, to use the terms of the trade, "randed" up, and not "slewed" up ; that is, the withes should be put in singly (the lateral withes), and not three or four together, as in wine hampers. For one dog this basket ought to be three feet six inches long, twenty inches high, and two feet wide. The opening is best made at the end, and there should be a hole at one corner with a tin or wooden trough, by means of which contrivance water is easily furnished. I have baskets, with a partition, for two dogs, and then the doors are at opposite ends. The single baskets, made stout enough, cost from twelve shillings to a guinea each, but boxes cost a little more. They are to be had of deal or elm, the latter wood the best, and the door is an iron grating. I have no double boxes—they are too cumbrous ; and except that they are, when properly made and banded with small hoop iron, more enduring than wicker-work, they are for the transport of dogs in every way inferior to the basket.

There is no doubt that dogs (and their masters) will do well to travel or start at night ; for pointers, and especially setters, suffer more from the heat than anything else : and, supposing that there are one or two empty carriages, it is possible to take one or two of your especial favourites with you, by the judicious application of your finger to your waistcoat pocket, when the vigilant super-intendents are in the arms of Morpheus.

Arrived at the end of railways, it is always best to take care that the boxes or baskets go on. It is very common for the coachmen and drivers to plead that they may be left for the return journey, that the dogs will best follow for the few miles of posting, and that it is "impossible" to carry those large packages "anyhow."

It is a lamentable fact that Scotch accommodation is generally best upon paper, and that the lodge, the stables, the keeper's house, and especially the kennels, are frequently the result of imagination on the part of the landlord, wholly or in part.

I have met with excellent Scotch keepers many a time ; but I have also come in contact with men who could not be brought to think any dog deserved better lodging than a pigsty, or choicer food than carrion ; and if they had the care of Hamlet—the best pointer, I think, in all England—they would tie him up with a halter, to hang himself if he liked. Of keepers, about one in five may be trusted to take charge of setters at home, and about one in five hundred to work them. But you mitigate all this evil much if you see that dogs have proper lodgings, plenty of water, and that their chains are secured in such a way that suicide is not possible.

Let your dogs travel in baskets *all the way* to their destination. Arrived at their journey's end, each basket (and the double baskets also, if made according to my directions) will answer for dog kennels until they are wanted for the return home, if the following advice is complied with : They should be raised with stones or a couple of faggot sticks from the ground, and a trench should be cut to carry off the rainfall. The sides may be protected with heather or turf, and a heap of the same material will make a very effectual roof.

It is true that some dogs are much affected by a railway journey. I once bought a setter of Lord Shrewsbury's breed, which did not recover his railway panic for more than a week ; but sympathy and a little patience on the master's part will generally put all this to rights, and I have not found the nervousness *permanent* or hard to remove, which it almost always is when produced by an injudicious introduction to the gun.

Unless dogs are sent to the north by rail, they must go up by sea, and they are exposed in steam vessels to greater risks, and for a longer time, whilst the master or the servant in charge remains in such a prostrate condition that they receive no care or attention from their natural protectors.

I come now to the second question proposed : "What is the best mode of packing grouse, to keep the birds and prevent pilfering ?"

Let me say it is of chief importance to get a moor which is accessible by some public conveyance. Packing grouse and sending it away are the great labours and annoyances of Scotch shooting, and these are aggravated beyond endurance when you have to send a horse and man daily eight or nine miles. A Scotchman is a very independent fellow, and won't come to you just when you want him ; so that it is indispensable, under certain circumstances, to have a conveyance of your own set apart for bringing what you want, and taking away the game you send to your friends.

If grouse are well packed and sent away in good time, a London dealer can give (as I am informed) ten shillings a brace the first ten days, and after that five shillings a brace. But it is very unfair to him to send game not worth the carriage (or mauled like the pheasants in French game shops, which have been fought over by four men and a dog), because he agreed to take good and bad together.

Much depends upon the way game is handled and carried until it is cold, upon the spot it falls on being a grey boulder or a bed of heather, and upon the feathers being wetted and not dried, as they ought to be when the guns stop for rest and refreshment—in other words, whisky and the cold spring water off the hill side.

If the keeper and gillies have the proper cleft stick, or, better still, the light iron " game-carrier," so that the birds hang by the neck and are exposed to the mountain breezes, and if when they are transferred from pannier or the saddle bags they are carefully arranged and neatly packed, grouse are almost certain to carry well ; but to put one bird cut all to pieces amongst them is certainly to taint the rest.

It is not generally advisable to send grouse to your friends directly you reach your moor, for at that time everyone is receiving presents of game from the north ; whilst you are able *at your leisure* to select such specimens as best bear carriage, to choose a cool day for packing them, and to put aside all " broken game," or such as " *ought* to be cooked," for the stock pot or digester.

I have seen systems of all kinds adopted for packing grouse. I have known the Russian material used—I mean oats or barley— but I have learnt that the system is not infallible ; and I consider heather the worst material—why I cannot tell. Hops are very commonly used for the purpose, but I think they are best when connected with malted barley by an experienced brewer.

I don't think anything answers so well as Scotch fir tops—the common pine, which you can find anywhere and everywhere in Scotland. Over and over again I have known birds thus packed and separated to travel in first-rate condition from Sutherland to St. Leonards, and I have heard of no failures.

It is best to take to Scotland, or to get when there, an eighteen-inch hand saw, an inch augur, a few bradawls, and a claw hammer. There are not many places where you are far from a sawmill in Caledonia, and you can get plenty of fir board. It is not a very hard job for the gillies or keeper, or all combined, to knock up a dozen or two of boxes on a wet day, and they can keep you well supplied, especially if you give them an occasional ounce of tobacco and a stoup of whisky.

If you add to the nails, when you pack the game for delivery, a couple of strips of narrow hoop iron, you baffle all attempts at " lifting " the game *in transitu.*

The usual prices of boxes, which are often supplied by the keeper as his perquisite, is sixpence per brace ; and this *toll* becomes an unbearable burthen, the more annoying because, like a tailor's coat box (price 5*s.*), each grouse case is useless as a brown paper wrapper when it has served its purpose, for you cannot ask your friends, like the game dealers, to send back these boxes, even if they would return carriage free, which is not now the case.

It is best to have the boxes large enough ; much game is spoilt by their being too small. Two holes should be bored with the augur at each end, and one at each side, for the circulation of air ; the turpentine in the pine wood and branches, and the interstices formed by the use of such coarse material as the fir boughs, will do all the rest.

PAPER XXVI.

A BRIGHT OCTOBER.

IT matters not how delightful the home may be, you will find the educated classes rejoice in a change even for the worse. My lord duke leaves his grand old palatial residence for a dingy square, and I, in obedience to the dictates of the powers that be, make my annual visit and do my accustomed penance in lodgings by the sea, at so much a week and extras for what is facetiously called " waiting " (on my part, not the overworked maid servant's), and 2s. 6d. per week for a small partnership in the kitchen fire. At the end of six weeks it is time to think of home again ; we are wearied of the German bands, the peripatetic organ, the dyspeptic monkey, the adulterated milk, the sloppy boats, and the dogs-eared novels, which from first to last possessed no novelty, and we turn homewards to " sweet Auburn," with Goldsmith's " lengthening chain."

Hunting or shooting, however, there *are* charms in a fresh country. Here I know every inch of the manor. I have an intimate acquaintance with the flight of every covey, and their line for miles. In " the bog "—that deep and difficult ten acres of grass hassocks and rank verdure, interspersed with pools and sloughs of mud and ooze, whence Billy Butler declared he had seen issue every kind of British game—I have a pretty fair know-ledge of all the stepping places, and have seldom gone far astray as I groped my way at night for the hut where I waited for day-light and the wildfowl ; and I know few places which possess more attractions, or for a stranger, more perplexities. Then there are the long wide reaches of rape and swedes, the seed clover, or, better still, the santfoin (the best partridge covert left us in Old England), and the fern now (in this month sacred to the mys-teries of Bass, Allsopp, and their brethren) changing from green to chrome, and so to burnt sienna and " Payne's grey."

It needs, one would think, some strong inducement to pack up and leave this glorious range of varied shooting, the wild black heath and rushes, even for a few days, especially when, any day now, the first woodcock may flip through the dark hollies and pitch again, wearied with his long flight—whence shall we say? Well, perhaps from Iceland—when, having found him, my old Clumber quickens in his pace, and is animated by the hope that half a score or more may have dropped in amongst the scrub, to take wing at dusk for Exmoor or some of the deep woods of Devon. But the love of change is strong upon me, when I get a hearty invitation for the Wiltshire open country, and I arrange my little matters of business speedily, and determine to take the train at once.

I deeply study *Bradshaw* as I finish breakfast; for don't I know that, unless I make what painters call a "finished study" of the various changes, I shall pass half the day at cross stations, pacing to and fro like a Crimean sentry? And having made all these arrangements, I find myself with forty-five minutes "to the good," sacred to the *Times* and my cigar. Not a bit of it. I must put up with the usual interruptions, which are not fictitious. Here they are:

A man with thirty pence to be changed by me into a half-crown, the said half-crown to be made into a ring and worn as a remedy for fits, the pence contributed by thirty sympathetic unmarried vestals. The tax collector, who called twice before but didn't leave his business; and, by the way, I can't for the life of me find my cheque-book. A woman with a bottle demanding medicine for a neighbour's child, of which she knows neither the age nor the disease, but will "go and ask." Lastly, a load of straw, requiring all my available hands to stow it away; and a man with a county directory, to which, in a moment of aberration, I subscribed, and who now waits for the money and "has no change."

At last I discharge these various suitors—all but the woman with the bottle, whom I behold making the pace as I drop down the hill—and, glancing at my watch, console myself with the conviction that if I send the dark chesnut along I may catch the train; and what is more, I do it, with one minute and three-quarters left. As it is, the prudent gate-keeper at the crossing shakes his head and won't let me through, telling me, as he makes an extempore speaking-tube of his right hand, "she's signalled;" but I get my ticket and go on.

After the usual complement of "shuntings," waiting on "sidings," and changes for which this line is celebrated, I disembarked, to meet the whitechapel and "iron-grey with the tanned muzzle," of whose knee action and pace I had frequently heard so much ; and, yielding myself to the pilotage of the clean-shaven groom, I was soon at the iron gates which admitted us to the beech avenue and state entrance.

I had heard of this fine old seat before; but, as it had but within a year or so been formally handed over to my friend after a Chancery suit, of some two or three centuries for what I know, I had never seen it until this time. Until we came close to the large quadrangle and the ornamental gates I could see but little of its form. I then observed that it was an old structure, pro-bably of the time of James I. ; that it was made up of gables and projecting windows, to which, not being an architect, I can give no name : whilst the porch was formed by a vast bay window of stained glass—a part of the upper drawing-room—and carried up two or three stories to a sort of tower. The fine old hall of many windows was well carpeted, as all halls ought to be ; and fashion had not interfered with the glorious old large fire-place and chimney-corner, with a log fire and quaint " dogs " to match. Thence all the rooms were entered, but modern civilisation had placed thick red curtains to each door ; so that in the evening, when the more gentle sex ascended the old black-oak staircase, and the smoking and the whist began, a more delightful chamber it would be very hard to find. Ample room in this " thirty-five feet by forty-six " for the large table spread with every periodical and letter-writing gear, the large rocking and easy chairs, and that dumb waiter furnished with strong waters, coffee, cavendish, and best brands of Havannah, which, following that old, pale, dry sherry and champagne, put all of us in good humour, in spite —yes, in spite—of the prospect of bills and Christmas. One at any rate of that company had well earned these comforts and this luxury in the last great war, though he thought more of the long tails which fell to his Boss gun that morning.

I am not going to paint Crimean charges, or give a page or two of Jackson and Graham, gloating over villa-haberdashery or cracked china. I hate a chair you may do anything with except sit in it, or a sofa which declines to receive my head without that cotton mystery persistently shrouding my shoulders when I rise, or disdaining to be used as a couch if I so incline. Nor am I diffi-cult to please in the choice of a bed chamber ; if waterproof, it's comfortable. Be that as it may, I was fresh enough next morn-ing after spending (it seemed impossible to believe it) eight and a half good hours in that capital panelled bedroom sound asleep.

What a bright glorious October morning shone upon me as I drew up the blind! The curtains I discarded the night before. I anticipated this glorious weather as I, half awake, traced the shadows of the rooks crossing and recrossing from the two rookeries forming the background of these bowling greens (or alleys) and those green terraces which, tier upon tier, bound the large flat plot, now sacred to croquet, or, as some one hath it, "The Feast of Curates." I must be late, for there, on his blood chesnut ("a West Australian"), half a quarter of a mile away, sits my host, his dress a dun shooting jacket and very coarse cord breeches, his legs from the knee downwards encased in tanned flax gaiters broached with leather at the wearing parts. All this I ascertain by means of my field glass just before he turned away to look at his kennel, for which he sets forward with a racing seat and canters down the valley, on one side of which you may see his best covert of 900 acres.

My watch reassures me; I have half an hour to spare, and between the duties of the toilette I can observe the lines of scarlet geraniums, the coloured-leaved edging plants, the dahlias, and, what I like better still, a few spikes of hollyhocks still spared, and coming out in strong contrast from the wall of yew trees that, with doubtful taste, screen off the fine newly-restored church from the parterre of flowers and fragrance.

Just then a rap at the door, and one of our party gives me the tip, "A knickerbocker breakfast, and we are going to kill partridges to Clumbers." "Make haste, he has been riding the young 'un ever since six this morning," So down to the hall, where, on the side table, are the guns all ready resting on their backs, poised on their hammers and muzzles. Through the window, on the old stone settle, I see the old keeper, whose face prepossessed me at once in his favour—and correctly impresses me, I subsequently discover—whilst his granite suit of tweed makes him look as though he were carved in stone, a part of the seat he occupies. The delusion is strengthened by that peacock, which, tail erect, shows his gaudy plumage to the sun, but a fathom behind old Hammond—that's the keeper's name—and, walking daintily, displaying his ugly feet and legs upon the gravel, calls up the remembrance of my old godmother (rest her soul!) in her Indian shawl and black silk stockings, picking her way to Lewis and Allenby's across the London pavement.

To the right, and in the breakfast-room amongst the old portraits of Delhi chiefs and warriors, beneath whom I observe our host busy at the "buffet"—his arms as busy with the carving-knife, and almost as dexterous as was that sword hung above him when he rode a mere stripling close to Lord Cardigan in the charge of the Light Brigade—and grouped round him I see another or two, one of whom rides straight and well, and trusts to Providence and his horse, for he can't see far before him except in Westminster Hall, when no place is too big for him.

Breakfast discussed, we turn out and make for the turnips and rape, alongside of the various coverts, as yet scarce showing a sign of autumn, excepting those poplars by the trout stream, where you may now and then see the spraints of otters and track them to the beds of osier by the mill.

We take out one brace of Clumbers, for whom the Captain pleads, "Give 'em time, if you've no objection," and we put them in the hedgerow for the chance of some wandering vagrant pheasant, one or two of which I see running ahead already. The dog takes the other side with his owner ; the bitch is on mine with Hammond, and busy in the long grass and fern. Whirr ! down she drops, and up whirls a fine old pheasant on the other side, and falls with a thud about fifty yards away.

"All right," from the other side ; and I hear the black retriever, who has brought it, rolling in the leaves, as he watches the Clumbers going on, head and stern down, and trying every morsel of covert where a bird can crouch and avoid their vigilance.

"Hammond ! "

"Sir ! "

" Get on to the gate at the end of the hedgerow, and stand there."

To hear is to obey ; and, whilst we give the old keeper law to reach his point, I notice the scent of a mild cigar coming through the hedge, and at the same moment two shots at the bird, both misses, acquaint me that smoking sometimes is hostile to good shooting.

Two or three more rises ; but the birds went for the hare covert, and were, of course, allowed to go there scatheless. One, a pied bird, was to be let off anyhow, go where he would ; and then began the walking up partridges with this pair of spaniels ; and, let me observe, as good a brace as it has ever been my lot to see.

I am speaking of a pair, perhaps four or five years old, used by the same men from their entry, and one of the best strains in

England, and therefore in the world. As yet they have not the trick of breeding sporting dogs ("smell dawgs," the Yankees call them) anywhere but in the British Islands. Wolf hounds, sheep dogs suited for their localities, Alpine mastiffs, and some such breeds, you may get abroad, and, with some reservation, nowhere else so well ; but England for the English dog—at any rate for the gun or horn,

Then what besides ? Firmness and discretion, the utmost kindness and appreciation of his weaknesses, caresses and rewards when he makes signal use of his great faculties, and inexhaustible patience on your part under difficulties. When he knows his work, let him be spaniel, setter, or retriever, *trust him;* but if he wilfully does wrong—above all, if he imitates a wrong doer—correct him. Above all things don't let this keen observer detect you shirking *your* work, or he will copy you. Always give him the wind, aye, if you walk miles for it. Dogs hunting by the nose can't do without it.

At any rate, this October morning we did not throw a chance away. We were three guns, and all of one mind to give these beauties—for I can call them nothing else—full time to show their faculties and their training, delighted more with them than with that mere knocking down of the bird kicked up by the foot which obtains with some the name of sport. To me it is on a par with gipsy snuff-boxing, and of the two sports I prefer the last. As concerning birds, no " Aunt Sally " game for me.

If we could manage the ground no better, we took one strip up, then walked back *over the same ground,* and took up the next piece, and so continued until all was finished. This we did in extreme cases only ; generally we were able to get a cross wind, and beat it exactly as any setter would quarter, if left, as a broken dog should be left, to work out the dictates of combined intelligence and education.

It was a very pretty sight to see these Clumbers, sometimes in the rape or swedes, invisible, coming up to sight, busy with the scent, but never ranging more than half a gunshot off ; then waiting for the guns, half dropping their tails, going all the time, and looking anxiously for us to come on, saying as plainly as they could, " This way, my master ! " and then down as still as death until they got the signal to be up and on again ; sometimes, not sure, waiting that the sign might be repeated ; whilst the retriever behind was silent and solemn, and like her master's shadow, until sent upon that errand from which she seldom returned without the bird or hare. No matter how long the search by this black slave for a winged runner or a crippled hare, there lay these Clumbers, silent, of course, and patient as statues, until they got " the office " to move on and find some more.

It was a very trying country; no hedges when we had left the neighbourhood of coverts, but a wild range of wolds and close cropped common, where the last bustard, or nearly the last was found.

By the way, I have a notion that the last bustard was killed in Devonshire, sold for a shilling, and eaten by some commercial travellers.* But very likely, in 1794, or a few years before, the taking of this bird on these bleak hills would have been no rare thing; and, by the combination of the landed proprietors amongst these Wiltshire downs, it might be even now acclimatised and restored.

On this ground I was somewhat astonished at the flints; broken flints covered the entire surface of the soil, and where the grass was laid down it grew over them as by a miracle. If it wearied us, how trying it must have been for the dogs; but the spaniels seemed little inconvenienced, and perhaps got over the effects of it by custom, and were led on by their love of sport. Occasionally these flints are most disastrous. I have several times had setters' feet cut by them, and one pointer of mine was ruined.

At last we finished our day's beat, and made for the side of a down partly covered with junipers, thorn bushes, furze, and a tangled mass of brambles. Here I had an opportunity of seeing the steadiness of my two dumb confederates, which put up the rabbits and turned them to the gun with marvellous intelligence, now and then pointing them, and to all appearance watching them in triumph, as I have ere now seen a cat pointing in a hedge; no chase, no riot, I need scarcely say no babble or noise whatever—in fact, a pair of as good general servants as it ever was my lot to see.

* In 1804 a great bustard was shot in Devonshire, and taken to Plymouth market, where a publican bought it for a shilling, and cooked it for some "riders." These gentlemen perceiving, on dissection, the difference in the colour of the pectoral muscle from the other part of the breast, voted it improper food. A writer in the *Sporting Magazine* (1817) describes these birds as confined to the Wilts Downs, unfrequented parts of Norfolk, and the high wolds of Yorkshire. He also states that Col. Thornton Hawkes could not catch them, and ridicules the notion that they could be taken with greyhounds.

I don't hesitate to say that pointers or setters are my strength (my weaknesses if you will), and that no pleasure on earth is equal or superior to mine when I see a pair of high rangers crossing each other independently and bringing up well on game ; but at times I am delighted with such a bit of discipline and intelligence as I saw that October morning, and kept up till dark, in spite of severe walking and that flinty soil.

PAPER XXVII.

VARIED SHOOTING.

I have in former years—perhaps five-and-twenty years ago—
more than once enjoyed a wild day on what was described to me
as "no man's land." In Hampshire a boatman took me across
the water to shoot snipes on a capital marsh several times, near
Christchurch, when my favourite pointer and I enjoyed ourselves
prodigiously, and the sport was interspersed with wildfowl, or
perchance an odd partridge or some foreign visitor, making a
capital because an eccentric bag. Many years after I was visiting
those parts, and casually mentioned the swamp where the one-
armed boatman (drowned, by the way, at Mudiford) and myself
disported ourselves, and I found that I had been unwittingly
trespassing on the grounds of my then worthy host.

It was quite a common thing to see boats "hauling off" at a
wild tract of land, where I had the sole right for a dozen years or
so, with a freight of gunners in the bow and a black dog
"forrard;" and I knew very well that the boatmen at a neighbouring town were at all times ready to land any number of
itinerant sportsmen if the coast was clear. I once picked up a
capital powder flask, nearly new, and a well broken active young
spaniel, on that same ground just after daylight, for neither of
which I could ever find an owner, though the boat which I suspect contained him was in the offing, and running with a fair
wind for home. That was just as the daylight broke, and none
of the ground had been disturbed.

A neighbour of mine had some good wild shooting joining this,
which has now passed into other and better hands. It is bog,
moor, heath, and fir-tree plantations, with any quantity of peat
and sand, and a vegetation of rushes. You could preserve rabbits
on some parts of the ground, and keep the plantations quiet for
woodcocks ; occasionally (if you whistled, not otherwise) a tame
pheasant would run to meet you, or possibly a dozen guinea fowl.
You could shoot them if you like—they were bred on purpose,
and, together with the pheasants, were thoroughly domesticated.

My neighbour used to say whistling up birds was so much easier
than beating; he would blaze away at them until his gun was
dangerously hot (and generally kill them, too), and I have
waited for it to cool. He was not a *thorough* sportsman. We
never knew his antecedents, as he persisted in going to sleep after
dinner. I always thought he had been a paper-maker, for when
some one handed him the *Times*, which contained startling news
from India, he didn't read it, but, having put his tongue to the
margin, gave it as his opinion it was "animal size," and passed
it on; and I have seen paper-makers test their goods in that
way since.

He always wore a frock coat, even with his beagles; tried to
catch wild ducks on their passage out to sea with nets hung on
clothes' props: trapped the foxes or poisoned them, cubs and all;
and eventually departed for a cheerful town in Warwickshire,
named Coventry, No, he didn't *go*, he was *sent* there.

He was quite a representative man. He didn't enjoy his wild
sport; though it might have been made excellent at very little
expense. With a gun punt on that grand old tidal river, and
access to the rushy islands, where, watching the wind, you could
land yourself, sculling with one oar in absolute silence, and kill
teal, widgeon, ducks, or diver, and frequently get a good specimen
for your museum, I can't imagine a better sport; but this
unsportsmanlike bird of passage didn't care for boating, saw
nothing admirable in a dog's intelligence, and was not only a bird
of passage, but a bird of prey.

It is the same with hundreds of men, who have the power to
exclude from such ground as this, though they never go over it.
Many a thousand acres, the "tag" to some large shooting or
other, remains unbeaten by the owner; and, without exaggera-
tion, there is enough of such wild ground preserved, unused, and
unavailable for all that, to form a little county.

I don't believe there is such a thing to be found as a tract of
land presenting sport for two guns, unless you are prepared to
have a millstone tied round your neck in the shape of a house—
possibly damp and badly drained, or with a queer roof, the dry
rot, or an exorbitant rent, and such a snob for a landlord,
and such a tyrannical, grasping, mean, poverty-stricken, "poor-
rich" devil in the shape of a game preserver over the nearest
hedge, that all your efforts and your keeper's to get up a head of
anything but weasels, rats, snakes, and hedgehogs would be
thrown away.

You must have the house. The shooting is only "let" to get rid of it, unless you can get the widow of a "civilian" to come there with her paraquet and monkey, or the civilian himself—an old bachelor, you know, with six dark-complexioned, bilious-eyed half-castes who call him "*uncle,*" and quarrel over his coffin by and by.

That's the bore! The better the shooting, the bigger the house. Put up with that embarrassment, and you will always—unless things alter—be able to get the domain of some bankrupt duke, or plunging marquis, whose accounts are dislocated—purposely sometimes—by his sleek steward, and as often as not by that set of sharks who are always ready to "renew" the bill.

My good-natured critics will call this "padding." Well, perhaps it is; and, if so, mine is not the only article adulterated.

As to wild and varied shooting, it's a marketable commodity; it can't be got without money, and vexatious conditions, and burly keepers who are for everlasting wanting "something to drink," or their wages "raised," or a new gun, or a couple of dozen of traps, or a new ferret box, or "some help" for night work, or their cottage thatched, or keep for a cow, or in fact anything that can be had by simply asking for it. And if such shooting is accessible and within a certain distance of London, it is worth half as much as the yearly rent, or any sum that the owner likes to ask.

The majority of occupiers prefer preserving to letting; and when the farmer has it, it forms a pleasant recreation for himself and his neighbours, which seems to cost nothing.

I was in North Devon a few weeks ago, and from a new watering-place near Bideford, which struck me as the most dismal swamp I ever visited, a boatman showed me Lundy Island, about ten miles from Clovelly. "Lots of shooting there," he said. "rabbits and all sorts, and anyone may go. I takes people in my boat, and they bring back as much as the boat will hold—gulls, woodcocks, snipes, and all sorts." I believe in ten minutes we might have been "under weigh," but that I remembered my Hampshire experiences, and could not but reflect that at my first shot possibly I might be interrogated by a keeper "with a deputation," and detained for "being in search or pursuit of game, or woodcocks, snipes, quails, landrails, or conies," and have to hear a learned pundit read from a legal document, "For that you, the said Idstone (or Hidstone), on, &c., &c., unlawfully did

P

use a certain dog, to wit, a setter, pointer, or lurcher (not being a greyhound), and a certain gun or engine, for the purpose of then and there killing or taking." &c.

Now this would not have mattered to my red-faced friend in the battered hat and blue jersey, who would have simply rowed back again without me, unless I had "made it right" with the gamekeeper aforesaid, or shown I must be detained twelve hours, and therefore could not be legally detained at all—which I believe is law, equity, or some such jargon; but I was backed up in the opinion that shooting *is* to be had at Lundy Island by an ex-keeper at my own place, who was born opposite to Lundy, and declares " anyone could shoot there fifty years ago; and," he adds, " good shooting *tew*, I can tell ye, sir, for them as likes it wild." However, I have since been undeceived on this point, as Lundy Island is as strictly preserved as any nobleman's domain in England.

Good cheap wild sport *can* be had, I believe, far away in the north of Scotland, and nowhere else except in Ireland, where there is this to be remembered, that they may take you for some one else and pot you, unless you " drive sharply down the avenue "—a caution bestowed by an Irish squire upon his guest as he got into his carriage after dinner. Then there are both Norway and Sweden, where you *may* get capercailzie, black cock, woodcock, duck, snipe, curlew, partridge, and "a few hares," whilst lake and stream furnish salmon, trout, pike, and perch ; duck shooting commencing early in July, and other shooting one day earlier than in Scotland.

You may get tempted to take a day's shooting, a week's, a month's, where there is "room for one gun," and dogs, champagne, claret, and domestic society are all furnished—only *beware*. Don't take a ticket for more than one week until you have seen your host and are on terms of intimacy with his capital shooting pony, his industrious fleas, and his terrible " pot luck." His occasional day's rabbit shooting, with a variety of plover (never nearer than 400 yards), his scared sample of *one* partridge, and a stray pheasant (apocryphal!), may rather disgust you ; and the hilly walking, tough cheese, stale bread, and inferior perry (bottled and metal-labelled) may prove unpalatable.

I have heard of men going to these places *once*, and one very tough army surgeon actually repeated his experience ; but at the end of the fourth day he came home half dead from starvation, and with his cartridge pannier full as when he left. " They didn't know I was come away for good," he gasped out as he got down at my door ; " I should have been starved in another day, and I believe that they had arranged to sell my body for dissection."

There is one chance for those requiring rough shooting. It is *to advertise.* Now and then a man wants a gun or two to share the expenses of his ground. You may drop upon a good fellow, which habitual renters of moors are not. They divide themselves into two classes, hawks and buzzards. They shoot for profit, just as some men get packs of hounds—subscription packs—for profit.

Did you ever know a good fellow who made it pay ? Well, between ourselves, I don't think *I* ever did ; nor is there any class of men " going North " of whom owners of moors have a more wholesome dread than those who sublet to "guns" on the hill, and find dogs, ponies, gillies, and other things "not in the catalogue."

I have known moors stripped of all game, and the shooting lodge *defiled* by the goings on of those greedy speculators—men without honour, conscience, or common decency.

.

PAPER XXVIII.

THE END OF THE SEASON.

THE advent of February is, I confess, to a certain extent, a melancholy event to me. Although I do not always take advantage of the leave and licence I purchase to go in pursuit of game, I feel a vague melancholy as I drive to the last assembly of guns, clumbers, and retrievers. As we get to the end of the last copse, and the shades of evening fall, I wait for the fiat of the head keeper, always delivered in the same Norfolk accent, and with a total absence of all feeling except an impression of relief, as he touches his hat, and, looking around him, expresses his belief that it is " all over for this season."

"All over " with game-destroying, doubtless, but not "all over " with me, nor with my companion here—not a professional man, nor one of broad acres, but of that vague genus known as " connected with business," whatever that may be.

I have known my young friend for years, and his father before him knew me, and both *père et fils* were of the same business, though now the older has retired.

It concerns none of my friend's acquaintance what his business is. He has no guns but Purdey's. His brandy-flask is of sterling silver, richly gilt within. His watch is a "compensating duplex three-quarter plate, jewelled in every hole, and goes fourteen days without winding up." His chain of 18-carat, and hall-marked. Grant made his gaiters, Poole "superintended " his coat. His knickerbockers are unique, and made by some one in Bond-street ; as he describes the place vaguely, I must do the same. All he can or will tell you is, "it's on the left-hand side." And as for a retriever (he always has one close by his side, but, unless appealed to in a difficulty, never lets him go), why, he is the envy of all his friends' keepers, and of the masters too.

And then his "loader ! " A neat, clean, sober, active fellow (six feet at least, like his master), and silent as the grave, never touching his master's elbow as the ground game is running, nor letting the muzzle of the second breech-loader be on a level with anyone's ear or heels. Down in a minute if anything heads back, so that his master can get a good shot over the velveteen jacket of his vassal, and at once be refurnished with breech-loader No. 2.

My companion (I must disguise his name, or I may get him laughed at in the City, and so I will call him Robinson, though his name has really a more aristocratic sound and flavour)—my companion thoroughly enjoys himself down here, or at his own place in Norfolk. He appreciates the pleasures of youth, good health, easy circumstances, and the best and largest cigars you ever tried. It is an understood thing between us that we never attempt to penetrate the mysteries of his City life. I have heard that he is a stockbroker, but he isn't; that he is an importer of Noah's arks, rocking horses, "and sich;" that he is the Assam Tea Company ; that he held some thousands of Rantoon shares, and had an interest in that wonderful single barrel with no stock, with which in the picture the keen sportsman was flooring wild ducks. The envious said he was in the pork and sausage trade, and that he was once seen in a Norway fishing smack at 4 a.m. off Billingsgate ; but all this wants authenticating. The most that could be said against him was that twice he was seen driving in the Uxbridge road and making for Oxford-street (and probably Holborn), both times at 10.30 a.m., in a mail phaeton with bright chains ; a pair of dark browns with tan muzzles were stepping well up to their bits in front of him, and going, as John Tollitt expressed it "within themselves." But then the Uxbridge road leads to so many places that it's hardly fair to insinuate he was going to the office ; and had he been about to thus sacrifice himself, I see no harm in it.

He was either a sleeping partner, or he had some capital representative ; for I never knew him relinquish any opportunity of taking his pleasure because he was otherwise engaged. He did everything so easily ! —no fuss, or as he called it " bother." " If I have not plenty of partridges," he said to me one evening after a brilliant day's shooting at his Norfolk manor, " I dismiss the whole lot. I get a head keeper, and I let him get his own men, and he has all the blame if there is any, and takes the consequences. I can't be coming here to look after them ; they must ' superintend ' themselves." As soon as the shooting is over I am off to fish, and perhaps I shan't see their faces until I take down my cousins to have a day's rook shooting whilst I see the young pointers out; by that time the governor wants me to go yachting with him ; and then there's the grouse."

And this brings me to where I started from—" the end of the shooting season."

A few years ago I was returning from a large party. We had been beating a celebrated covert of 1000 acres, full of fat pheasants quite as tame as fowls.

I took up three " guns " in my dog cart, and my men walked home. One of my companions (he on the box seat with me) seemed over-melancholy on the subject, and said, with a sigh which would have done credit to an undertaker, that " we must put our guns into their coffins now."

It seemed to me that he was almost inclined to order one for himself, and, knowing that he was of a morbid turn, I tried to cheer him up a bit. For my part, fated as I am to live in the centre of desolation, with no neighbours who can " drop in "—a wild heath on one side of me, and a vast deer park on the other —I have been compelled to find out some employment and occupation, and thus carry on the war.

My old breaker will as surely be at my door the 2nd or 3rd of February as the collector of income tax. and takes off instalments of young pupils about every three weeks. I know where to find him any morning if I reach his cottage at half-past nine, when he will have given them a preliminary canter ; and if I don't care to take a young Irishman from Ballinasloe Fair for an eight miles' drill in my Whitechapel, I can loose my young retriever and give him a bit of waiting discipline amongst the rabbits in the fir plantation yonder.

There is plenty to do in a country place without spending much money, or going salmon fishing, yachting, and so forth. With a couple of ferrets, a few yards of line, and a spike collar, I can make a young retriever, check the depredations of vermin, and ascertain their haunts. I have no sooner finished one year's sport and exercise than I prepare for the next. The setters I shot over last year in Perthshire will probably be next season backing and pointing in Indiana, or standing snipes in Russia. I like new tools, and to see young dogs develop and reward my patience, labour, and self-control. Robinson wants it all done for him. Here goes! I'll do it.

A good walk in the early morning with my breaker, another after two hours' rest, luncheon, and then what Jem calls " a two hours finisher to put the polish on," is more to my taste than human pupils and so many inches of a Greek play, especially when, dropping off to sleep at half-past eleven, I seem to hear Jem's last words : "Well, if he do go to Stafford, sir, and they have a judge as is a judge, and can count his marks up after he've a give 'em, up wind or down wind, they will have a job to beat him."

" You promised to come and weed my kennel," says one of my old friends. I throw my portmanteau into the railway carriage, and go and do it. Hard if on that march I don't learn something to be done or avoided. It's not so very long ago that I learnt on one such expedition the way to make a good, portable, light shelter for a keeper out of five wattled hurdles, combined with cheap hinges, something like an Indian screen. At the same time I got a good hint or two on dog breaking, and saw a dog-cart which was new to me, and rode in it, and it went down at once in my indexed note-book. Item, I saw a good way of detecting trespassers ; and such a clever pitfall, that it took in my friend who made it. and as he explained it to me we disappeared together !

It is far more pleasure to Statter's breaker, or my old Jem, or my " apprentice " to Jem (a wiry young fellow with more muscle than experience as yet) to see dogs *perform*, than it is to the swells who merely write big cheques for them to-day and spoil them to-morrow ! The genuine sportsman, who can make a dog and hunt him—which is a far more scientific thing than the " shooting man " supposes—who can superintend game rearing, set a wire or trap, and outmanœuvre a poacher to whom woodcraft is a plain open book; who can detect the presence of a stoat or weasel, and even decipher a foil, however 'cute the vagabond or vermin that made it, has ten times the enjoyment of ordinary men who turn their hundred-guinea dogs adrift without studying wind or scent. think beating a field means crossing it at right angles, and are as proud of seeing their names in prize lists at dog shows as though they had made their animals, about which they know as much as half the picture collectors, or those *virtuosi* who buy every rare violin that gets into the market, though they could not for the life of them put even the second string in tune or screw up the bow !

It will be apparent to those who read what I write that I am decidedly inclined to " dodges," and so I am. One dodge I have found invaluable in a dull place—to be always occupied somehow, wet or fine weather, the whole year round.

PAPER XXIX.

ON BEATING FOR GAME.

OUR ancestors shot for sport and health, *and enjoyed seeing their dogs work.* They went to the moors, in the days of flint and steel, and for the greater part of "the percussion epoch," to enjoy the exercise of hard walking on the moorside, with the charming interlude of the luncheon spread on the grey boulders of the Brawl, and another walk after it ; then home to a wholesome dinner, with a good appetite, on a sure-footed Highland pony. I cannot say whether the grouse in those days were more approachable than they are in these. I fancy they had wild seasons and wild days ; and that the laws of scent were as mysterious as they are now, *with this difference,* that whilst *they* could get a point with "a southerly wind and a cloudy sky," *we* must have some east in it, or the dogs are at fault. If birds were less shy, I am inclined to think it was because fewer men shot grouse—they were not so frequently disturbed, and there were not half so many discharges of the gun as in these days of breech-loaders with snap actions and rebounding locks.

A revolution has gradually broken out amongst renters of moors. Many a man now "goes north" without any team of dogs, or, it may be, without a retriever. Ostensibly he requires exercise and change of scene : he secures the last, but the first he does not get. He may do all his shooting in Regent-street patent-leather boots, and his knickerbockers will come back to his London chambers unsplashed if he so wills it, and yet he may have slain his thousands. He has done it in a way of his own. He may even knock over his birds without moving from his rocking-chair, keeping iced punch and thin sandwiches within reach of his languid arm. He may be dallying with the *Times, Morning Post,* or the *Field,* his head supported by an air cushion, and kill his right and left with the most cool indifference. Meanwhile he is within speaking distance of one or two companions, and at any rate he can telegraph by silent signals to his observant man that he requires fresh refections. Strong exercise, climbing hills, and " that sort of thing " he leaves to gillies, who are driving the grouse over his head.

Now and then these proceedings are enlivened by a sweepstakes, and then you want to throw a little more energy into the work. " You must exert yourself, you know,"—which means you must have an active Scotch lad to pick up the birds after every flight and raking shot, without caring whether his employer or his neighbour killed them ; and it is a capital joke to have a clever retriever in this case, who will " fetch the other fellow's birds " (or at any rate pieces of them), from the grasp of the other fellow's dog. One rather heavy sum was honourably won last season by making up a winning bird from fragments thus obtained, and it was allowed as perfectly fair and the right thing to do, " under the circumstances."

This system has become fashionable, but it must not be dignified by the name of sport. Men shoot now for " the bag," which is not altogether shooting for " the pot." Once the birds are counted, Young England cares little who has them. The pot is always " going " to receive " broken game," which means game blown to pieces from over anxiety or want of calculation ; and the rest, after " the house " is supplied, is dispersed in deal cases by the iron roads. And oh ! the bore and trouble that it is ! If Young England makes a good game-book he is satisfied, though he may do it in an inartistic manner. All the writing in the world won't stop him ; it is no exertion, and there is less probability of missing.

He finds his shooting pony (low to mount and a safe one on the heath) waiting at the door on a fine bracing August morning, and his companions equally well provided, each of these sturdy little horses held by a sharp, intelligent Scotch lad ; and possibly a " sweepstakes retriever " or two may be of the party. The provender has been sent ahead (the gigantic grouse pie frequently carried on a man's head, by the way, and kept hot with blankets), and it may be a folding chair or so, to the spot over which the grouse are to be driven. This place may be a sudden fall below a hill, or a range behind a bank ; or, now and then, permanent huts are erected for the purpose, so comfortable and weather-proof that something far less hardy than a Crimean hero could survive the night in them. It may be one o'clock before even the breakfast is over, letters are answered, gossip at an end, and the lords of their time are prepared to—aw ! shoot ! The more energetic of the class will have a little walk beforehand, and perhaps a brace or leash of setters. But, unaccustomed to the poetry of shooting, they won't give the dogs time to hold their birds or quarter their ground ; and having half ruined their breaking and brought the keeper to the verge of apoplexy by suppressed wrath, they come empty away. By this time the crowd of gillies and helpers have driven whole packs of grouse to a given space, almost as certainly as a boy can "herd" turkeys, and when the guns are placed the driving begins.

It is but moving the *battue* northward ; the slaughter is positively delightful. "If it hadn't been for the cripples we should have had a tremendous bag." "Ever so many went away with their legs hanging down." These are the remarks you may overhear as you ride along, which means simply that, as we saunter home smoking our cigars, a number of inoffensive birds are pining in anguish and dying by inches because we shoot *into the brown of them.* Unhappily, some cripples will be lost, shoot how you will, for "driving" I am sure not only increases the bag but augments the suffering one thousand fold.

The old system was far more laborious, but to my mind, beyond all comparison, superior. *It required talents of no common order,* and every man was not calculated to take the lead. One man, the best sportsman, was required for that position, and possibly to work the dogs. The keeper ought to be competent to do this ; and any intelligent man might learn how to *keep* dogs right in one day's shooting, although not even-tempered or persevering enough to "make" them—which is another thing. If the keeper *can* do this, he relieves his master and improves his shooting, for *handling dogs and killing birds do not go well together.* And if the dogs are well handled it will probably be by the man who broke them, and to whom justly belongs the credit of the display, though something is due to the discernment of the man who bought them, and more to the breeder who sends out a good one.

The head of the party has sometimes to choose between two evils—giving his dogs the wind and driving grouse off his moor, or taking his dogs up and walking that beat without them. The latter is perhaps the best course ; but under any circumstances he will lose no time by beginning at the lowest point down wind, and giving his dogs the advantage of it all day. If the wind is light, or imperceptible by other means, he may ascertain its direction by throwing up a few of those downy feathers which are always lying *perdu* in the game pocket. Having arrived at his starting point, he should place a sharp-sighted boy or two in commanding situations, to mark and try, as he beats with his setters, to drive the birds towards some favourable " laying."

He will effect this by *keeping that outside gun well forward, which he wishes to head the birds from him*, and, indeed, by beating in an oblique line. He must not go right ahead, for thus he could not command a wide beat ; but he must take a side wind, and then come back. But all this will depend upon the nature of the ground and the covert he tries. If he works the dogs, he must know precisely when to whistle and signal them, so as to control their quarter if they range too wide of his party ; and none must interfere with the dogs except he to whom that responsible office is assigned. In hunting dogs for the gun the wind is everything. Let the scent be blown *to* them, and, if the piece is wide, it must be given to dogs by diagonal or oblique parallels.

In ordinary cases, when dogs want blood, follow birds marked down, having first called the dogs to heel, but if the dogs are doing well *never think of the bag*, and, above all, never think of your last miss, or of the possibility of missing.

The whole line must move gently forward, and not fast. There ought to be *no talking*, but at any rate no noise ; and when the dogs point and back they should be approached *with perfect silence and the greatest deliberation.*

To one or two " outsiders " the duty falls of marking the birds killed ; to another marking those unscathed, which are certain to flap their wings before they settle, and probably fly farther than a novice would suppose. Any of the party first observing the dogs pointing may call the attention of the line to that fact by raising his hand, when the leader will signal how they are to be approached.

A brace of dogs will often be enough, but when the ground is severe, a leash or two brace may be used with advantage : and, provided they are clever and well broken, *the more the better.*

When the birds have fallen to the gun, the retriever may be set to work. He should be close to his master's leg, or at the downcharge, and *one dog only* can be used at a time. The dead birds ought to be recovered without him, but if they are lost, he should be taken to the place where they were supposed to fall *after the runners are secured*, and his owner, pointing to the place, should let him work deliberately, and *give him plenty of time.*

Then he may be put upon the winged, or sent after the towered birds, and when all are retrieved he must resume his place by his master's side; the setters may be signalled to hunt again, and the sport proceeds.

This retrieving—the deliberation required for enforcing the downcharge, the contemplation of a magnificent point, and the steady pace of the line of guns—gives a little time for rest and enables us to contemplate the wonderful instinct and sagacity of our dumb companions; and it is something to talk over when we sit by the great fire at night. To my mind this method is far to be preferred to the insane scamper of a line of guns who take their chance of grouse, or very likely walk over the majority of them, lying hidden where nothing but a dog could detect their presence. But those who shoot will have their own way, and amuse themselves according to their fancy, whilst, so long as fashion dictates "driving" men will drive.

I anxiously expect the time when men will hunt foxes without hounds, or possibly without foxes. The latter feat I accomplished verily when, in pursuit of "aniseed" and with a few mangy hounds, I hunted "the drag" at Oxford, and ascertained the depth of Waterperry Brook.

Still I will not believe, as a recent writer has stated, that the pointers and setters bred by such men as Mr. Garth, Mr. Whitehouse, Mr. Francis, Mr. Meir, of Tunstall, Mr. Comberbatch, the blue blood of grand old Hamlet, or Queen, or Beau, or Bounce, or Jill, or the mighty Drake, will be lost or undervalued in the future, or that the setters bred by Mr. Statter, Mr. Bevan, or last and not least, "Stonehenge," will ever glare wildly from glass cases in the British Museum, as specimens of an extinct race.

The steam horse has done wonders, but the steam dog will never range the moor. There are limits to young England's speed, though I hope not to his endurance, when he moves northward to the land of whisky, new milk, and heather.

I.—FLAPPER SHOOTING.

Many excellent sportsmen would not go a hundred yards to get the best river shooting which is procurable in July, because, having plenty of money and time at their own disposal, they can find abundant amusement suited to the time of year. Like my friend "in the City," their excellent keeper will take care that "the best retriever in England" is at concert pitch when they fly northward in August; and, until they hand over all business to the bailiff, steward, or "agent," who now dubs himself esquire, they have London and country amusements galore from "morn to dewy eve."

Those with whom "ponies and monkeys" are abundant, and who do not object to bidding them adieu for ever, have the range of all the race meetings one after the other; but to the uninitiated in handicaps and the Racing Calendar the croquet lawn presents much the same excitement, whilst at any rate the danger of losing cash or notes is reduced to a minimum.

Not having a yacht myself (unless I may dignify by that title my duck punt and spritsail); being beyond the range of ices, where refrigerators as yet have not penetrated, and a water cart is as uncommon as "the noted" black swan of Latin Grammar celebrity—I have to seek for a change of temperature by the river's brink, and to escape the chances and dangers of sunstroke amongst the shady poplars.

Sydney Smith it is, I believe, who accuses the Englishman of always desiring to kill something on a fine day. I don't feel that myself; but I do know that a gun in the hand, and a good dog behind or in front of one, changes a wretched constitutional walk into exhilarating and healthy exercise.

At Oxford we had two descriptions of summer birds: first, he who did the High-street in a new glossy hat, a frock coat, patent leather boots, gloves of the most delicate tint, with a tie the gods might envy, and perhaps be persuaded to wear about the hips. He was generally attached to a *confrère* as exquisite, who, if his right hand were free, brandished an Algerian myrtle or "clouded cane." The other sect were to be found on the Isis or the Cherwell, or having a bit of practice off Lillywhite's bowling at Bullington Green; whilst the faster lot, whether the ground was good or bad for it, got up a scratch race of Oxford hacks, or sent them flying at the hurdles by way of practice. The last division, by far the most numerous, form the nucleus of the coming sportsmen; and having one of the lot staying with me last month—a period of the year when there is little going on—I was glad to show him somewhat of rural amusements, most of which are now to be had by the river side.

We had a bye day with the rats, which are always thick about kennels, but the sport was meagre, so we gave it up until the corn should be garnered, and these wary rodents betook themselves to their winter haunts again.   In the nick of time I got a hint that there were lots of young ducks amongst the flags and osiers, about a mile before you got to the old church and that overshot mill beyond it.   Next day (the interval seemed twelve months to my young comrade) we put up the breechloaders, and started for the river in the valley yonder, where they are trying, but I fear fruitlessly, to preserve, or rear, or breed salmon, and reduce its price from 2s. 6d., stale and tasteless, to 8d., fresh and with the curd.

The boat, moored under the old Monks-bridge, is awaiting us, and the surly blacksmith, who knows every twist and turn of the stream, and every hole where with the cast net he can get "bait," gives us a frowning welcome.   Although he would make believe that we have kept him waiting, he begins with a morose gesture to bale the water out.   By way of making things pleasant, my young cub, who is quick enough at discerning any human being's weakness except his own, affects an extreme intimacy with Vulcan, though until then he had never seen him, and offers him a few grains of consolation, which in reality are only chaff.

I see at once that it is best to cut matters short, and placidly direct the smith (whose countenance grows darker as the suspicion is aroused that some of his finer feelings are being played upon) to go down stream and show us where he last saw "them eight ' flappers ' as could fly like old 'uns."

Loosing, with a twitch that manifested extreme impatience, what I suppose, to speak nautically, I ought to call the painter, but what my stable boy persists in calling the halter, our boatman signalled with his head in the direction of some bullrushes, and intimated, in a few by no means well-chosen words, "That's about where they was last Sunday when the bells was going for morning church."

At the spot he showed me, the bullrushes, six or eight feet above the water, were as thick as they well could be, and, though the water was four or five feet deep or more, a dog could almost walk upon them, especially where the young broods had been in the habit of roosting for the night, and had beaten them flat down like the old-age rush-strewn floors.

A few patches of what decoymen call "bright water" could be seen as we walked along the banks, bored by water voles for miles, and whereon in one place I could see the spraints of an otter, and the grassy knoll where he had curled himself round to

enjoy the sun, after well beating down the grass, that nothing
might obstruct his view or shelter an enemy.

From the boat, which he thrust through the tangled mass of
weeds inch by inch, the blacksmith was thrashing the strong
rushes with his punt pole, and making those inarticulate sounds
which from time immemorial have been supposed to rouse woodcocks or hares, rabbits and other prey. He had just beaten a
flowering rush to pieces, and its pink petals were drifting down
the stream, when there was what he called a " scuttle " amongst
the stalks and weeds, and something—as yet it might be moor-
hens—was " playing back and forrard," as he told us with an
excited countenance which for the moment made him look positively handsome. True enough, his was a countenance that
looked best when lighted up—which means, observe, that at no
other time was it fit to be seen. " I suppose," he suggested,
with a confidential wink, " the young gentleman on the bank
yonder knows these flappers don't fly so fast as old uns." And
then, in a sort of Surrey Theatre " aside," he roared to my
academic friend in a slightly vindictive way, " I say you, shoot
slap at 'em when they gets up, and mind you don't mull it."
" Won't your dog go in the water ?" he continued, looking at my
retriever ; " why, he ought to go and hunt these rushes like a
spaniel "—advancing the opinion, which he offered to corroborate
by a bet of " any money " that Mr. Somebody had one, a sort of
mixed breed, that would drive every duck between that spot and
the next five miles, to dry ground or the heavens as sure as anything. " At any rate," he added confidentially, " they musn't
hide in the water." This was no news to me, for I have seen
an Irish spaniel do wonders in such water, and a good terrier or
small spaniel, when fond of swimming, is an excellent animal for
the sport, but curly retrievers, as a rule, are the best of water
dogs.

I had hoped to have the assistance of a couple of good water
dogs, and so I explained to him ; and I did not depend upon my
usual retriever to do anything except fetch a cripple or dead
bird. For river shooting you want a dog especially adapted to
the sport, and fond of it ; and unless you have one, in wide
rivers as this was, you lose half your labour.

When a river is thirty, forty, or (at the bends) fifty yards wide,
and one mass of weeds, which make the surface of the water dark
even in a glaring sun, and, when to this is added the shadow of
thorn bushes, alders, tall poplars, and the obscure nooks and

crevices formed by old pollard willows "askant" the brook, it is very easy for the dusky brood of young ducks to get *back* without splash or observation; and this they will do unless they are pressed hard to fly, because they know they are safe in the water, and as yet have not made sufficient proof of their flight to trust to their wings unless you force them. I myself saw several "head back," and, plunging into the osiers, they were seen no more; but of the lot our boatman saw we sprang three or four, and yet, owing to bad shooting. killed but one of them. Two, turning to the right, deserted the stream, and, making across the meadow, got moderately high up in the air; then, drawing up their feet as ducks do when preparing to ascend beyond the gun's range, they made for a bend of the stream behind us, into which we marked them.

Whether because we had no dogs, or because there were few ducks or many to pursue them, our bag that day was small, and much inferior to what years ago I used to get with a famous liver-and-white spaniel and an old muzzle-loader, which, though an undoubted killer, was, as my old boatman used to say, *hardly* safe for a gentleman unless he insured his life. There we used often to walk the birds up in the deep grass, or the spaniel puzzled them out, for they left the river at the sound of our boat; and I have now and then shot six or eight of them in a four-acre water meadow, and missed as many more.

There is some very charming river shooting not far from Stock-bridge, in Hampshire, where they shoot the flappers in this way; nor does it materially influence the winter wildfowl shooting, or disturb the "lead" as it is called—that is, the tendency and disposition of birds to harbour there as they come from (let us say) Iceland or—but I leave this to naturalists and "professors."

This last July I was most fortunate in seeing such river and rushes and wild country as I don't think I ever saw before, and scarce expect to see again. The land—part of a manor of nine thousand acres—is wild as in the days of coracles and ancient Britons, and presents doubtless precisely the same features as it did in the olden time! It would have been, as Royal Academicians say, "in keeping" had a herd of Chillingham cattle charged us in that valley of water meadows, or if a naked savage had scuttled across the "broad" of one of those rushing streams in his wicker boat.

I won't anticipate further the flapper shooting I went to see, but, without aiming at effect, "loose my shaft," as the gentleman archer said in the play.

Certainly the men of old well knew the line that separated the sterile and the fertile ground; and I have noticed this positive knowledge all the way where heath land cuts in, from Dorchester to Woking. As I crossed the heath road leading to Moreton station, and came upon the lodge gates and shrubbery, I was much struck with this fact; outside the entrance the ground would starve a peewit, but inside you came upon good oaks, fine old beeches, and white-barked birch trees which form the commencement of a thoroughly shaded avenue of about two miles. It is but occasionally that you can see the light overhead—for which I had no need to look, as in that hot July day I was thankful for the shade, only interrupted now and then for a yard or two as I drove along. I was of course too late for the rhododendrons, which were making their seed pods now, their green leaves charmingly contrasting with last year's autumn leaves, that hid the ground, except where the bright and rare ferns were growing luxuriantly.

Here and there was a fine holly many a foot in girth, and now and then larch and lime. In such a situation larch does no harm, because, although pheasants will roost in them—or, indeed, in any tree they can see their way well up to—the covert is well guarded by a thick, impenetrable belt, in which at dusk hardly any poacher would care to entangle himself. Along the wide drive I kept on at a slow pace, grateful for the shade, and glad to know that I was twenty minutes before my time, for I had to get over a good many miles before I could say my day's drive was done. At last I came to an old wide short bridge, with a rapid shallow steam of clear water shooting under it, so clear that I could count the pebbles. A turn to the left, and I am told by my guide—a little girl with a physic bottle, whom I picked on the heath, for she held up the said bottle with its white tippet of instructions, and begged for a lift for the sake of the laundress at the House, who, she said, had got "the rescivelas " (erysipelas) —I am told by my guide, I say, that as soon as I get through the next gate I shall see the Squire's great house beyond the bridge, and the church on the right hand opposite.

I find her description true enough; for, emerging from the dark drive, crossing two rivers, I am in a fine old park stretching away, so far as I can see, for miles. To the right, almost hidden by (I think) plane trees, are the old hunting stables; beyond,

high up on, as it seems to me, an artificial mound, one of the
most highly decorated churches in the country; and all of this
mirrored in—what shall I say?—eight or ten acres of broad clear
water.

As my wheels grate upon the gravel, up rise a flock of wild
ducks from this sheet of shallow water, and, circling over my
head, almost near enough, as it seems, to knock my hat off, they
drop into the water like a charge of grape. As I rise the hill I
come upon the old mansion—but not so very old, for opposite
the dark stain on the grass shows where the old one stood a
hundred years ago.

Be that as it may, the present house is of old Purbeck stone,
grey with age and weather-stained; well contrasted, on the other
side, with that line upon line of scarlet geraniums which, a mile
or so beyond, intimates the garden walk, and separates the well-
mown pasture, where otherwise the eye would fail to distinguish
lawn from gravel.

As I thought more of the outdoor attractions than of what the
owner could offer me inside, I was glad to get at once to the side
of these two rivers, which run parallel, and, being admirably
skirted with rushes eight or ten feet high, form the best shelter
for wild duck which it has ever been my lot to see. Of course a
straight river is little better than a pond for ducks. The best wildfowl shooting you can get by river sides is in those streams which
run zigzag and at sharp angles, as do the Frome and Piddle.

The shooting begins about a quarter of a mile from the house,
and, by commencing in the middle and starting in opposite
directions, it would be easy to make two or even four parties for
July or winter duck shooting. Only let them be composed of
men who won't talk, or cough, or sneeze, or call out, or whistle
(*sotto voce*) to come here or go there, or stop a minute, when it's
out of the question, and can't be done at any price.

I should say the stout keeper whom I met by appointment,
and who was described to me as a fund of information, must
have got his supernatural taciturnity from "biding" among the
ducks. But that his master kindly went with me, I should have
been utterly in the dark as to the best points and the choice
snipe bogs and trout holes, all of which interested me. Although
I am ignorant, to my sorrow, of the art of fishing, I am glad to
be made acquainted by an experienced hand of the salmon
hatching and rearing going on here, and of the best place for a
plunge on a sultry day.

It was with no slight gratification that I saw the charming double bends and high rushes of the Frome (and to describe one river is to describe both), and was shown by the stout old keeper in dumb show, and by the master in a few words, the way they manage to kill almost any number of flappers in summer or mallards in the snow and ice.

There must be five or six miles of walking by the river side, and if you shoot both together the guns would be a quarter of a mile apart. Two guns to each river is the usual thing, and these take it in turns to go to the head or end of the piece beaten, which always is a bend. As you walk along the young ducks flutter on, and there is little weed to hide them. At the bend they see themselves headed, and up they go at once. When the stream is weedy the old grizzled retriever will put them up, but he is seldom required, except to recover dead birds floating down the stream.

In a sort of amphitheatre formed by woods descending to the plain I saw a capital locality for a decoy, and I heard that some huts had been put up there successfully. There were also some admirable clumps of osiers and alders, and, what ducks especially enjoy, water at different elevations, and consequently at varying temperatures. One reed bed, an especially favourite piece of lying with the silent keeper, held a number of flappers, some of which we got to fly, but most of them rushed into the green reeds and disappeared. As we returned they got up at nearly every bend in threes and fours together, and, stretching out for a flight, as it seemed to me, whirled round, and pitched in again close at hand.

All this first-rate duck shooting was one continuation of water weeds, with "spear," as they term the reed left when the grass is cut. This "spear' used to be the ditcher's perquisite, and he sold it to purchase his new water boots for the ensuing winter. Of course this spoilt the duck shooting and the duck breeding, and it is done away with.

I am very glad to find hereabouts, at any rate, a strong inclination to preserve wildfowl, and to encourage their breeding by keeping their haunts secluded.

True enough, they will never furnish the sport pheasants afford—if battue *is* sport—for at the first discharge they are on the wing, unless the place, like that I have endeavoured to describe, is adapted for the mallard by nature. Then I honestly believe that a couple of good guns might bring to bag as many

Q 2

head as any thorough sportsman could require, and meet with some such shooting as would pleasantly vary the monotony of the warm corner, and give even an old hand plenty to do as he calculated pace and range.

I know of but one place that equals Mr. Frampton's (above described) excepting always Mr. Drax, of Charborough's varied ground, in Dorsetshire and Kent, and that is the Longstock flapper shooting, situated near Stockbridge, in Hants, and lately the property of Mr. Joseph Anderson, of Piccadilly. There the natural advantages offered by the river for duck or trout could with difficulty be rivalled or excelled, except in extent and variety.

II.—PARTRIDGE SHOOTING.

Very little trouble is taken in the preservation of partridges, considering the sport they afford.

They are left to shift for themselves, and provided their eggs are neither broken nor stolen, most game preservers consider that they have done all that can be required of them.

The lordly pheasant is the aristocrat of the manor, and if he has "a good sprinkling of birds for breeding," the keeper never troubles himself about them.

A good deal might be done to increase the stock, I mean beyond the ordinary custom of putting those eggs which are mown out of clovers and grass under hens, although they cannot be bred in confinement like pheasants (at any rate only one or two instances are recorded). For instance the birds might be continually driven out of the clovers, and the fields might be "brushed" which they frequently are not. The keepers too, might give a *general* attention to the destruction of running vermin, or the prowling of stray dogs, especially towards the end of June, and they would in wet seasons add largely to their stock of birds by making scrapes in the wheel ruts, or water holes for the escape of the young birds which constantly fall in when their feathers are wet and "draggled."

But, partridge shooting is not so favourite a sport as it was, when very few men comparatively emigrate to the north. "Lor, bless you," a friend of mine said to me as we were lunching one September afternoon, in the shade of a vast beech tree, with thirty odd brace hung up to cool among the branches. *"Lor bless you, after the moors these birds seem no better than biggish beetles! I always think of a cockchafer when I see one get up."* He was no exception to the generality, who, after they have passed the meridian of life "go out for an hour or two," and leave the most of it to the lads home for the "long vacation" or "the young 'un on leave."

I know cases where the old keeper has had simply to supply the house season after season ; and, too indolent to do it in any other way, he has potted the majority of the covey as they "juked" in a cluster under the new ricks.

In the old times the sport was excellent, I mean when you were dependent on good dogs for all you brought home, and unless you were a sportsman, you came empty away.

To succeed in the legitimate way you must be to the *manor* born, and possess most of the talents Beckford pronounces indispensable in a huntsman.

Patience, perseverance, coolness, quiet, perception, all of these gifts *were* required to achieve success, and it took half a dozen seasons to make a finished sportsman. Now, all the wearied Londoner need do will be to bring his breechloader, his cartridges, his boots, gaiters, and knickerbockers, to walk in line and blaze away.

The keeper will manœuvre you over the piece of turnips or clover, and you need not even wait your dead birds or cripples, all the Metropolitan need give his mind to will be not to shoot friend or "beater." The rest is a matter of "condition." You need not give dogs the wind—probably there are none on the manor save the keeper's retriever in a string, and you can keep your coveys off your neighbour's country.

They began this system more than forty years ago, but it has become *general* during the last dozen years. Five and forty years ago " the Paper Hawk" was in common use " to accommodate the gluttons," many of whom desired to rival " Sir Charles Cuyler who, on the 1st of September, 1825, bagged, in two hours and thirty-five minutes, 103 partridges."

Twelve or thirteen years before this, a man was a wonder who could shoot flying.

Guns, too, were fabulously dear. Colonel Thornton mentions one of his as costing 400 guineas. This was in the time of the First Consul, who frequently gave as much as 800 guineas for a gun, when he desired to make a present to a foreign prince. It is said that a pair of pistols from the Versailles manufactory would cost 400*l.*

Old Joe Manton not uncommonly got 100 guineas for a double barrel, and I believe, old Westley Richards was the first man to make a thoroughly good article at about a fourth of the money. Nowadays you can get a plain, and I believe, a safe breech-loader *for a ten pound note,* I don't recommend these guns because I don't feel enough confidence in them to use them myself, but many do use them and don't complain, but what would be a man's reflection, supposing he found his hand blown to pieces by the bursting of one of these bargains made by inferior workmen, ground down to the last farthing of wages, and harried in their work by the rapacity of middlemen.

If you want sport use pointers or setters. If you are solicitous about your own eyes and limbs as well as those of your companions, use good tools which can't be sold at less than twenty or twenty-five guineas, buy Eley's blue cartridges ; and if you simply want birds or a walk, or exercise, or anything but sport, you may walk in a line and kill what gets up or miss it.

III.—HARES.

If harriers and greyhounds were extinct, I should heartily wish there were no hares to be found.   They have frequently made the stitches of my shooting jacket "grin" when I have gone out for a quiet walk with a gun and a brace of dogs ; and very frequently they have imperilled the steadiness of a canine pupil, and given me occasion for extra vigilance and strictness for weeks to come.   In fact, nothing bothers you like the hares ; and frequently we have left them to take their chance on a hot September day, hanging them on the forks of trees or hedges, preferring the chance of losing them to the trouble of carrying them about.

Worst of all, in my opinion, they are not worth carriage ; nor are they presentable at the table except as soup.   Tastes differ, however, and puss was a favourite with the Roman epicures. The only part of the quadruped I could ever tolerate is a slice down the back ; but old Horace preferred the shoulders, and says,

Fecundi leporis, sapiens sectabitur armos ;

whilst Martial declares her to be the best of all quadrupeds for the table; but much he must have known of gastronomy, who gave it as his opinion that the thrush was the best of birds!

The laws of Moses and Mahomet forbid Jews and Moslems to touch the flesh of the hare; the ancient Briton considered it an enervating diet, and eschewed it lest he should become timid and cowardly. Cato, however, declares that hare soup provokes peaceful slumbers, and Pliny states that to feed on hares for seven days in succession will make the victim "beautiful for ever," and prevent, I imagine, any occasion for Madame Rachel and her Arabian balm. Various properties are ascribed to the animal. The hind foot worn in the pocket is said to cure rheumatism. The only real use of it is, in my opinion, to paint the cheeks of the funny man before he "goes on," for which purpose he keeps it in a hole in the wall with his pot of rouge. It was considered capable of foretelling events by its course and other signs in the days of Boadicea, who, just before her last battle with the Romans, let one escape from her bosom. It took what her soldiers thought a lucky line, animated them with courage, and perhaps tended to their success.

The chest of the hare is formed so as to give the lungs an abundance of play, and advocates of coursing argue from this that the hare was formed to be hunted; whilst it would be more in accordance with fact to say that greyhounds, from the very earliest days of which any record remains, were bred and educated to catch the hare. In her form she can take in a large *circle* of observation, but she has difficulty in perceiving any motionless object straight before her. Thus, if a hare is approaching in a direct line, supposing that the sportsman remains perfectly still, she will almost to a certainty canter close to his feet, and offer a capital shot as she turns to the right or left. Her hearing is most acute, and as she flies over a down or fallow, with her ears laid back, she is sensible of the exact position of her pursuers.

We had been talking of hares all one evening in November before the large peat fire of a friend's billiard room, and had searched Daniel's "Rural Sports" and many quaint old authors in the light of the large French "moderator" which lit the billiard table, and made all the *salon* as light as day. The truth was, we had assembled to discuss the first truffles of the season and a roasted turkey, and to arrange a party to kill down the hares before the frost drove them from swedes to young wheat and grass, and injured the farmers considerably.

We had killed a good many all the season. It had been a capital partridge year, and the hares were numerous also—two things which don't always go together. A couple of brace of birds don't fill a basket without a hare; and sometimes we killed two or three hares to every brace of birds. Then, if we had to go down a long hedgerow to get the wind, it was a continuation of sport to take up the pointers (which I always ran in leather collars and " D " links), couple them, and try the ditches and hedges with clumbers as we go on. Many a straying pheasant we put back into the woods by this system, and many a partridge we got with the spaniels, which never came within the range of Major and Peter, who were as wary of a hedgerow as if it were made of "wait-a-bit" thorns.

But, compared with what we found in the open at the first part of the season, the hedgerow hares were scanty. They seemed to enjoy a form in the short stubbles when the day was calm ; and perhaps in the extreme heat the shadow of the large, vigorous turnip leaves, where it was difficult to shoot them in the head ; or the rank mustard, in which they escaped frequently with impunity, unless we got a lucky snap shot as they vaulted over "the thick."

" Shoot all you can, sir," said old Bertie to me one of these delicious September mornings (as he, by my desire, was preparing to administer correction to one of the most resolute young setter bitches it was ever my good fortune to possess, and who persisted in following a hare for twenty or thirty yards in spite of the punishment which she knew must succeed) ; " shoot all you can, sir, they are all witches, every one of 'em."

I made no answer just then, for I don't like talking when dog-breaking and shooting are going on, but when we got to a fine old yew tree where luncheon was waiting for us in the shade, I called him up from the respectful distance at which he had posted himself with the keeper and the dogs, to ask him what he meant.

There was no shyness about him, for he had always been used, as he said, " to talk to gentlemen," and as I furnished him with tobacco he filled his pipe, and at once gave me the information wanted.

" As to their being witches or not," he said, " all I can say is, if ever I got into trouble it was a hare as done it. When I was

quite a youngster, and work was very short at home, I remember
going off to get a job for a few weeks, and, as I hated idleness, I
thought I might as well try and catch a few of Squire Drax's
hares. So I stayed at home one day and made a lot of wires,
and borrowed my mother's maiden name (Summers it was) until
I came back, in case I should be caught. It was the end of the
harvest, and they had just begun to be busy thrashing, for the
farmers said they were short of straw, but we all know what that
means, and that many a farmer is short of other things at Mile-
mass (Michaelmas). So I soon got a job where there was a lot of
barley thrashing ; and as I was a stranger, and terrible strong, I
took the straw away, and out of pride, like, carried about twice
as much as any of 'em. The second day I was there the young
squire came along and his keeper, and got talking to my new
master about the hares, which it seems were rather too thick just
over the turnpike-road where the wide grass rides and the
keeper's lodge and the fir plantations were. Well, I thought I
could shorten the stock for them. So, not that night, but the
next, I went and set six wires in the fir copse, and I got five
hares next day. It's always been my motto, a poacher will do
best close to the keeper's house. There's most game there, and
the keeper thinks no one will have the impudence to trap and wire
close to his door. I waited a day or two and set more wires—
twelve or fourteen this time, and, as I did before, when the
machine stopped for dinner, I sauntered up the hedgerow, and
begun at the lower end. There was nothing in 'em until I came
up to a large, thick old fir tree, and there she was all right and
dead ; but as I took her out, I fancied the wire was very slack
round her throat, and her head wasn't swelled a bit. However,
I sets the wire again and was just getting up, when I heard some
one in the tree sing out, ' *Think it will do now, Mr. Summers?* '
and then I was caught. I was only fined, it's true, but I lost my
place, and the lawyer charged me as much as I was ten days
earning ; and all through a hare ! The same with a lurcher or a
gate-net; they gives that ghastly scream and startles watchers,
and brings everything down upon you before you can get out of
the way, directly you drop upon 'em, if you don't look alive and
break their necks. I recollect that Mr. Smith, as lived at Ted-
worth, who never was afraid of nothing, used to say that the
scream of a hare went through him just like a knife, and if ever
you had seen him ride, as I have years agone, you'd say *he*
wasn't squeamish.''

According to the old man's theory, hares made the "bonds" for faggots break, caused tipsy carters to fall from waggon shafts, and were at the bottom of all the evil in the parish, Whether or not, I knew they had broken up many a homestead, and I killed and always will kill them early—*very* early in the season, for you get more of them, and you prevent all mischief, and, what is of equal importance, all grumbling. Indeed, no landlord can be guilty of greater cruelty and injustice than he perpetrates by keeping a stock of hares until the middle of January, when, if the weather is hard, they feed on agriculturists just as the Roman lamprey was fed on slaves.

If the hares are well shot in the partridge months, and subsequently hedgerows are beaten and shot also, the first brush through the coverts, what I may call the cock pheasant shooting, may be conducted without reference to ground game. You may have two lines of guns (one forward) with impunity ; and if you care to kill hares then, the first row of guns can kill them, provided they don't shoot back, or the guns posted at the end of the wood may kill them as they scour across the fields, for other coverts.

In hare shooting you require wide rides and open weather, as in frost you cannot fix the net stakes ; and when the shooting is deferred until late in the season, careful keepers take care to put their stakes ready in the ground two or three days before. You must then have the beaters pretty thick, and take care that they keep their sticks going and their tongues quiet. You must place good shots on the outside in the open, and men who will not, of course, shoot into covert or at hares in the hedges, or some of the parties may return home minus their usual complement of eyes. When you have experienced covert shots shooting together, they will know how to take advantage of the ground—when to get forward to the bare places beneath a wide-spreading oak, for instance, or when to go twenty yards or more in advance of the beaters to where the dead fern is flattened by the snow and offers no obstacle to the gun.

In all covert shooting it is desirable to wear dark or "pronounced" colours. Anything like grey or shepherd's plaid assimilates too closely with the stems of trees or old gateposts, and I once nearly became a victim to this invisible dress. In driving hares it is desirable, too, that the ground game should see you, as it is less likely to go back, and thus be left for breeding.

The slaughter of hares is to me so uninteresting that I shall not inflict the particulars of the day's sport upon the readers of the *Field*. It is redeemed from all idea of cruelty by the knowledge that hares increase, and that they must be killed, and that every dead hare is so much saved for the agriculture of the country.

One of the best sportsmen I know does as I advise all to do where there is no public coursing; and as that is, I belivee, generally confined to open country, hares there do but little harm. He kills his hares close down in September, he well brushes his coverts for them the latter end of October, and then gives his tenants such an amount of coursing as he can spare and as they require, which is neither more nor less than they deserve for the care they take of his game; and when he finishes his shooting, killing cocks and hens, he takes care to have the best covert shots, and no others, and kills what hares he wants.

"I lived with him once," said Bertie, "and we used to say to the head keeper, ' We must have good guns for mixed covert shooting, Windsor ' (that was the keeper's name); ' no London lawyers and parliamentary agents; I'd as soon go out shooting with Esther Took ' (that was the squire's old nurse)."

I will add one hint to those who desire to get up a good stock of hares. Let your keepers drive the clovers at dusk and send your hares into covert. They are safe for that night at all events.

IV.—PHEASANT SHOOTING.

The system of shooting pheasants has been almost entirely changed since dealers have been allowed to sell game. The birds were neither bred in such profusion nor killed in such numbers in the old days ; and, if they had been so killed, our forefathers would have been puzzled to know what they should do with them.

We used to begin pheasant shooting in October, and to find them occasionally with pointers and setters. Not that I at all countenance such a proceeding : it makes a setting dog hang to the hedge, for which fault no other excellence can atone, and it also teaches him to " keep drawing," which is not like an artist.

The land was not cultivated on scientific principles, and any old postboy or coachman turned farmer. The hedgerows were wide, the margins of the small inclosures deep in grass and weeds, forming admirable laying for every description of game, and there could be no more enjoyable sport than walking with a couple of clumbers broken to hunt, one on one side of the fence, the other on the other, and to furnish occupation for a pair of guns, or perhaps two pair, the additional pair by turns taking the outsides or going to the ends of the strips or thick boundaries of the fields.

These days were not concluded with the vast bouquet of pheasants, some escaping to furnish sport for next year, others going off with their legs hanging down, and perhaps the majority blown to fragments and falling a tangled mass of bones, blood, and feathers; but there was the exercise, the talent of the dogs, the keen appetite, and far more excitement than we obtain under the present system.

Battue shooting is the sport of wealthy men, and it would be better named " something to do " than sport. We must agree to an enormous outlay for a few hours' sport. *I state deliberately that I have frequently formed one of a party where I believe the sport to have cost little less than one hundred pounds an hour.* I put the outside value upon the pheasants when I say they were worth £40, the hares £12, the woodcocks £6, and rabbits there were none worth mentioning—all of which game was given away. I have commenced shooting this large covert at half-past one or later in the day with some such results as those I name, and the staff of keepers, the barley, and various expenses were never met by the sum of 600*l*. per annum, Occasionally the covert has been shot a second time, but not with equal results. This, however, would reduce the cost of the sport per hour by one half, and I am, I admit, putting an extreme case. I am alluding to a pheasant preserve on which no expense was spared, to give some notion of what these large bags cost.

When the battue shall take place depends upon the will of the preserver of pheasants. The true friend to the foxhounds manages that his coverts shall be shot as early as possible that he may not interfere with " the noble science;" others finish on February 1, without reference to fox-hunting, which possibly is not patronised in their vicinity.

A moderate sportsman can manage to beat a small covert so that it shall form a part of the day's sport—that is, to beat it with reference to several other small coverts; but it is not every man who can manage a large pheasant preserve. This can be accomplished by a good sportsman and a man who is something more, and by no others. Many an excellent gamekeeper can rear and protect game, but he wants the skill to *show* it. He lets his pheasants run back, or he " flushes " them badly, or in the wrong place.

I could name many men who possess the faculty of beating coverts (let me say of directing the beating) in an eminent degree, and I have heard, and I know, that the noble owner of Holkham is at the head of this class.

You must have men well disciplined and well protected, and you must expel all babblers and skirters from the pack. If they are not well protected from thorns by long leggings, they not only will not go through them, but they cannot. Every man should have a white " slop." This protects his clothes and shows him to the guns ; besides which, the ground game see and move from him more readily than if he were in dark clothes.

He ought also to have gloves and a stick. He must use his stick and not his tongue ; and on the silence of the beaters, the constant rattle of their sticks, and their keeping in line and not shirking " the thick," the success of the beating depends. The under keeper should be at one end of the line of beaters, and an intelligent man—a night-watcher, for example, who knows the wood, or some one who comprehends the arrangements—should be at the other. Frequently the under keeper is required to superintend the running of the nets, and then the beaters are left with a very inferior head or leader, unless the owner of the covert or some friend who knows the ground walks with the beaters at the end and keeps them in order.

The head keeper has to " place the guns," and (according to John Leech, himself a good sportsman and unrivalled satirist) to order " two lords on the right, two more lords on the left, a couple more forward, and the commoners to walk with the beaters."

Three or four men are required to carry the game ; they walk a few paces behind the beaters, bring the game out at the end of each strip, and consign it to the head keeper, who places it in a row, counts it, and consigns it to his cart in waiting just beyond —sometimes not beyond—the guns.

Some head keepers (I am supposing the head keeper to be the general manager of the sport) place stops at the end of every important strip ; and if the strip faces the open, or is contiguous to an enemy's country, they should be so placed. This function is generally performed by an old ex-keeper, an invalid or a cripple, who keeps tapping the trees with his stick as he walks to and fro ; and any small boy is equal to this situation, *provided that a man is left to take care that he performs it!*

In this battue shooting it is desired to drive the pheasants to a particular spot where they may be easily shot, and where an *abattoir* has been prepared from which they will rise a few at a time. This is managed in various ways. Sometimes the underwood is cut and " splashed " down into a mass or mat about two feet high. Sometimes long fir poles are fixed horizontally at intervals, and fir branches are leant against them so as to form a sort of large tent, beneath which the birds will run.

If you " go in " for this " sport," a great deal depends upon the way the birds are flushed ; and there is need of great experience to get them to the place and to put them up for slaughter when they have reached the shambles.

Some men are indifferent as to the day's sport provided they get a good finish, which, by the way, often is put off until it is too dark to distinguish cocks from hens.

When this good finish is desired, no nets are placed at the ends of the squares of covert into which the preserve is marked out, and numbers of birds and hares run on, never presenting a mark for the guns, which are posted in front of the beaters, and are shooting towards the advancing line. I need hardly say that when the beaters come near the guns, and rabbits are thick and pheasants fly low, or are shot by " snap shots " directly they appear above the scrub or brushwood, I have frequently envied these men their position, especially when I have observed a little group around one or more of their body who owes his life to the thickness of his head, and is made fit to be shot at again by a half-crown and a pull at one of the gentlemen's flasks. It may be want of taste, but I confess that I consider no cock-fighting could have been equal to this—especially when the gun that " potted " him is very severe with him for being "in the way when he pulled."

There is always some danger from the jealous shots who shoot across each other, and, as it appears to the disinterested observer, shoot *at* each other. There is considerable amusement in contemplating the greedy shot trying for the best place, and endeavouring to appear indifferent as he walks by the guns posted " by authority,"—which is not considered a polite thing to do. There is always one man or more who, in spite of warning or advice, runs on before the beaters, by which means he puts up game which no one is at hand to shoot, and escapes uninjured by a miracle. There is frequently the man with the last new thing in breech-loaders, which won't go off, or from which he can't get the cartridge, or which won't shut or won't open, or of which an important part breaks, or is left behind, or does not " act ;" and there is always the man who can put it to rights, and who probably breaks or bends a vital part of it, and beats a precipitate retreat. There is generally a victim or two to " converted guns." One of these I met not long ago, who appealed to me in doleful accents. " My gun," he said, " wont shoot, and the fellow charged me 15*l.* for doing it ; and now, when I complain, he says he can't help that—he had done all he can to make it, and so I must put up with it. I have lost a good muzzle-loader, and I possess a bad breech-loader, and I am minus 15*l.*" (By the way, I should like to see a class for converted guns at the next " *Field* trial.") Then there is the old man who wears "stick up" collars, and shoots with a single muzzle-loader, which he possibly lectures upon at lunch ; and there is sure to be the man with the new gun which "won't kill,"—the "swell," as the beaters call him, with his pair of Lang's or Purdey's, and his loader, who is a hybrid, being a gentleman with kitchen grammar, a valet, and a footman all in one. The rest of the party is formed by the man who, having a reputation, and knowing it probably, misses all day long, to the delight, perhaps, of the next gun, who kills every time by a sort of " fluke." Yet we must not forget the class for whom this *battue* work is best fitted—I mean the old and inert sportsman, who has not lost the love of sport, but possibly wants the power of locomotion. Consequently, he has his camp-stool at the end of the beat, and his shooting pony and Somerset saddle close at hand. I have seen an old earl, now no more, take the field like a boy (an old boy), with the fattest of all loaders carrying two guns, and a vast umbrella slung behind him, wrapped in an old shepherd's plaid cloak, which he left for twelve months on the floor of a Scotch cabin a year before. Poor dear old Earl ! He had been one of the very keenest and best of sportsmen in his day, but then he was in everybody's way, and grumbling at the younger men who were killing the birds of whose whereabouts the poor old octogenarian had but a vague idea.

Now there is a great difference apparent as to the manner in which *battues* are managed. One man does quietly and well what another fails to do with any number of " cursory remarks."

Beaters can be managed by firmness and kindness, and they should be shown as clearly as possible where they have to go ; nor should they be hurried. In some situations, if they go fast they cannot drive the game. I do not think that, with the very best and most masterly beating, we ever see two head of game out of three in any covert. Hurry the men, and you don't see a quarter of it. Noise and clamour are destruction to all sport either in woodland or the open. Thus it is that one good gun alone, or two good guns, kill more in proportion than any larger number of guns combined. They come upon the game without being perceived. At the first roar of a beater's voice every hare is on the alert, and the old cock pheasants who have heard the heavenly voice before immediately begin to run, *for the pheasant is quite as fond of his legs as his wings.*

Occasionally, however, good "sport" may be obtained without gamekeepers, barley, vermin-trapping, or any of the expenses attendant upon *battues.* You may have a bouquet to order of cocks or hens, and all this independent of anything or everything but money.

I remember a wealthy purple-faced millionaire taking a place in the country some years ago (at which place he soon drank himself to death), and, as he had been invited to these festivals of pheasant slaughter, he determined that he would ask his friends in return. He had qualified himself for "sporting," as he called it, by purchasing Purdey guns in pairs, a duck punt and gun, about half a mile of netting, eight or ten brace of pointers, and a magnificent team of Clumber spaniels ; and of the way to use these guns, nets, and dogs he knew about as much as the hippopotamus calf which perished the other day. He told me confidentially, however, that he had seen the thing done in the manufacturing districts, "Like confectioners furnish suppers, you know,—they take back what is not coot" (cut). He explained that these gamedealers would take back the "dead 'uns," except such as were too much shot ; and these, he said, would make capital soup. Accordingly he had down about two hundred pheasants, mostly cocks, but with a sprinkling of hens, which the dealer told him "made it more like nature "—in the same way, I imagine, as hairdressers faintly streak the wigs of old gentlemen with grey in order that their demands upon our credulity may not be too large and exhausting.

The hampers or crates, each holding about a score of pheasants, were placed among the laurels at convenient distances, and into these laurels none of the guns were allowed to enter. This was the preremptory code of my wealthy friend.

I forget whether the Clumbers were used, or whether beaters aided in the deception (I was not there myself), but I heard it spoken of as magnificent sport, for whenever a hamper was opened there was a capital rise ; and as good open spaces were selected, few birds had a chance. Many, of course, were blown to bits, and these were a dead loss ; but every bird clean killed—except a few for presents—took three or four shillings off the cost price.

But the grand affair of all was to come at the last moment—the bouquet ! As described to me, it took place in an enormous bed of rhododendrons, and well in view of the bow windows of the drawing-room, within which Mrs. Millionaire and her friends were stationed to enjoy the spectacle. The butler had been sent down to superintend this *feu de joie* of pheasants ; but, alas ! he had not calculated on one fact. The bouquet pheasants came from a different dealer, who had fastened his hampers with wire ; so "Bottles" had to fetch his champagne nippers ; and whilst that plethoric individual was toddling to and fro, the guns were all waiting for the captives to be set free and shot at for " sport."

A keeper who was there, when alluding to this scene some two or three years after it occurred, concluded in these words : "Sir, you never see such a thing in yer life." I devoutly hope I never may !

V.—WILD FOWL.

Going to look for wild fowl has a peculiar charm for me ; and the harder the weather, the darker the night, the better I like it. Whether widgeon, teal, mallard, pochard, scoter, shoveller, or smew, the bird is so thoroughly wild, so absolutely distinct from the tame-bred bird, that I stalk the flock or wait the flight with feelings as different to what I entertain at a *battue* as those which actuate the buffalo hunter of the prairie or the butcher's slaughterman.

Many an evening late on in the summer, possibly just before the annual migration of pointers, setters, and retrievers by the Great Northern, I have followed the windings of a deep river,

R

whilst my black spaniel or my young Clumber has beaten the sedges in a quiet way, and put up the young flappers one by one. I remember once overcoming the difficulty I had with a young bitch of the same family as Mr. Price's Bruce, by constantly taking her to beat these river sides. I never saw one so averse to water, and the example of my black dog, who preferred swimming to walking, seemed to have no effect upon her timidity. However, I persevered, and one warm evening I cut down a couple of flappers, right and left. The black dog got the dead one, whilst the Clumber watched him nervously on the bank, and then he tried to overtake the cripple, which was swimming in a circle and beating the water with one wing. However, when he did reach the bird he could do nothing with him, and I tried to *silently* encourage the young Clumber to go in. My second attempt was successful, and, to my surprise, she swam well, not beating the water with her fore feet, nor making much fuss about it; and when she had fetched that bird she took to water, and gave me no more anxiety about retrieving from it.

We cannot all go to Norway, nor could we all catch a salmon if we did; and before the grouse shooting comes it is pleasant to have an opportunity of trying a new gun or a fresh retriever. Flapper shooting enables us to test both, and perhaps a strong old mallard going right away and killed handsomely at fifty or sixty yards is as satisfactory a proof of a gun's performance as any man could desire.

When this sport has come to an end, I have often waited between dark and light, in that soft twilight which all along the southern coast is known as "duckish," for the flights of young ducks going "stubbling."

Perhaps, as I rode along the lonely road, skirted on one side by a heath, which is to all appearance boundless, and on the other skirted by the sea, I have heard something whistle over my head like a charge of shot, and far beyond the range of the best Lang, Purdey, or Westley Richards ever made. I have seen a skein of ducks sailing away in a straight line for my neighbour's barley or mine. Poor innocents! they scarcely noticed me as they sailed over the road, and occasioned my black Labrador to assume that morgue expression as he wistfully looked over his shoulder at their retreating phalanx.

Well I mark their line by some conspicuous mound in the purple outline that shows out against the clear pale yellow of the setting sun, and I note the time to a minute. Next evening I unchain my black retriever, throw my leg over the brown cob, sling my gun, and, leaving my nag tied to the most convenient gate or fir-tree, post myself where I can best conceal myself in their last night's line.

As the exact minute approaches I begin to feel almost nervous, and wonder if my watch has been performing any of the freaks which make teeth and watches alike abominations—without which we cannot, however, get on in life. Within five minutes of their time! Surely it was not so dark last night; and now time drags as slowly as though I were lolling with assumed indifference in the dentist's "uneasy easy chair," whilst behind my back that skilful operator selected a brighter and more hideous "Clewdon stump forceps" than heretofore.

How the minutes drag! And yet I cannot learn patience from Sam, who, curled up well out of sight, with his nose close to his hock, "knows the game" well, and calls to mind, no doubt, his experiences a year ago. After a time I look again; one minute —it seems an age—and I shake off the suspicion that perhaps I have a bad cartridge which won't go off, and I have barely time to assure myself that both barrels are at the full cock, when I see a pale lavender-coloured line rapidly enlarging, bearing down for my ambush, and, drawing up my feet, I prepare to spring to my legs and give them the body of the charge, and a second shot during their momentary confusion. In less time than it takes to print off these words I have put this design into execution, and I hear simultaneously three, four, five ominous thuds amongst the heather. Sam, who has raised his head, looks at me with a wistful glance, which says in plain language to me, "All right, Idstone," and at a mute signal, as I load again, he lies down at full length, with his head between his paws.

The exploded cartridges have not done smoking when the second school appears. These laggards, however, fly rather wide of me, and I have to run pretty well ten yards. My dog creeps on to me, and is observed by some of them, and just as I pull they are mounting higher, so with both barrels I get but one, and he flutters in his fall, and pitches on his head two hundred yards away.

All that I have described does not take two minutes, and I take Sam by the collar and lead him back to his first "form" and reason with him two minutes more. Then I send him for one duck after another, and he brings me four of the first lot, the fifth I cannot find. He waits patiently, and once I make sure

Sam has him. I see him standing at a bush, and his tail stiff. "Go in and get him, foolish." But he makes a plunge in vain, and when he comes back to me there is nothing in his mouth.

I saunter to about the place where I think the last duck fell, and after Sam has trotted about in the slush and ooze, and smelt many a tuft and mound, he stops suddenly by an old alder root, and I hear that he picks up something, which proves to be a mallard.

I then go to the cob, which I have left tied to the gate, and find him none the worse, except that he has got the bridle rein over his leg, and that he has pawed the earth all round him with impatience, and I pick my way through the track in the fir wood for home. Sam stops before I have got twenty yards on this dark path, and when I snap my finger he goes into the bush and dark brown water on my right, where I heard him panting keenly, and evidently busy on a scent.

It gets rapidly darker now that the sun is down, and as I know well the unpleasantness of blundering over the fir-tree roots, I am half inclined to call him in. Before I can do this I hear the grating quack, quack, of the fifth duck which fell to my first shot, and Sam brings him in triumph to my saddle girth.

Watching and timing the flights, I have had many and many an evening of this sport, which, though it lasts but one or two minutes, has its attractions for me, especially when two or three of us post ourselves, perhaps a quarter of a mile apart, on good points or pieces of rising ground in the "flight's line," and have a blaze at the birds one after another. You may get another shot at them of course just before sunrise, as they return for the sea; but although I have done it successfully, I do not think it so pleasant or convenient as the dusk of evening.

A hard frost-bound winter, such a one as comes but seldom, brings ducks and waders of all kinds in profusion. Wild geese, black ducks, pintails, smews, shovellers, mergansers, shieldrakes, golden eyes, mallards, pochards, teal, widgeon—all these were to be seen—some of them in profusion when the soldiers were in the Crimea.

I remember one bitter night the snow was nearly a foot deep, and crisp and dry with intense frost. We had been out snipe shooting all day, and had been much perplexed by the lameness of my setter bitch and the retriever also, for balls of ice had formed upon their feet between their toes, and the setter had gallopped sometimes in agony, stopping to bite her feet, to my surprise, for at first I could not make it out, and when I did I was in doubt whether to cut the fur off her feet or not, but I did it and it answered. As we drove home, with a dog on the footboard to keep our feet warm, I observed the wild fowl making out for sea and some coming inland *in shoals ;* and as we passed a little frozen pool, the teal were sitting on the ice as thick as sparrows at a barn door. As we passed they rose, swung over us and before us, and made for the ground again, and I made up my mind to drive round by a large piece of water, of which I had the shooting, and to make my observations.

When I got to the margin and was peeping over, listening to the incessant clatter of these fowl, just on the move for the night, I observed a white head rising from the furze to my right, where a rise in the ground gave the best facility for observation, and I recognised old Bertie, who was also taking an observation. As we drew off together I observed that he was accompanied by a stealthy, clever-looking, smooth black bitch, thicker set than a large pointer, with small ears, and eyes and head very like a seal, but by no means "a gentleman's dog," as he himself observed in anticipation of any deprecatory remarks from me. "However," as he observed, "you musn't take her by her looks, nor gentlemen neither. I was once taken in that way," he added, as I signalled him to get up behind, where he stood up, and receiving encouragement from me, continued his story, for I thought his tale would shorten the road.

" I was a groom once," he said, " and my master sent me over to an old lord's who lived about ten mile off. So I took the note. It was from our young ladies to their young ladies, and I went into the stable to wait, and there I saw an old man, with shaggy eyebrows, sitting on the cornbin by himself. As I thought the young horse would be none the worse for a feed of corn, I asked the old boy to give me a bit. ' Help yourself,' he said, as he got up rather ill-humouredly. So I fed the horse, and he sat down again ; and says he, quite sharp, ' Whose servant are you ?' ' My master's,' says I, ' and I should say I have got a better place than you have, judging by your clothes.' Well, he got up and looked at me, and just then in came a swell servant with a note, and the old man says, ' take this young fellow into the hall and give him some beer.' ' Yes, my lord,' says the flunkey. ' And,' says the marquis, for it was him, ' Don't you judge by appearances again, young fellow. I've got the best place in the 'establishment.' I touched my hat, and begged his pardon, but the servant pulled me by the sleeve, and I was glad to get away from that ' establishment,' I can tell you, sir.

" Now," said he, in continuation, "this dog came from ' the land ' (Newfoundland), and if she gets into a hole on the ice she can get out, and, you know, sir, very few can. She belongs to the old Decoyman, and I thought if (he said this with a very knowing look) you would get up to-morrow before light, and have a shot at the ducks, she would be very useful."

" You call me in the morning, Bertie," said I, " and I'll go."

"That," said the old man, " is easy done ; " and by this time we had arrived at my stable gates.

" I wish you good night, sir," said Bertie, as he turned for home. " Come on, Diver ! I'll throw a charge of shot at your window, sir ! "

Dead beat ! This is a feeling I have seldom experienced, but this night the wood fire and peat upon the top, the white table-cloth, the armchairs, the " kidney table," the bright lamps, the fragrant soup, the good companions—now, alas ! two of them are dead and gone—all these failed to give their wonted pleasure after our weary walk, and I believe we all envied the red-and-white setter when she walked in and " flopped " down on the rug. But what dinner did not do, tea did, and after we had rested in the easy chairs, and smoked some of a naval friend's cavendish, we thought bed superfluous. However, we all " turned in," and then I could not go to sleep. I got some short naps, in which the setter bitch was constantly " setting " before my eyes, and in the longest of these I heard the ominous shower of grape against my window. It was hard work to rise, I was stiff as a ramrod, but I managed to crawl out of bed, where, by the light of a Palmer's safety candle, I looked rather uncertainly at my bath. However, that refreshed me, and I was soon downstairs, where my friends had preceded me, and after a cup of hot coffee we lit our pipes and climbed into the German waggon !

This took us to within half a mile of the pond, which was about a hundred acres of water, all frozen over except a small patch. There was no sound to be heard, nor could we have found our way except by the help of a small lanthorn, which we carried in case it should be required.

Bertie placed two of us full length upon the ice behind some rushes, having first with his hook cut a goodish bed of them for us to lie upon, and then he proceeded to place the other two guns.

All these events took place in absolute silence, and we were left in the darkness alone, Bertie telling us our position, and bidding us to be sure and fire when we could see the line of water black with them.

In what seemed a sea of ink before us we could now and then hear a moorhen scuttle through the water, or an old mallard quack two or three times as though suspicious, and once I imagined I heard the otter "blow" and drop into the flood of unfrozen water. Just as I could hardly tell whether it were darker or lighter, there was the quick whistle of wings, and a duck, as it seemed to me, fell like a cricket ball into the water just before me ; another, and still more, then a good flock, all striking the water like bricks thrown from an eminence, and then began the morning ablutions—the ducking and quacking of the whole brood. Then came the teal whistling round four or five times, now close to our heads, then off suspiciously and beyond the fir trees, now gradually looming dark ; and now I could just see the silver of their under wings. At last, in they go, and I can faintly discern the water black. It is no metaphor—black with wild fowl.

I touch my companion and he touches me. Even this movement awakes suspicion, and as I push forward my big Westley Richards, loaded with green cartridges, and my friend gets his splendid Lang into position, I see a little uneasiness in the flock. One, two, three (in whispers). Bang go the left hand barrels, and we both give them the right as they rise, cutting two lanes through them ; and at the instant they get the cross fire of two Purdey's placed to our left. We load and fire at the teal as they whistle over, and now we get, perhaps, one or two stray ducks, but most are off to sea. As the light breaks we see the water thick with dead, lying on their backs most of them, and some to all appearance alive, but with their heads in the water. "Come on with Diver, Bertie ! "

"Look at them, look at them !" said my companion, in a loud whisper, for, although I hardly raised my voice beyond its ordinary pitch, my appeal to Bertie for the black Labrador caused a flutter of wild fowl (teal especially) from the sedge, rushes, and little islands of dead reeds, and I had another opportunity of observing the pernicious effects of the human voice on game of all kinds.

If you want to signal anyone, use some other sign—a bird call, such as a lark whistle, or a pigeon call, which I know could be got at Tunbridge Wells, and which I think can be procured at

Davis's, the saddler, in Piccadilly.   It is rather a cumbrous thing,
being about 2½in. in diameter, and about 3in. long.

I once knew a gamekeeper who could " do the woodpecker" to
perfection, and I have already noticed in *The Field* that some men
can and do signal to each other by mimicking the owl.

My exclamation in this case did little or no harm, for the teal
whirled over us and gave us one or two famous " pot" shots
directly, and as we instinctively stood back to back we could
inform each other, as they swung like so many winged Leotards,
now over the large fir trees and out of sight, presently half a
mile away, and before they dropped whirling in front of us and
turning up their wings with the precision of a flying brigade.
If they are within range, that is the time to give it them,
and the crack duck shots of America do most execution at that
instant.

There was no reply from Bertie, and I was too "warry" a bird
to repeat my indiscretion ; indeed, there was no immediate hurry.

As we stood well concealed in the bullrushes and hanging
alders, we could scarcely have been better placed, and all we
wanted was exercise, for although the excitement of this grand
morning's sport had perhaps accelerated one's circulation, now
that we had only a shot at intervals of time we began to feel the
chilly morning air.

Excitement makes us forget pain, and for the time removes it.
I had a personal proof of this once, as I waited on one of
the Thames bridges the coming of the Oxford and Cambridge
crews.   A punctured wound in the wrist from a blunt screw-
driver had kept me awake two or three nights, and the pain was
increased by the keen, fresh, cutting draught of air which swept
down the river.   But this throbbing ceased when two dark specks,
accompanied by a silent yet moving crowd, appeared in sight, and
as I watched the dark and light blues forging up the river with
that solemn, steady, determined, regular swing, all pain vanished,
nor did it return until the boats, to all appearance locked
together, had rounded the bend, and after a few minutes' interval
the name of the winner had been passed along the shore.

Before I could think of a plan for noticing the duck and teal
amongst which we had made such havoc, or signal old Bertie, the
day broke and clearly revealed our exact position.

To my right were alders, their stems deeply embedded in the
frozen waters and almost within reach of my hand.   All round
me were the pale dead yellow rushes, breast high, and hassocks

of grass standing a foot out of water, possibly a yard apart. The hard, smooth, black ice is below me, and, with the exception of the patch of bright water to which the ducks had pitched, all the water was hard bound with frost and more or less covered with snow. Black spots in the distance gradually revealed themselves with the coming light as wild fowl, which had fallen after a short flight; and when the sun shone out full before me I saw the winding brook—the outlet of the pond—black compared with the snow-covered meadows in which it lost itself, and the teal hovering over it like swarms of bees.

As I was looking at the beautiful forms the snow had taken, and calling my companion's attention to a network of ice over an old bramble, which interfered with a little stream of water as it had run over the bank, I saw a movement in the sedges, and presently the black head of Diver, who was steadily hunting up the margin of the ice, and lashing her tail with that "sword exercise" movement *which I must have* in pointer, setter, or retriever ; at the same moment old Bertie pushed through the bed of osiers with a mallard and a "pintail" in his hand. " This one (he said) fell close to me, sir (at the same time he held up the ' pintail'), and the mallard, I saw him drop five hundred yards off ; so I took the dog and put her on, and I should think she was a quarter of an hour getting him. When you called she was so hot on the scent I could not bear to call her off, and I've left her now on a teal. There are lots " down" on the heath, and a good many will be lost, for they runs like lapwings. Now (he continued), if you thought well to go and walk among the rushes all round the pond, I could try and get these out with Diver, and I dare say you will get some cripples, and you are sure of more teal ; that we do know. Hullaw, Diver ! " As he said this, the decoyman's retriever pushed through the sedges with a male teal in her mouth alive, and looked up for further instructions.

" Let us see her get one out of the water, and get on the ice again, Bertie," I said ; and it seemed to me that this cunning, smooth Newfoundland understood what I wished, or perhaps she observed the direction of my glance, for she carefully stepped from one hassock to another, and at last was slipping and sliding on the ice. When she got to the unfrozen water she ran all round it two or three times, and at last dropped in where the sedge and peaty earth made it comparatively easy to get out again, and, having secured a duck, tried hard to bring two at once ; however, she gave that up, and *having put the first bird upon the ice*, went back for a second, without leaving the water.

To all appearance she forgot the good place for getting out again, and was a considerable time trying, the current drawing her hind legs under the ice, so that I began to think Bertie had overrated her powers. " Let her alone, sir," said the old man, touching his hat in reply to my opinion, " *she* won't be drowned ; you might as well try to ' stiffle' a otter ; " and, as though to corroborate this flattering notice of her, the bitch dropped into the water and tried the ice on the opposite side, where the current carried her hind legs *from* the ice instead of under it, and was out with the duck in about the time it takes to record her dexterity. She then tried hard to bring both birds at once, but gave it up, and returned with them singly ; not very fast, it is true, for, except when she trotted *stiffly*, she could make little way, and was, as Bertie called it, " all of a sprawl."

Next time she went in at the same place as before, where getting out was easy, and she did not again attempt to bring two at once, or to get out upon the ice, always going to the place where the water joined the peat mould and hassock.

When she had brought out ten or a dozen, I recollected that there was an old Poole duck punt, decked fore and aft, at the end of the pond, and I begged Bertie not to let her go in again, for it would be easy to get the rest with a cripple net which I had at home, and to collect the other birds upon the ice by pushing the boat up on the top of it ; and after consideration he thought it would be as well. We therefore picked our way to the firm ground again, where I was glad to see a boy with my two companions holding my black spaniel and a clumber, which some of my friends at home had, with good forethought, sent down in case they should be required. Two of us had to go at least half a mile round to get to the other side of a long sedgy " lake," as they called a strip of marshy land with a deep brook still running in the middle of it, and marshy, deceitful swamp on both sides of it—now safe enough, for it was hard as an oak plank. Whilst we waited for them to get round with the clumber, leaving us the " darkie," I noticed two kingfishers shoot the arch of the bridge on the parapet of which I sat, and which divided the long lake from the frozen pond. Now and then there was the faint sound in the distance of the heavy shoulder guns which the punt-shooters were discharging at their cripples and the " scuds" of teal at sea. I had heard their stancheon guns to the south-east and west of us just after we fired our first shots before daybreak. Diver had coiled herself up at Old Bertie's feet, apparently asleep, comfortable although wet, and gave an occasional shiver.

The bright sunlight, although it gave but little heat, made this situation endurable until I heard that faint whistle which was to be the signal for us to move, and which immediately aroused Diver and dispersed her dreams. As though to show us the necessity of prudence, even this cue was the means of startling one or two ducks which had pitched into the long rushes up the vale, and a duck and mallard came right for us, but when about seventy yards off, whipped over the fir trees and were hidden. A few seconds and they appeared again over our heads, but now far out of range of any shot gun, and this they evidently knew.

Nothing learns the range like wild fowl. An old cock pheasant is 'cute enough, but he never seems to know whether I can knock him over or not. I have often felt convinced that, "a rocketter" believed himself perfectly secure as he sailed over my head, and that he was never more sold in his life than when up went his tail and down fell his head, and he came crashing through the branches like a bag of shot.

Wild fowl, ducks especially, soon learn the range of the *long* guns, and, as it seems, transmit that knowledge to their offspring —at least so the old gunners tell me ; and it is a tradition that Hawker, "the Colonel" they call him, never made such practice as he did the first year that he shot his oval charge. However, this is another digression ; but I can't control my pen with a curb and chifney, and it would be dangerous to do it unless I had better hands.

If Bellerophon had given Pegasus his head, he would never have got that nasty "purl."

As soon as we got the signal from the other side, we started to try the deep covert, and the Clumber bitch almost trod upon a shieldrake. He flew right for me, and I shot, as I always do, for the head, when he turned, but my eye was attracted by that broad band of orange which contrasts so exquisitely with the white plumage, and I don't think I touched a feather. The next bird was a pochard, which got two barrels from the other side, and was pretty well riddled too, and then a black duck and a shoveller (female) got up together. The shoveller got off, but the Clumber I saw jumping through the reeds with the black duck in her mouth.

Farther on the water had sunk in from the ice, which was no thicker than a penny piece, and the noise it made in breaking was a great hindrance to our sport, as it put up the fowl a long way out of shot. I saw a beautiful tufted duck and two mergansers escape us in this way, and when we got nearer together, and hoped to be on better terms with the teal again, we were so puzzled and weary as we stumbled along, that I was almost disposed to try back and give up that beat; but as my companions, though excessively polite, would not hear of anything but going on, I had no alternative but to follow the course of the stream. A little further on, the walking, though tiring, could be effected without noise, for we came upon dry ground and dead fern. Here, from beneath an old pollard oak growing from the bank, and from the top of which, as it falls aslant the brook, I have often dropped to the other side of the trout stream, up sprang a couple of ducks. The mallard fell thump upon the bank, and the black spaniel fetched it, while, as I thought, the duck fell also, but although I hunted everywhere with the spaniels, find her I could not. So we loaded and went on, Bertie, by my directions, remaining behind to beat with Diver, and promising to join us at "the mill."

When we left him we fell in with some widgeon, and my black spaniel was very busy round a large thorn bush close to a deep trout hole, and would not leave it. When I came up I saw a duck sitting quietly by the very brink of the water, and at the same moment my dog observed her also; before I could lift her the duck and dog were in the stream, and dived together, and he came up with her in his mouth. I therefore signalled Bertie, who had, however, some idea that we had got the bird, and he and Driver came on.

One of my companions, and a good shot too, gave unmistakable signs of knocking up, and called to Bertie to take his gun, "for," said he, "I can't kill the birds, and I'm getting tired of it." I may add that since firing into the brown of them at the first rise, according to his own account, he had done nothing, and so Bertie, delighted, went to take his gun. "You had better shoot, Bertie, if anything comes your way." "All right, sir," he said, as he struck a light for me before we started to cross by the old pollard. "I remember once a lawyer came down to shoot at the ducks here, two guns and all regular, and he had a little chap to load for him named Billy Baker, who, when he was sober, never missed, 'specially ducks, for he and his father got a living at it.

So the lawyer says, 'You shoot next, Billy.' 'All right,' says Billy, who was half sprung. with a confidential wink to the gentleman , whom he never see afore that morning. 'You stick to me, little lawyer, and you'll soon have a " bred " (bird) in your pocket.' "

Before we got far away Diver hit upon something. and old Bertie, who heartily enjoyed seeing a dog work, forgot all about the gun. "That's he, Diver," said the old keeper, as he stooped and pulled aside the sedges to help the retriever, who was standing stiff and all alert in a piece of dead fern, and presently jumped once or twice, all her feet off the ground at once, and then ran round a tangled mass of fern and brambles. Something moved and arrested the attention of Bertie, and at his signal in she went ; up got a mallard, and sailed away ; hard hit, however, and before he could reach the fir wood on the right we saw him "lower." "I think I know where he is," said Bertie ; " we'll take the bitch and try," and as we finished that bit (which led us to the turnpike) without further incident or adventure, he and Diver disappeared. As we clambered up the bank and stood looking at the milldam on the other side, we saw him coming to meet us down the road, with the retriever behind him, carrying the mallard in her mouth.

" Got un," said Bertie, touching his hat with that look of fun about him, which he could no more control than his natural inclination, unfortunately, for beer. " *Got un*, sir, our old squire used to say, was the best word in the English language. I think," he added, " this Diver wouldn't be a bad one to buy, and I believe the old decoyman would sell her ; he has another coming on."

" Well," I said, "*perhaps* she would not do for my work after all " (I confess I had not much doubt she would, though).

" I don't know why she shouldn't, sir," he continued. " Of course you know best ; it puts me in mind—"

" Stop, Bertie," I said, " who is for going on ? " All thought we had done enough, and as we were going out to an evening party, so agreed to stop, and thought we might as well go home.

" Now then, Bertie," I said, " let's know what Diver puts you in mind of ? "

" Well, sir, I think she would do all her retrieving just as well as she does for ducks. I heard a story once of an exciseman as used to take too much in Staffordshire—perhaps you have heard it before—and once he and his wife fell out, and to mend matters he went and got quite stupid and went to sleep. Some of the colliers as was on the ' night turn,' as they calls it, thought it would be a good joke to take him down the pit ; so they puts him in the thing they goes down in, and takes him down. Well, he slept all their turn, and they went up and forgot all about him ; and when the next lot went down, one of them, as black as my hat, give him a shove and woke him up, and says, ' Hullo ! who are you ?' Well, when he rubbed his eyes and saw the dark place he was in, and this here black standing there with the candle, his teeth began to chatter, and he thought he was dead and buried ; so he touches his hat quite civil, and he says, ' If you please, Mr. Devil, I was an exciseman upon earth, but now I will do any light job you'll please to set me.' "

" I suppose, sir, I'd need to go and see to picking up all the rest of them cripples on the ice."

" All right, Bertie, we will go home. Call round at the decoy-man's and tell him to come and see me, if he will sell the bitch ; and say I should like to come and see his decoy. I hear it's the best in England. I heard something of his taking £300 worth of duck in one year."

" I'll give your message, sir," said Bertie, as he disappeared over the bank, " and I'll bring you word to-morrow morning. But "—and then he hesitated.

" Well, Bertie, but what ? "

" Well, sir, I was going to say the decoyman is terrible jealous. He won't tell you nothing. He got took-in the other day, though. A gentleman as had been all his life in the navy came into a swinging good property and sent for him. Well, off he goes with his son, thinking he should leave the son to make a new decoy. The gentleman asked him to show him a thing or two, but he would hardly say a word. At last the gentleman says to him, ' Well, my man, how many pipes must I have to the pond ?' The old decoyman looked at him out of the corner of his eyes, and tapped his forehead with his forefinger, and, says he, ' A sealed book, sir ; a sealed book.' Well, the gentleman took it very easy. As they walked home he smoked his cigar a little faster, but he never said a word more about the decoy business till he got to his hall door, and then he pulled a ten pound note out of his pocket and says to his butler, ' Take this to your mistress and ask her to send me a five, and *seal up* the rest. The five is for your railway fare, my man,' he said, ' but we will *seal up* the other. Good morning.' The decoyman didn't say a word at first, but as he turned away he said, ' If I'd a known this I'd have acted different ! ' "

" That is the morality of others besides decoymen, Bertie. Let us know what ducks you pick up."

He touched his hat and took a short cut through the plantations, that he might, as he called it, " save the light," and Diver, after a moment's hesitation, followed him as we turned for home.

The thick clouds and the general stillness seemed to foretell more snow ; the wind was piercing cold as we faced it and turned for home, and we all felt 'glad to gather round the logs, before which we found breakfast had been spread about six hours in anticipation of our return, whilst the unopened post-bag gave the whole of us the notion that we had been dreaming, and that the clock had either stopped, or, as one of our number (well known as a handicapper) observed, had been making the running " hands down," for it was twenty minutes after three when the hour and minute hand assumed some such position.

VI.—A BYE DAY WITH THE GUN.

My next interview with old Bertie, I am sorry to say, was by no means satisfactory. I mentioned in my paper on duck shooting that we left off early, to have a few hours' rest before we started for one of those evening parties popularly known as " at homes," which, like picnics, are fated to take place in inclement weather. We proposed to start about ten o'clock, and at a quarter to that hour the carriage lamps were burning, and the coach-house doors wide open—a plan adopted frequently to apprise the villagers that the coast is clear, and " master's a-going out. I saw this as I pulled aside the staircase window curtains, and the light blazed full upon old Bertie's back, loaded up with mallard's the green of whose necks shone like emeralds. I could discover no more than that he was in very earnest conversation with the keeper, emphasising his remarks with much animation and solemnity. I had not reached the bottom of the last flight when I met one of the maid-servants, who, half-concealing her features with the corner of her apron, told me that "the old man was come with the ducks, and he wouldn't go away until he had seen me."

The real facts of the case never struck me until I reached the back door, and, looking towards the coach-house, up the path which had been cleared of snow, I saw old Bertie standing very much "over at knee," his hat on one side of his head, whilst a dishevelled look about his hair, a peculiar heaviness in the eyelids, and a tendency to balance himself upon his heels, betrayed his condition at once. I was not quick enough to shut the door and decline an interview, for before I saw him I believe he saw me, and staggering up towards me with the ducks upon his back, assured me, with a sort of solemn drollery, that he was not "tight; nothing of the sort," the last part of which sentence he contrived to run into one word.

I have always thought command of countenance to be quite as great a gift as command of language, and I felt that all the household (by whom such a spectacle is regarded as a farce which they can see for nothing) were waiting to take their cue from me. When, however, he had reached me by a few most cautious steps, closely resembling "the outside edge" upon the ice, and, after balancing himself for an instant, fell down backwards in a heap of snow, remarking that it was "mild weather for the time of year, and we should soon be expecting the ' vilats ' " (violets), I signalled my keeper to take the ducks, which were frozen as hard as logs of wood, and see the old man home.

I turned into the house in anything but a good humour, and observed a dark frown upon the faces of the cook and housemaids, which I felt was a reflection of my own cheerful countenance. The coachman, who came out at the moment with the "off-side 'oss," scowled at poor Bertie (who was making efforts to rise, which very much resembled a fly in treacle) like a sober Pharisee, which indeed he was.

Before I reached the "at home," I had recovered my equilibrium, and, as one of my companions remarked, a child might have played with me. I had been questioning myself whether I had not treated old Bertie with too much familiarity, and whether he was taking advantage of my doing so. Looking back now, when he has long, poor fellow! been nothing but a few bones, I cannot lay any such charge at my own door, and I believe that my acquaintance with him was the means of preventing him from indulging in a vice which, long before I met with him, laid the foundation of that disease which shortened his days.

It is not always easy to provide shooting at the fag end of the season, though you can always manage a walk and a little dog manipulation, which I prefer ; and as my two friends were enjoying the dancing, which is beyond my ability, unless I have some one always at hand to "catch my horse," I was wondering what I should do with the solitary friend who stayed another day with me! I was talking in the glowing heat of the hall stove to a country rector—a nervous man I recollect he was, with a bald head, over which he trained and bandolined a few straggling hairs—when we were joined by one of our neighbours, who unconsciously broke in upon some plan of the divine's for the taking of Sebastopool, which was there and then lost to the world at once.

A man this of many amusements, a tenth part of which I cannot at this distance of time call to mind. First he occupied himself with a Holtzapffel or Evans lathe (I forget which), by the aid of which he was always making something new and decidedly ingenious. Having a little spare time left, he "went in" for photography, and travelled the country in a cart or van, having a dark room and all convenient. He broke out next with dissolving views and a magic lantern—photographing his own slides and painting his own scenes with such success that the lady's maid had fits, and only one man (the pad groom, unmarried) could hold her. He had passed then through the microscope stage, and had proved a valuable client to Beck and Beck. His bells rang by electricity ; one scuttle of coals a day warmed the mansion ; an hydraulic ram raised water for the fountains; Veitch had no better conservatory ; and his peach-houses ruled the prices of Covent Garden. The best of everything was good enough for him, and nothing short of it; and without seeming to have anything to do, he looked to everything himself. Go to any place of amusement—croquet, archery, picnics, coursing, shooting, the assizes or county sessions—there he was ; tall, dark, well-bearded, and at home. A mutual friend once made a bet, as he took his children to the Pantheon, that he would not be there ; but, singular to say, there he was. Having just purchased a piping bullfinch, he was engaged in dealing for the blue macaw !

"You," he said, touching the rector's waistcoat button with his forefinger, "you don't shoot ? A good thing, or you would very likely kill somebody." And then, turning to me, he continued : " I've got a new gun, and I'm going to try it tomorrow. A rough day. You have a friend with you ? All the better, so that he does not pot us ; and if you have a good spaniel, bring him. We can shoot something in the turnips ; then I want to try the heath, and, if we have time, I want to dig a badger. There is one in the chalk pit, and do bring old Bertie *to drive him home* in a string. I want to see that."

I explained the " excited " condition in which I had left my old friend, but accepted the suggestion that I should have him in and talk to him, and eventually, if his health permitted, bring him in a penitent state to assist in the amusements of the morrow. I felt bound to take him, as, if I worked my liver-and-white spaniel, he could make him downcharge, having a wonderful and mysterious power over dogs, which seems a gift to an occasional poacher, keeper, or shepherd, and one they appear to be able to exercise no one knows how, and least of all themselves. I witnessed this gift in Lord Poltimore's huntsman, Evans, who in the kennel (I never saw him out of it) seemed to influence hounds and direct them without word or signal ; and I know a shepherd who never strikes a dog or seems to take much notice of it, but who never has a bad one, and at the present moment possesses a sort of colley which will push the lambs along with her head, or shove them out of the hedge sides with her nose, with all the care and tenderness of a " Nightingale " nurse.

The morning after the ball was dull and foggy ; but before we had finished breakfast we could see the circle of the sun ; not bright, it is true, but like a disc of white paper ; and before we could start he had broken out through the mist, and on the south side of the house the snow was melting into " ice candles," which festooned our gables. Long before this I was left with but one companion ; the rest had dressed by candle-light, and caught the early train.

I had sent for Bertie, who did not wait for my messenger, but had been loitering about ever since eight or nine o'clock ; and we had him in. and gave him a severe lecture upon his love for beer. Receiving those promises of reformation which are older than the Mendip Hills, we gave him absolution and his breakfast, and started for my neighbour's manor, telling him to bring Denny the terrier. and the spaniel. Late in the year as it was, and the scent indifferent. I tried to beg off the turnip beating, but with no avail : so we had a leisurely stroll through them with Bob, under the presidency of Bertie. I had all the season made him lead this young spaniel whenever we went shooting, and down charge him to every gun ; and we had let him range a few times, or hunt for us even amongst hares and rabbits. He was one of those dogs which combine use with beauty. Perhaps for thick covert he would have been more serviceable with shorter ears, but in all other respects he was perfect. A long body, short, large legs and close feet, the Clumber head and style of work, mute, patient, and *thrusting*, he was such a dog as I should keep if the laws of the country forbade me to have more than one. He was a good retriever, nearly all white, with a few spots of liver. I did not breed him, but bought him young, and I have been fortunate enough to never entirely lose the breed. He " entered " naturally, and, though active and bustling, he dropped very soon to rabbits, and ranged close. In a hedgerow he was perfection, and he only failed in one point—he hated water from first to last.

This morning we had a saunter through the swedes, and some very pretty shooting. I think we got four brace of birds, a hare or two, and up the hedgerows we killed a pheasant and flushed a " cock." He made straight for the covert we were going to, and had been boring in a warm spring. There were but four beats in this wood, and they were small ones, so I had a good opportunity of noticing whether Bob, the spaniel, would take liberties in covert. I rejoice to say that, except attempting to chase a hare, which offence Bertie met red-handed (I never beat a dog myself), we got on very well. Just after this I heard the whirl of a cock as he tried to get up and free himself from the hazels, and I saw him jerk himself behind a dark spruce fir tree. Directly after I heard a gun " snick," or miss fire, and the next instant there followed what perhaps was the second barrel. As I was " going on with the beaters " in the thick, I waited until I heard some one shout " All right ! " and I was struck at seeing Bob running round a fir tree, as I have seen a young retriever before now watch a squirrel.

" There's the bird," said old Bertie, who had been particularly subdued. Without raising his voice, he pointed to a branch about four feet from the ground, and holding Bob up he let him lift it from the branch in which it was entangled, then taking it from his mouth caressed him for his 'cuteness and observation. " Whoo-whoop ! " said Bertie, as he broke off the legs of the bird and drew the tendons.

s 2

Just as we got to the end, and had given up the woodcock to
my tall friend, who was in high feather at having killed it with
his new gun, I shot a hare which had jumped the fence and was
making for the open, and at my desire Bertie sent the spaniel
after it.   " Stay at this end, please," said the master of the cere-
monies ; " we shall drive this piece to you, and I am cold standing
about."

As the beaters went to the further end, Bob came dragging the
hare to us, and whilst Bertie took it from him he said, " We call
these ' Jack Fancy's deer.'   Jack Fancy stuttered a good deal, and
was a terrible fellow to poach, but you couldn't catch him out,
and he had liberty to shoot on a little heath farm, having got it
entered in his writings in this way.   Just before the lease was
granted he met the young squire and his lawyer, and said, in his
hesitating way, ' One thing I do want, if you please, zur : if a
hare comes into my garden or ground, may I "pot un ?" '   ' Yes,'
the lawyer said, ' there is no harm in that.'   ' Then,' said John,
putting his finger on the lease where there was a vacant space,
' Will you write down there " pot un ? "

I see no objection myself to letting tenants shoot rabbits from
the 1st of February to the 12th of August.   If they are worth
keeping as tenants they will do no harm with a gun then, but a great
deal of good, and they might ferret many months in the season,
too ; but *traps are ticklish things, especially amongst the vixens.*

The last beat was not successful.   We got one cock pheasant ;
we let the hens go ; and perhaps five or six hares went out, but
only three were killed.

We now crossed the moor after lunching under the hedge, and
were very soon partially blinded with fog and drizzle, in the midst
of which I heard a golden plover whistle, and saw one jump up
and settle again right ahead.   I have never found a good way of
getting at these birds, which seem to spring from the earth as
Bedouins arise in the desert.   Many a time I have seen them
high up sailing away, in the form of their bodies like so many
sparrow-hawks, but of course easily distinguished from them in
their flight, and after marking them down and stalking them
they have baffled me at last.

I have done best on a pony, and have sometimes got as near
as I dared, and running up to them have given them both barrels
as they rose.   I never had any luck with them, and on this
occasion I think we got but two, and four or five full snipes, which
lay well in the reedy bottoms close to the river.

Our snipe shooting disturbed the first and nearest part of this wide stream, now happily preserved for salmon ; but when we had passed the old white mill, with its overshot wheel now being converted into the best form—I mean the "breast shot," to be followed by its destruction altogether, and the substitution of steam—we dropped into some pretty wild-fowl shooting, and killed, amongst other birds, the golden eye and an Egyptian goose. As old Bertie was hooking this bird off the frozen margin of the river (the bird had fallen on its back), he pointed to the horseshoe on its breast, and said,

"I declare the gentleman has shot one of the squire's tame geese ! It's as bad as young Trencher did. Our squire turned two kangaroos into his park, and one of 'em got away, and they shot him in the next manor, about the last shot before they left off. Well, they never see such a thing before, and sent it to be stuffed. The lawyer as shot him (a family lawyer they called him ; he's got the whole property to manage now, and makes the gentleman an allowance), he thought it was a cross between a rat and a roebuck. However, they had it stuffed, and our squire, as it belonged to, went to law about it."

We got a good many teal after this, and then, turning over an old bridge, climbed a hill and were close to a chalk embankment, which looked like an old fortification, as indeed it was. We met here with the labourers who were digging at the badger's earth, and also the rest of the game, for we had made a half circle, and were close to the little covert where Bob found the woodcock in the fir tree. The two men who were digging stopped when we came up, and at once recognised old Bertie, who as an earthstopper was well known, and also knew everybody.

"Just try with Denny," said the most intelligent of them. "Let's see how far off he is."

"Oh, not far," said Bertie, without approaching the hole. "I can tell without the dog, or yet putting in my arm," he added with a sly look. "I could hear him ' snoffle ' when you moved the spade," and taking the spade in his hand he dug "up hill." (The hole was on the side of a sort of chalk mound.) He had opened the earth a good deal, when a white-toothed urchin said with a broad grin, "I thought I heard him querk "—a provincial expression denoting fear on the part of the creature pursued or unkennelled ; and just after we saw some dun or grey mass move beyond the spade.

"Clap the spade against the hole," said one of the men standing by.

"Nonsense!" said Bertie, as he fumbled in his pockets for a small line, adding "I wish one of you would go and cut me a 'rice'" (the name given by covert beaters to a long taper stick); then, making a slip knot at the end of his tether, he caught up Denny, and showed the badger to him.

Master Denny contemplated him in silence, merely struggling to free himself from Bertie's arms; and as soon as the badger showed his head, which he had been hiding like the ostrich, old Bertie loosed him. He went in without hesitation. With dog or man, this is half the battle; and Bertie, catching the dog by the hind legs, drew dog and badger clear.

"I would have let him enjoy hisself a bit," said Bertie," only it's getting late;" so he watched his opportunity, then lifted the badger by the tail, meanwhile holding him at arm's length. "Now, then," he said to a young fellow who stood by, "slip the noose over his hock, and draw it tight. That's right," he continued, as he got Denny off, and dropped the animal close to the leg of a soft-looking young man, and after dragging his prize a little way from the hole, took the long stick or rice in his hand, and drove the badger in front of him with far less trouble than he would have driven a pig. Touching his hat to my friend, on whose manor the badger had been dug, he said, "I suppose you don't mean to bait 'un, sir?"

"Well, being a county magistrate, and expected to act as an example, I rather think not!"

"If I did," said one of the bystanders, "I should break his teeth first. That's what they does in London, and then, when gentlemen tries their dogs, they thinks how game they are."

"Ay," said Bertie, "most dogs will go at a badger in a tub, but they don't like calling on 'em at home. A badger's a harmless thing enough. I think it was Evans (now Lord Fitzwilliam's keeper) had two which would run up his arm when they were young. He sold 'em to a travelling showman."

"I suppose, sir," he said to my friend, as he guided the badger up the avenue, "you won't beat any more to night?"

"Not any more to-night, Bertie, nor this year. We will put that badger in the large covert, now we have finished 'beating for game.'"

VII.—DRIVING DEER.

Since the days of Nimrod hunting has been the occupation of man. He has had recourse to every expedient in order to obtain a supply of food, destroy noxious animals, or possess himself of creatures either useful to him when domesticated, or valuable on account of their producing fur, feathers, or even supposed curative medicinal qualities; and he has attained his superiority over them in the progressive stages of civilisation by various means. The weapons of every savage tribe (the arrow and bow) differ nothing from those used by Esau, eighteen hundred years before the Christian era. Occasionally either the natural pitfall, or a cautious encircling of the vast group or herd, has been adopted, and numbers have been wantonly driven down a precipice, after the fashion employed by the North American Indians. The artificial pitfall was used solely for the destruction of beasts of prey, but the net was in common use more than fifteen hundred years before Christ.

It is doubtful whether we have reliable information as to hunting by the aid of dogs of more ancient date than the " Cynegetics" of Xenophon or Arrian. Even in Xenophon's prime and manhood he had discovered that " this noble science" increased the health, strengthened the sight and hearing, and protracted the approach of old age ; whilst the encouragement given to all his officers by Wellington, in the Peninsula, to follow his hounds when they could, told them more plainly than words that he considered the pursuit of the fox an excellent apprenticeship for war.

Falconry, alike the sport and the system of the Persian and ancient Briton, required but the *rousing* of the game, and it is impossible to form any notion of the antiquity of the pursuit. Probably it is coeval with the use of the hound or dog. At any rate, the *beating* for falconry was the mere flushing or rousing it ; and the hawker's chief desire would be a find on an open and unenclosed country.

In later days, and as civilisation increased, the pursuit of game was developed as a system or science ; and the line of beaters drove coverts ages ago for the Celestials, somewhat in the manner adopted at the present time by the proprietors of large pheasant coverts. A close observation of wild animals leads us to the conclusion that the human race imitate them in their chase and pursuit of each other to a great extent, and that the weasel, the hawk, and almost all birds and beasts of prey have their allotted hunting grounds on manors, driving off intruders upon their manorial rights with the activity and malevolence of *Christians.*

After an experience of more than twenty-two centuries, mankind has seen no reason for disputing the truth of Xenophon's assertion as to the health-inspiring, invigorating effect of hunting the beast of the forest (which is true woodcraft, hunting, or venerie), or to repudiate his notion and sentiment as to the effect field hunting or the chase produces upon the mind and body.

"Hunting" is the term applied to the hart (or red deer of mature age), the hind, the hare, the boar, or the wolf. By " the chase" we mean the pursuit of the buck, the doe (that is, *fallow* deer), the fox, the marten, or the roe. Other means are adopted for bringing wild animals to hand besides the net or pitfall. These are the " stalking" or creeping up to deer, until we are near enough to serve the rifle ; and waiting or lying in ambush for the different waders until they " pitch" into their feeding ground, or water left " bright" or unfrozen in the depth of winter.

Driving the deer is a sport within the reach of few sportsmen. It creates a panic and confusion in the very largest forests, is a system seldom adopted, and probably never would be adopted but for the charm of excitement, and the *fête* it gives rise to in the hunter's home. The owner of the large domain and of unnumbered wild acres has probably collected beneath his roof a number of hard working men devoted to the government of this great country, to letters, arts, or commerce, men who have thrown aside the cares of state, or have determined to forget the frowns of critics or the heavy balance sheet, as a duty they owe to the state or their own families. They require some distraction, and to be taken away from themselves and their cares. Perhaps they have lost their relish for the daily walk with pointers over hill and moor, or they may be jaded with the constrained posture and the hard physical exertion of protracted " stalks " after royal harts—" a stalk " meaning the serpent-like following of a forester for hours. The drive is a very different affair.

The preparations are interesting, *especially interesting* to the novice. He witnesses a great deal of activity, as unintelligible to him as the rapid motions of a ship's crew appear to the unlucky landsman who stands by his nautical friend on the quarter-deck in a gale of wind—a position I never desire to occupy again.

The apprentice to deer driving finds himself thoroughly ignored, sent to Coventry, and expatriated, if he makes his way into the courtyard or attempts to overhear, still less to comprehend, the Gaelic vociferously uttered by the leading spirits of the chase. The whole establishment is grouped in little knots of conspirators. The very billiard-room is full of "consultators." The keenest glances are directed at the slightest clouds; the barometer is surrounded by "clients," and the various staircases display as large an amount of hurrying to and fro as a metropolitan bridge at noon. Next morning (if his window looks that way) he has a half-conscious, half-dreamy recollection that he was awoke long before sunrise by the tramp of many feet. He heard the beaters leave for their several stations to begin the drive miles away; and, at the solemn breakfast, he is conscious of an unwonted silence and stillness in the courts and rooms. He is shortly on his way to an ambuscade behind some rock or secure hiding-place, where he will be left alone for hours. He will receive the most stringent commands from the head forester who places him in the pass, with his rifles convenient to his hand, and some provision for his creature comforts, that he is on no account to show himself under any possible condition before the deer have passed, and that until he is fetched from his retreat he is "just to bide quiet and load again if he can."

Meanwhile the army of beaters has not been idle. Under the direction of several experienced chiefs, they have managed to get to the farther side of the stags, and have commenced the difficult task of driving them gently with the wind, a process at direct variance with their instincts. Sometimes the greatest skill and prudence are required. Occasionally one individual forester, in a critical position, must merely let the deer have his wind; at another time he must boldly show himself. Now he must turn them with his voice, and frequently he must hide himself from their keen vision with the speed of lightning. He must change his tactics according to his best judgment and experience, He must be quick to understand the position of affairs, and he needs a considerable amount of patience, courage, and endurance. It is not easy to collect together a number of men calculated to drive the deer down the passes in which the rifles are posted, or to command success when you depend upon the scientific contraction of a circle.

At a *battue* of hares and pheasants, with coverts netted in quarters. and under keepers to maintain the line and restrain the

tongues of the beaters, and to insist upon a perpetual rattle of
sticks against the hazels or young trees, you may put up with
the frozen-out gardener, the hodsman, stable helper, boy in the
garden, or the blinking watchman, who has not seen sunlight
through his lodge window for weeks of winter. All the odd men
of the place may be called into requisition for the simple purpose
of driving a wood, provided the men are formed into line in the
right place, and managed upon a proper system. In fact, success
does not depend *upon them;* but in driving it is frequently a
matter of individual skill. One "jack-daw amongst the rooks"
may overthrow the most artistic arrangements, and "mull" the
whole day's sport irrecoverably, for driven deer are not to be out-
generalled a second time: they do not forget the manœuvres of
the human race for weeks, and before they are to be "had" the
whole household will have emigrated to the metropolis for
that year.

There is some danger of alarm being given to the deer from
want of caution on the part of those men who have the hounds
in the leash. A struggling deerhound, or a youngster giving
tongue, or showing an inclination to "riot," as it is termed,
would scare every head of venison from the rifles, and when the
herd are seized with panic they will not be turned by any body
of drivers. Occasionally this instantaneous fright seems to run
through them all, communicated probably by some signal from
the leader, for reasons we cannot fathom; then no expedient
will keep them within bounds. I have observed this fact in large
parks containing both red and fallow deer, and under these circumstances no human power can turn them.

In English parks the owners have resorted to various expe-
dients for driving them within a netted inclosure; and one
English squire, as good a hand with deer and as fearless amongst
them as any forester of the north, has resorted to the expedient
of riding out the buck and shooting him when he is wearied
down. When, however, it is necessary to confine the whole herd
of fallow deer, no means appear to us so efficacious as the
moderate use of a clever old shepherd dog, and a few intelligent
labourers with poles and little flags.

I am not aware that the dog has ever been called into requisition for driving on the larger scale, or whether he would be of
any use with herds of the dun deer among the wilds of Scotland,
nor can I *guess* whether it would be successful; but I think it
would be quite worth while to make trial of a skilful, temperate,

well-broken colly for that purpose, and that he *might* be made an excellent coadjutor to the men, provided he were *well in hand*, obedient to signal or whistle, and possessed of that surpassing intelligence, and showing that implicit obedience, for which he is conspicuous and celebrated. A patient, well-disposed, good tempered sheep-dog is capable of understanding and appreciating the motions and intentions of a herd of deer almost as well as a Scotch forester, and we have some grave suspicious that a few dogs might be found whose movements would show that they developed their talents with great rapidity, or that they had been previously connected with the business. I know I am comparing great things with small, but I repeat I have seen a sheep-dog do wonders with a large herd of fallow deer and about eighty red deer, in a *very large* park, a great many times ; and I should not have believed it possible unless I had personally witnessed the sagacity and intelligence of the dog, and the gentle control and influence he exercised over the herd.

After all, it does not appear to me a more extraordinary feat than the coaxing an old crafty mallard into a decoy tunnel by a trained spaniel, or the intelligence of the "Sau-finder" in Saxony.

VIII.—THE END OF THE SEASON.

Bertie and the badger had scarcely disappeared, when we walked up the bank which overlooked the river, and saw the farmer, whose own land and house stood on the other side, crossing in his boat. Six feet two and about seventeen stone, he carried in his hand a double-barrelled nine-gauge gun, which weighed quite nine pounds, but which in his grasp seemed a handy little gun enough.

" I heard you shoot two or three times," he said, as his man put him across the stream, " and I thought through my parlour would be a short cut for you, so I have told them to mull some claret, and take the chill off the beer for the men."

It was quite useless to contend against this frank and genial invitation, so, without any pretence to apologise, we stepped into his boat and crossed with him.

On the other bank his garden wall was built in the stream, and we entered up three or four stone steps and through an iron gate,

above which projected the bay windows of an old ivy-covered
fishing-house, built on the wall, and commanding from the side
lights a view of the wide stream on both sides for miles. Thence
our new friend—at least, my new friend—led us up the gravel
walks of an old garden, the walls of which were covered with
trees admirably trained, then up a terrace and into the old
Grange, for so it was, remarking, as he ushered us into the old-
fashioned hall, that it had been in his family for centuries, and,
so far as he knew, never had been mortgaged,

"That old spear head," he continued, in reply to some remark
from me, " one of my ancestors, or what you please to call them,
carried when he went with Queen Elizabeth to Tilbury ;" and,
throwing open the door of the large but rather dark dining-room,
he added, " here is what you don't see very often—a set of
Apostles' spoons, dug up in the days of my grandfather, in the
old moat."

On the table, most likely coeval with the house, we found an
old peg tankard of spiced wine and several long glasses, and it
needed some resolution to resist the warm invitation of our host
to sit down before the beech-log fire and make ourselves at home.
However, we got off at last, and after seeing the dovecote at the
back—an old circular stone building, not unlike a large limekiln,
round which flocks of blue rocks were sitting, preparatory for the
night—we went up the avenue of beeches leading to the road,
and made for my friend's house. This we reached just before
dusk, in the bright moonlight, and had an hour to spare before
what my neighbour called an early dinner—I mean half-past six.

That hour before dinner is a pleasant time after a hard day's
work ; you have a sense of independence, and can take your time
Plenty of hot water, a good fire, and dressing by degrees after
hunting or shooting, is, a refreshing process, and when you
gave the last fillip to your hair (if you have any), you feel as
if you had just mounted your second horse.

The first bell (electric) was ringing as I experienced this sensation, and when I opened the door I saw old Bertie below me in
the hall, with a hamper, surrounded by the drawing-room establishment, to whom at my friend's request he was exhibiting the
badger, whilst a footman with scarlet plushes and the approved
balustrade legs stood at a respectful distance.

Poor Bertie had somehow lost his way, and had been rather
baffled by the obstinacy of his prisoner, which, as he explained
to me, "turned unked," or contradictory, and he thought, he

said, as he wiped his forehead, he had been "a matter of three miles round."

"Poor man," said the wife of my host; "if I were not afraid it would hurt you I would give you a glass of beer."

"Thank you, ma'am, I'm sure," said Bertie, touching his forehead with his finger, and with a droll look of humour in his eyes, which always showed something was coming; "If you will only be so kind as to give it me, I'll risk that." At the same time he opened the hamper as unceremoniously as though it contained a tribe of puppies, and showed his captive to the assembled company.

At this moment the second bell rang, and we went in to dinner; but before they left I saw several slip coins of the realm into Bertie's hand, and I must say I dreaded the consequences, and not without reason, for I thought his resolutions to be sober were by no means strong. There was no chance of his being able to have more than what the butler thought good for him, as he had received a hint from me, and I thought no more of him until, at about ten or half-past ten, we prepared to leave; then I noticed that the old man was slightly flushed in the face, and exceedingly clever with the bags containing our shooting gear and guns, all of which he had piled so as to inconvenience the driver (meaning me) as much as possible. However, we remedied this and started, when his hat fell off and he "barked" his leg, as he called it, against the steps of the waggonette in getting up.

We got home without any adventure beyond those I have mentioned, and the old man had departed, when, allured by a bright fire and two easy chairs, my friend and I sat down to talk over the events of the day, and indulge in the pernicious habit of smoking as a preparatory measure for a night's rest. We had got upon the usual topics—dogs and horses—and did not notice that it was nearly one o'clock, when the hall bell rang sharply, and my friend observed that he thought he had heard the sound of wheels.

"Don't hurry," he said (he was the most deliberate man I ever knew), "let them ring again: perhaps we're dreaming." I prepared to go and ascertain who this new comer could be; meanwhile my opposite neighbour began to speculate. "I shouldn't wonder," he said, speaking very slowly, "if my grandmother is dead. When I came away the homœopathists had got her in tow to finish what the water-cure people began." And now

there was an unquestionable ring again, quite a peal, followed by
the blast of a post-horn or some such instrument execrably badly
blown.

When we opened the hall door the mystery was solved.
There was a pile of luggage at the entrance, a large gun case, a
bag, a portmanteau, all of which had been thrown down in that
apparent haste and recklessness which I have observed in case of
fire, and when I looked at the high-wheeled bright red and black
dog cart, to which was attached a vicious-looking rakish chesnut,
I knew who my friend was before I caught sight of his glowing
red face and peculiarly ugly hat, which might have overshadowed the brows of the late Mr. Thomas Sayers. When I
add that the moon's pale light revealed a very large body clad
in a double-stitched overcoat of the old four-in-hand cut, and a
white kerseymere shawl with a scarlet spot here and there, and
that this large, long body was supported by a pair of very small
legs which a feather-weight might have envied, I have completed
the picture. The figure which thus loomed upon me I had
known ever since my schooldays. Now, however, increased in
width if not in wisdom, I saw the old companion whose delight
it used to be to illustrate the margin of his Latin verses with
horses and hounds, and who now enjoyed nothing so much as
dropping on his friends from the clouds.

" Have you got room for me ? " was his first greeting ; " if
not, the chestnut has ten miles left in him, though he has come
forty miles to-day, and I never should have found you, living as
you do among these cross roads, for I have passed the house,
only I met this old fellow staggering out of the public-house half
seas over," pointing meanwhile to Bertie, who was rocking on
his heels as usual, and holding on by the point of the shaft.

" All right," I said, " come in Frank ; " and having knocked
up a groom, who tumbled out so quickly that as he lit his stable
lantern he seemed in a dream, I left the wonderful chesnut to his
care, and began to consider how I must amuse this comer.

" I haven't," I said, as we together helped to get in his luggage,
in which Bertie assisted with tipsy alacrity—I haven't any shooting worth speaking of."

" Yesh you have, sir," interposed Bertie, " rabbits ! "

" Now, my good fellow," I said, " go home. This is what you
call leaving off drinking."

" Tapering off, sir," he replied, " tapering off. I couldn't
leave off at once ; the doctor said it wouldn't do." Then

wishing me good night he blundered through the door, and after looking up at the moon as though it were a new constellation which he had never seen before, and shaking his head as though grieving over the errors of mankind, he staggered up the road.

When a man slowly unwinds the scarf about his neck at one o'clock in the morning and looks round for something to eat, it does not say much for the night's rest of those upon whom he makes his swoop, unless he is most carefully handled. I therefore showed him the larder door and plate rack. initiated him into the mysteries of the staircase, chalked a cross on his bedroom door, and after finishing our pipes, retired, leaving him to contemplate his slippers before the fire.

Next morning the usual scene of penitence and promises took place on Bertie's part, his plea being that he was not intoxicated, only fresh ; for he was such a philosopher in drunkenness that he divided the stages of imbecility with the precision of a stage coachman.

" I don't mean to say I was not sprung, sir, he said, " but there, I knowed what I was saying ; I hadn't got my *crooked* stockings on."

" Well, Bertie, don't let me catch you in that condition again."

" No, sir," he replied, " I won't ; " adding (without altering a muscle of his face) " I didn't *mean* you to *catch* me yesterday— leastways this morning. If I go round and get some dogs from the people of the village, and two or three boys, do you think, sir, these gentlemen would like to have some rabbitting ? There's the large wood all ferreted, the keeper has just told me so." They assented, and having turned the conversation, he hurried off to do what he could.

In about an hour, before we had done with the letters and arranged a few other matters, he came back with a medley of dogs and half a score of ragged urchins, glad of a job in this hard weather, and the prospect of bread and cheese and beer. A strange pack of dogs it was. Mongrels of low degree, but some of them possessed of that marvellous intelligence which, in dog or man, is not always inseparable from blood and breeding. Most of them, from obvious reasons, had a dash of greyhound about them, although remote ; and Bertie accounted for it from a dog of very high caste having been years ago given away by a sporting clergyman to one of his fraternity who was not overridden with brains.

" You see, sir," he said, " old Billy Butler was a terrible man
for a good greyhound, and he threw a shoe just close to this 'ere
soft 'un's house when hunting, and so he stopped to lunch. Well,
the clergyman where he was lunching wasn't a very good sort ;
he was terrible proud of his learning, but I believe he wasn't
much. His clerk told me all the best bits of his sermon was
poached ; and as for visiting the sick, he was so frightened at
catching their complaints that he used, when they had fevers,
to have a ladder put outside and read his good books to 'em
through the window. Old Mr. Butler, let him be what he would,
was not afraid of anything, and, what's more, he hated a coward.
As he was at luncheon the soft clergyman says to Mr. Butler, ' I
want a dog to follow the carriage ; can you give me a young
greyhound, Mr. Butler ?' Well, old Billy Butler knew that the
parson's brother was a coursing man down in Wiltshire, and in
those days all the best greyhound blood was scarcer than it is
now. So he says, ' Yes, I'll give you one with only one fault,'
and got up to go ; for he said afterwards he was afraid that his
brother parson would want something else next. Some time after
the parson's brother wrote to Billy to ask what the one fault of
the greyhound was, as his brother had kindly made him over to
him. So Billy sat down and wrote to him to say he was a
terrible good dog, only he *wasn't hardly fast enough.* That dog,"
said Bertie, " has left a lot of his sort about here, and distemper
nor nothing won't shorten the breed."

He told me this story as we walked to the wood, about 100
acres, perhaps half of it cut and hardly showing any growth since
that operation ; the fern hiding the large " mocks," or stools,
which had been pollarded close to the ground at intervals for
years. Here and there were oaks, each of which might perhaps
have cut a couple of gate-posts, if felled ; and at the top of the
wood, which was a slope, there was a belt of dark large firs.

These firs were now continued all round the wood as a roost-
ing-place for pheasants, but except at the top of the covert they
were as yet small and useless for birds. There were three fox-
earths in this covert which had existed for years and years, and
in two of them the vixens had brought out their cubs, whilst, as
though to give a flat denial to all cavillers about foxes living
with pheasants, *we had killed more pheasants in this covert this
year than in any equal proportion of land where there were no
foxes, by about one-third.*

" Don't tell me," said old Bertie as he stood over one of them, "about foxes doing harm; see the good they does. Look at what I've taken out of a fox's larder. Rats' legs, hind legs of rabbits, and certainly some hares (but a hare puzzles a fox dreadful), and some ducks' wings I allow. But moles, mice, rats, and all vermint, that's the fox's dinner. It isn't long ago I helped take in a faggot-rick for a farmer, and when he see the hind legs of the rabbits in the sort of parlour inside the rick bed, he says, 'Well, I think a fox does more good than harm;' and so do I."

All this time we were steadily beating one square in line. We had it all netted, and the mongrels and lurchers were in full chase after the rabbits, very often tumbling head over heels, or half stunning themselves by running against the roots and stumps, whilst the shouting, and screaming, and excitement were something wonderful.

Bertie and my keeper both had guns, and I was the only one who did not take one. I wanted to look to a young retriever which had begun admirably, and to have my hands at liberty, as I did not trust him without a line trailing on the ground. It was well I did not, for once or twice he lost his self-control, and when he saw half a dozen dogs fighting over a rabbit, he tried ineffectually to dash in. Each time I caught him up sharp in the check collar, and once I threw him on his back; and as he was flogged back to me by my boy, and the last time Bertie gave it to him handsomely, towards the end of the day I was able to trust him with not more than half a dozen yards of line.

This was one of the few woods I have ever seen clear of vermin—I mean *running* vermin. Of course hawks hunt like spaniels, and there is nothing for it but post traps; except through the covert I could not detect the presence of a stoat or weasel. I carefully examined the gates and hedgeruns, and saw no trace of them. I thought we must have got the last, and it struck me that possibly these gentry may give the fox a bad name, and the absence of their fangs might be one reason for the good sport the wood had afforded.

When we came to the last beat, where the wood was oldest, there was some hitch in the keeper's arrangements that turned back the whole gang—probably a corner left unbeaten; at any rate, I went on alone and waited, rather impatiently, for some token they were coming. All at once I saw a roebuck's head, so exactly matching the grey lichens of the oak by which he lay, that I could hardly believe I was not deceived. As soon as I

T

touched my whistle he rose slowly and stretched himself, as un-concernedly as though he were a deer-hound, and trotting into the thick, cleared the fence and trotted across the open, turning his head from side to side like a young hunter that has thrown his rider.

By this time the rest came up, and we finished our rabbit shooting in style, for they had drawn to this end and we had scarcely time to load. Just as we were finishing I met with a nasty accident. I was jumping a narrow ditch, without observing an elm branch which was overhead, and the tree almost knocked me backwards. I felt a little stunned, and Bertie said I turned as white as his new smock (smock-frock).

" It puts me in mind," he said, as soon as he saw my head was too hard to be hurt by anything made of wood, " of a man whose wife had a trance, and was screwed up, and they was bringing her down to be buried. Well, they knocked the coffin against the bedpost and woke her up, and she lived and had dree (three) more children. Then she really did die, and the man was terrible cut up about it ; but when they went to fetch her down, up he jumps, and says, ' Let me come—don't you go knocking the coffin against the bedpost again ! ' "

"Ay," said Frank, who all day had scarcely spoken a word because his chesnut was off his feed, " I saw a fellow shot along with us in Gloucestershire, and he picked four shots out of his forehead and put 'em in his waistcoat pocket. Then he washed his face and stopped the blood, and when he got to the end of the wood, and they were at luncheon, some one said, ' What, have you scratched your forehead ? ' ' No,' he said, pointing to one of the party—the squire it was—and handing him the shots, ' you put these into my forehead.' ' Lord,' said the squire, putting them carefully in his shot pouch, and with no other apology, ' What a —— hard head you must have ! ' "

" Now, then, let us go home, I'm tired of it." (*Public*)—" And so say all of us."

PAPER XXX.

LAND VALUERS AND STEWARDS.

A CLASSICAL education is not intended to prepare us for the management of an estate ; and if a young gentleman declares himself as preferring agriculture to Æschylus, he is frequently suspected of seeking an apology for doing nothing. In other words, it is possible to be " crammed " with classics and mathematics to the exclusion of common sense, and that knowledge of the world which comprehends business habits and the control of property.

Many a man withdraws from a liberal profession to take the position of a country gentleman, or succeeds to an estate, possessing no more knowledge of land, or the duties of landlord and tenant, then the retired manufacturer who, late in life, has invested his capital in acres.

Large properties are generally committed to a steward, paid by a fixed salary, which is regulated to a great extent by the importance of the possessions he has under his charge, or the liberality and social rank of his employer. This steward has, in all probability, his house and walled garden, his pair of phaeton horses, and a hack, which at the proper season is caparisoned as a charger for the yeomanry, and pays no duty. He has some opportunities of *increasing* his income, and, unless a man of weak principles and avarice well disguised, he levies no black mail upon farm tenants, nor does he exhibit what our American cousins call "smartness" in his dealings. By the tacit consent of the Squire, he is often permitted to do little bits of quiet business for the neighbouring gentry, such as simply require the exercise of a farmer's experience, a common everyday acquaintance with Gunter's chain and the surveyor's cross staff ; whilst towards his proper chief, who, in racing phraseology, has " the first claim on his services," he acts as a sort of nautical fender or a railway buffer, protecting the lord of the manor from the jolts of dissatisfied tenants; or he may be said to resemble that imaginary

" Co." whom the sinking merchant puts forward to gain time in
his trade embarrassments, and thus postpone the evil day.   A
steward is a necessary though a rather expensive luxury.   He
receives the rents, examines the quarterly bills, gives plans for
drains, marks the timber, parades himself in broadcloth before
the working bailiff, and, in association with the family lawyer,
makes a good thing of the estate, whilst, with the honesty of an
East Indian "khansaman," he warns off a swarm of minor
harpies from the ancestral hearth.

Next in honour and dignity to the steward comes the working
bailiff we have just named.   His equipage, a rough pony; his
full dress, velveteen ; and for *very best,* those glazed leggings
which flash back the light.   A man this with no pretension to
grammar, no affectation of aspirates, nor inclination for gloves—
the man of a pound a week, a cottage, *and no vote;* carrying out
the steward's directions, if there *is* a steward, and doing "by
rule of thumb " what the amateur imitates by the help of "Rees'
Farmer's Account Book " and " The Agriculturalist's Calculator."

It cannot be denied that there are times when the experience
of a man acquainted with the value of land and the routine of
agriculture is required—in the purchase of an estate, for instance, or when a change of occupation is contemplated, and for
" valuing tenants in or out."   But before employing any person
calling himself a land valuer or surveyor, it would be well to
reflect upon the following legal opinion which we obtained a
short time ago : "Nothing has ever been done which can fix the
charges of a land valuer or surveyor ; and, having regard to the
work done, they are more extortionate than those of any other
class of professionals."

A case was reported in *The Times* a short time ago, where a
charge of 95*l.* was made by a surveyor, and, as far as we can
gather from that paragraph, the services rendered were simple
in the extreme.   The defendant paid 64*l.* into court, but the jury
thought the plaintiff entitled to all he sought to recover, and
found a verdict accordingly.

We have failed to ascertain the precise merits of the case, but
we quote it as one instance corroborating our opinion, that the
indefinite and extortionate amount of remuneration claimed by
surveyors needs legislation, and baffles the *proverbial penetration*
of a jury.

We bring forward without reluctance another instance in which
a steward (a gentleman's steward), doing a little valuing upon his

own account, showed a thorough appreciation of his own worth as a professional man, charging ten guineas for going over a farm of considerably less than ninety-three acres, and falling short of 200*l.* a year in value, the amount of work being easily performed in four hours, and within the power of any practical farmer to accomplish it. It is true that such a fraction of business can scarcely be worth the notice of a "professional" land surveyor, and we should scarcely quote it but as an example within the contemplation and easily to be understood by lower intelligences.

We present another picture by the same artist, wet from the easel.

For valuing an estate of 300 acres (more or less), of the annual value of 500*l.* per annum, and for *nominally* letting the farm, he made a charge of fifty pounds or more, charging a guinea for a letter, the same sum for giving a casual inquirer at his "office" a few particulars of the farm to let, and in another case "two guineas for such an appointment, and writing his employer that such an interview had taken place." Finishing and colouring a tracing of the farm is an important item, for it seems to have been repeated most wet evenings, and there is a separate charge for examining it after it *was* finished, possibly through a roll of paper, or as a magpie is popularly supposed to criticise a marrow-bone! We pass over the expensive interviews, the costly schedules, the vexatious charges, and we caution the public that unless they make a bargain with this class they have no remedy, and they must expect no consideration. Remonstrance in the case just alluded to was followed by the threat of a writ, and, under the wholesome fear of legal expenses, the whole sum was paid. Worst of all, the work was done but indifferently well!

Until the fees of these men are settled by law, it will be true economy to employ only such as are most eminent in their profession, and to eschew country practitioners, who have emerged from "the office" full-fledged land valuers without any examination, and who have risen probably by talent, but also possibly by luck, or something worse.

For the general business of a moderate estate it is possible to enlist into our service a practical educated farmer, plenty of whom may be found in every rural district; men of unimpeachable honour, of strict integrity, and cultivated intellect. Such a man as can use the spirit-level and theodolite, whose soul does not scorn an agreement as to terms, who can descend to the practical routine of common life, and tell the value per acre

of land, crop, or labour, the cubic yards of digging (in drains),
the contents of oblong stocks, and, without that wisdom of Solomon
which could "speak of trees from the cedar tree which is in
Lebanon even unto the hyssop that springeth out of the wall,"
can grasp the mystery of planting, and say how many draining-
tiles make a yard. Such an intelligence may be discovered, we
repeat, in the land of clay, shingle, flint, chalk, sand, or marl,
and we can state for the consolation of those who, seeking to
ascertain what their property is worth, desire the opinion of men
who are something far superior to good guessers, that a very valuable and reliable opinion can be obtained from men competent to
fulfil their task at five, three, or even two pounds a day!

PAPER XXXI.

SNIPE-SHOOTING.

When I drew the blind of my bedroom bay window the whole landscape was covered with a thick white mantle. The sun was shining brightly, but had as yet not power to melt the snow on the roof: it was freezing undeniably hard. I was prepared for such a scene from the glimpse I got of the outside world the previous night, when by the moonlight I could only detect a greyish line marking the boundary of my lawn—a hedge of five or six feet in height.

We adjourned after breakfast to the billiard-room and held a council of war, and, after a considerable amount of tobacco and reflection, it was determined to have a cut at the snipes in some lowland about five miles away. We therefore desired the groom to soft-soap the horses' feet and to have out the waggonette at once, or rather what we called the German waggon, for the waggonette of these later years was unknown. This vehicle, which is the most useful conveyance I ever possessed, much resembles a "body break," and carries six or more inside. It did not take long to put on the harness, and we soon heard the muffled sound of wheels at the front door. Into the dog-basket which is slung under the body of the carriage we put a capital snipe-dog I had bought of Bill George, chaining her short; and my retriever could jump in it or out of it as we bowled along.

As we hardly knew the boundaries, we picked up my odd man —the night-watcher, rat-catcher, earth-stopper, and loader all in one—and began to climb the steep hill that led us to the main turnpike road. We had to pass within half a mile of the lake, and could see the teal whirling about over the fir trees, and the ducks, singly and sometimes three or four together, flying from one part of the water to another. Our old mentor, who knew the "short cuts," suggested he should take a look at the water as we drove on, adding, he could meet us further on without causing us any material delay. We at once fell in with this idea of his, and he made for an opening into the plantation and disappeared. We had another hill to climb over—a steep one—and through a rude cutting on the crest of it we could see the wide heath stretching miles away, beyond the " back water" and the line of hills like a sheet of silver.

As we dropped down the steep incline cautiously, and got into the level ground again, we caught sight of a couple of roebuck which were lying under a hayrick to our right, and which, when they saw us, gave a leisurely stretch and trotted to the embankment of the turnpike road. This they cleared with an ease and indifference that appeared marvellous to me, considering the state of the ground, and making for the fir plantation to our right, they were soon in the shelter of the covert.

We had scarcely reached the old bridge at the bottom before we saw our emissary coming up the valley, making us signs of grotesque exultation at the success of his visit to the water. As he kicked the snow from his feet against the parapet of the bridge, and gradually recovered his breath, he informed us that there was only about twenty feet square of "bright water"—that is, water unfrozen—and that the rest was skimmed over, some of it an inch thick.

"There are lots of teal all on the ice," he said, "and some widgeon, and about ten score of ducks, but *they* are terrible wild, and they keep whistling over your head every minute," he added. "Hadn't you better go and have a shot at 'em ?"

As the frost seemed very likely to hold, we determined to go on to the snipe ground, however, where we were told it was not uncommon to find a good sprinkling of wild fowl also. Accordingly, we embarked the old loader again, and continued our journey through the snow. We found it was simply a heavy pull for the team, but that they did not slip at all. We had come the first two miles steadily, and though the horses did sweat and steam a little, they went well up to their bits, and were full of going.

We reached the farmhouse at last, which stands on the margin of the heathland, or rather between that heath and the swampy snipe-ground.

That damp, low-lying tract of land about six hundred acres, is one continued flat, and is kept in its present state, and prevented becoming an entire waste, by an earthwork running its entire length, called a "sea wall," and a number of dykes partially choked with rushes. Beyond the "sea wall" the back water is deep enough for a small steamer to run, and beyond the hills is the open sea.

The plain I have described as reclaimed from the ocean is thickly overgrown with rushes, and in many parts with reed, but in its whole length and breadth there is scarcely a place that will not bear a man's weight, and there is not one dangerous place within the boundary. The whole is mapped out by these wide ditches into fields, perhaps twelve or fourteen acres in extent, and one—the last—is full of little pools and ponds, which my experience (acquired since the day I write of by many an hour's good sport) tells me generally hold teal or duck, or perhaps some rare and valuable wader.

The little auk, the glossy ibis, the dusky shoveller, the black duck, the scaup duck, the smew, all have been shot near this locality, some by me and some by my neighbours, who hold a continuation of this shooting divided from me by a wide tidal river. The rushes form good harbour for partridges in September, and pheasants frequently spring from under the grass hassocks all the year round ; in fact, the shooting is varied and wild, and I think I have never been here without making a bag.

As we intended to shoot down wind at snipe it seemed useless to take a dog, but we had more than we could do without him, and I considered that, if he really was a snipe-dog, he would enable us to kill more than if he were not with us. For my own part I do not care to work without a dog at any sort of shooting. The sport, to my mind, is in witnessing the dog's intelligence. Knocking down the game is simply the dog's reward, everything else is "pot-hunting." If it is sport I don't see it. A steady point is a useful thing when you have a thin, frosty air. When the bird flies away with a loud scream and a twist, like the flash of a gun, it is just as well to know he is going to get up, and it gives the gun a chance ; which perhaps is not required so much when you can see the ash colour of his wing, and almost count the feathers in his tail spread open like a white-tipped doll's fan.

In this case it proved a success, and the dog was almost indispensable. She was a lemon-and-white setter, and as well made as any I ever had before or expect to have again. She had a long, lean head, and just the right amount of lip. Her freckled legs were as good as a foxhound's—I can't say more than that ; and though her hips looked rather ragged, I found, a few months after, that Bill George told the truth when he said she had been "worked to a stump and starved to death." I never saw her give up galloping, and I never knew her tired. Her deep ribs and loins, her good, firm wearing feet, and her quality, all helped to make her the best I ever saw, and the staunchest I ever possessed. She never shivered in wet and cold, nor showed anything like slackness in her work in the dry weather in a hot September day. When I took her, however, to the snipe ground on that snowy day she and I were strangers.

The only question I asked when I inquired for a snipe-dog was, "Does she know her work?" and receiving an answer in the affirmative, I paid the money and received a new chain and collar in the bargain. A few days after I loosed her from her kennel with my own hands, and took her for a walk with a brace of black-tan setters for company, and, provided the dog comes from a distance, I have generally found this a sufficient introduction between the dog and his master. I knew she turned to whistle and hand; that she dropped to hand, wing, and shot; that she did not chase or blink her birds; and this was all I knew, except that her style of hunting was perfect—head up and tail going, and plenty of speed; whilst the way she brought up when she caught the scent, stood as stiff as a biscuit, perfectly motionless (no shaking of the stern), and turned her eye towards me, showed she was a thorough good one, as the sequel proved.

As we started down wind I confess I was unprepared to see her gallop gently and sink the wind for each beat or parallel, quartering back to us, and suddenly pointing in a thick piece of rushes, putting the birds between us and her, and gradually sinking on her haunches. I confess it was my firm opinion that she was on a pheasant; and I was agreeably surprised to find, as we came up to her, that a snipe got up about six feet from her, and went right over her head. The bird turned and jerked twice when he had passed the bitch, and fell dead about thirty yards beyond her to my gun. About thirty yards on she ran into some partridges, but she dropped the moment they rose, and going down wind she could not help it. A north wind and a driving sleet came on, but the scent continued good, and she kept going on down wind as before, and working back to us, pointing every snipe and missing but one "jack" during the time we were beating this portion of our ground.

We then came to some watery meadow or marsh, but the water, being brackish, had not frozen, and though she continued her slow gallop it was so light and airy that she scarcely made any splash at all. However, it was too wet for the birds to lie there, and we took a turn up the rushy dyke. She beat this— she had the wind of it—straight up, and stood when half way up its entire length. Here we got a long shot at a duck and mallard, and killed the latter, and had but just time to load when another duck got up close to her and was dropped at once.

By this time we had come to some bog myrtle and a brook with a plank bridge close to the cottage of the dairyman, and here we had good sport. We got five couple of snipes in about five acres of ground, and, but for the ice cracking under our feet—for the water had dried away and left it like brittle sheets of glass— we should have got many more. Further on the water was out again and unfrozen, and we stepped from one dry hassock to another, but this ground would not do; the birds got up in wisps and were evidently sitting on the hassocks watching every move-ment of our party. We therefore jumped the dyke at the best place, according to our guide's experience, but old Bertie jumped short and got wet, to use his own expression, "as far as he could get wet until the luncheon came." It was to meet us here but had not arrived, and I sent the old man to the farm to get a glass of brandy and do the best he could, for his clothes began to freeze upon him directly he was *extracted* from the water.

For ourselves, we went on and found the brook nearly frozen up. I never saw so many snipe in one field before ; they were flying about in all directions, and pitching on the ice all round us. We could shoot them on the snow or as they flew by us, and instead of going right away, they flew round our heads and pitched again. There was no occasion to move far away, for as fast as we could load they came by us, and the dog was setting them and dropping all the time. Best of all they were in good condition !

Our luncheon reached us here, and we got over it as soon as we could, and lit our pipes and began again, but they now moved off towards the next piece, and we moved after them. Here the land was not so wet, and the furze grew moderately well. A good skein of teal rose from a small pond in the middle of the ground, and we got three of them, a fourth pitching on his head in the river, and breaking the thin ice in his fall. As my retriever was worth more than a dead teal, I did not try to recover him, for I once all but lost a retriever in a mere duckpond from the same cause. We foolishly sent him after a duck; as he caught it the ice broke under him, and I had my choice either to

break the ice before me, and wade for him, or let him drown.
As his breaking had cost me many hours' hard work, I fetched
him out, although I had to wade to my shoulders in the water,
but he was saved, and I am none the worse.

We got a "ring-necked pheasant" in the same piece of furze,
and fine dog fox broke from the end of it, Here old Bertie
pointed out the seal of an otter, and we could track him to the
bank and in the direction of the river, but soon after he must have
got upon the ice, and we could make no more of him.

It was now time to think about returning, and we got our
green-coated companion to show us the best way back. "Through
the copse and so back across a piece of heather, and it is not quite
a mile," said the cheery old man, who declared he was quite dry
and warm—an assertion I felt to be untrue—and we turned into
a good small covert to make our way to the old farm.

We got a hare and a few rabbits on the heath, and as we
passed through a sort of wide crevice in a sudden declivity which
old Bertie called a "droke," I felt pretty sure I flushed a woodcock, though I could not see him perfectly. However, the
assertion of our old guide that it was a brown owl was received
with acclamation by my friends, and I had to endure some joking
on the subject. When their mirth was at the highest pitch,
however, a woodcock was flushed by the farmer, who was coming
to meet us on his pony, and flying straight for my friend, fell to
his gun, and it was generously conceded that it was the bird I
had flushed in the "droke."

I did not keep an account of the snipes we got that day, but I
think it was about twenty-one couple—I know it was over
twenty ; and what is better still, we had about a fortnight of
this work. At one time we had seventy couple in the house ;
and I believe a farmer, a neighbour of mine, who has a famous
eye of anyone I know for shooting ducks by his river side at
night, and who is seldom equalled by anyone who shoots with
him by day, "realised" nearly as many with his own gun.
He is a Hercules in strength, and I think I am right in saying
he uses a 10-gauge Westley Richards, and puts in 5 drachms of
powder. But heavy guns and large charges are a mistake.

I once used just such a pair of guns myself, but I found it all
wrong. First there is a grave increase in the powder bill at
the end of the year; then, although you may kill at longer
distances, you are a longer time *getting on the bird* than your
companion ; and, lastly, there is the additional weight; for such

a gun generally weighs at least 9lb. The difference between 7lb. and 9lb. is not perceptible after the first half-hour, but it must tell in a long day, and, tiring the muscles of the arm, deteriorate from the nicety of the aim.

The gunmakers have fixed on the best weight, in my opinion, for average sized men ; and no guage is so reliable, according to my experience, as the *number twelve.* The proper regulation of the charge rests with the man who uses the gun, and no rules can be laid down for the quantity of powder or shot, but of the latter nineteen out of twenty certainly use too much.

Printed by HORACE COX, 346, Strand.

WALKLEY AND CO.'S
REVERSIBLE WATERPROOF COATS

Are made of the Finest Fabrics ; will fold in a small case for the pocket, and
weigh only a few ounces.

COLOURS DRAB OR BLACK.

LADIES' CLOAKS,

With Hoods, of the same Light Materials, also folding in pocket case.

Light Waterproof Knee Wrappers, Carriage Aprons, and Rugs.

FISHING AND DRIVING COATS,

Coachmen's Driving Capes with Sleeves, Fishing Stockings and Trousers, and

All kinds of Indiarubber Goods of best Manufacture,

WARRANTED TO STAND THE GREATEST TROPICAL HEAT.

THE RANELAGH,

For promoting the Health, Beauty, and Muscular Development of the Human Body.

Produces, by a few minutes' daily use, the highest form of healthy bodily development, with perfect safety, and without sense of fatigue, being equally adapted to the delicate child and to the strongest man. Their convenient size, real portability, and the facility with which they may be used, even in a very small room, render them peculiarly fitted for gymnastic recreation.

It is now made on improved principles, and embraces various degrees of strength.

MILNES'S PATENT.

With PRINTED Instructions.

PRICES:

	s.	d.
No. 1, for Ladies or Children	10	6
No. 2, for Gentlemen	14	6
No. 3, ,, ,, very strong	18	6

Or with metal work bronzed,
1s. each extra.

WALKLEY AND Co.,
WATERPROOFERS & INDIARUBBER MANUFACTURERS,

5, *STRAND* (*opposite Charing Cross Post Office*),
LONDON.

[1]

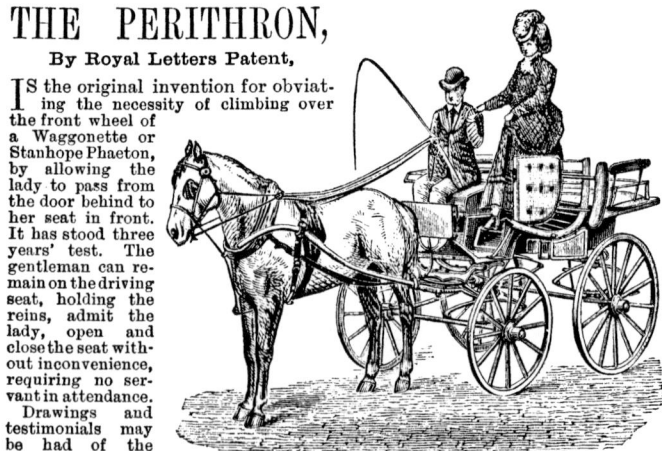

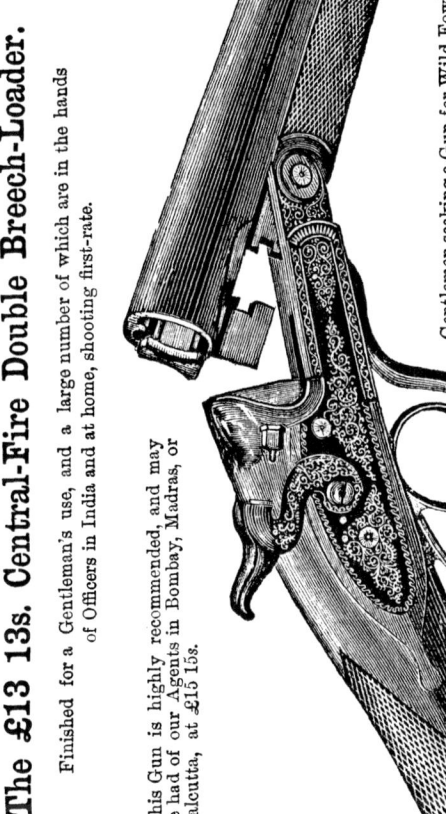

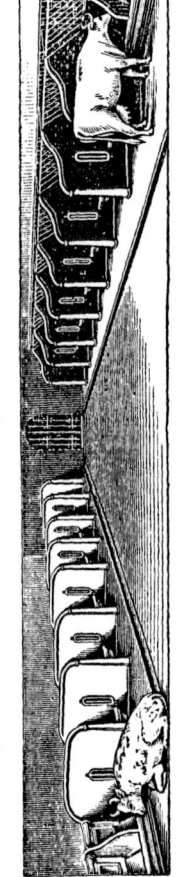

MUSGRAVE'S PATENT HARNESS BRACKETS,

With polished wood cappings, a new invention, which soon repays the first cost of the brackets by their preservation of the Harness.

MUSGRAVE'S PATENT SLOW COMBUSTION STOVES,

Safe, healthful, durable, and extremely simple; will burn in halls day and night for six months without relighting; used by the Ecclesiastical Commissioners for all the Churches in Ireland, and by all the leading Architects of the United Kingdom for Halls, Churches, Hospitals, the Corridors of Lunatic Asylums, &c.

For Illustrated Catalogues, with Prices or Estimates, post free, of the above Inventions, apply to

MUSGRAVE AND COMPANY, LIMITED,

ANN STREET IRON WORKS, BELFAST.

Printed in the United Kingdom
by Lightning Source UK Ltd.
116155UKS00001B/163